PROPHETIC PICTURES

"Meanwhile he had been painting with more and more eagerness. . . . He observed that he was just getting interested in the picture; and I could recognize the feeling that was in him, as akin to what I have experienced myself, in the glow of composition." (May 7, 1850, *The American Notebooks*, pp. 498-99.) Courtesy of The Grolier Club of New York. Portrait by Cephas Giovanni Thompson.

PROPHETIC PICTURES
Nathaniel Hawthorne's Knowledge and Uses of the Visual Arts

Rita K. Gollin and John L. Idol, Jr.,
with the assistance of Sterling K. Eisiminger

Contributions in American Studies, Number 99
Robert H. Walker, Series Editor

GREENWOOD PRESS
New York • Westport, Connecticut • London

Library of Congress Cataloging-in-Publication Data

Gollin, Rita K.
  Prophetic pictures : Nathaniel Hawthorne's knowledge and uses of
the visual arts / Rita K. Gollin and John L. Idol, Jr., with the
assistance of Sterling K. Eisiminger.
    p. cm.—(Contributions in American studies, ISSN 0084-9227
; no. 99)
  Includes bibliographical references and index.
  ISBN 0-313-27573-4 (alk. paper)
  1. Hawthorne, Nathaniel, 1804-1864—Knowledge—Art. 2. Art and
literature—United States—History—19th century. I. Idol, John L.
II. Eisiminger, Sterling K. III. Title. IV. Series.
PS1892.A66G65   1991
813'.3—dc20   91-9554

British Library Cataloguing in Publication Data is available.

Library of Congress Catalog Card Number: 91-9554
ISBN: 0-313-27573-4
ISSN: 0084-9227

First published in 1991

Greenwood Press, 88 Post Road West, Westport, CT 06881
An imprint of Greenwood Publishing Group, Inc.

Printed in the United States of America

(∞)™

The paper used in this book complies with the
Permanent Paper Standard issued by the National
Information Standards Organization (Z39.48-1984).

10 9 8 7 6 5 4 3 2 1

In Memory of
Manning Hawthorne, Norman Holmes Pearson,
Arlin Turner, and Hyatt Waggoner

Contents

Acknowledgments

For his tireless help and constant good will, the authors are grateful to L. Neal Smith, who was associate textual editor at the Ohio State University Center for Textual Studies when this study began more than a decade ago. The authors are also grateful to Dennis Berthold, Texas A & M University, for reading the manuscript and making many useful suggestions.

Rita K. Gollin expresses thanks to the Geneseo Foundation, the Berg Collection of the New York Public Library, and the staffs of the Rush Rhees Library of the University of Rochester and the Milne Library of the State University of New York College at Geneseo. She is also grateful to all those who offered counsel and encouragement during the long gestation of this volume, among them the four generous scholars (now deceased) to whom this book is dedicated, her colleagues at Geneseo and in the Nathaniel Hawthorne Society, and C. E. Frazer Clark. As always, her deepest debt is to her most stalwart counselor and critic, Richard Gollin.

John L. Idol expresses thanks to former Clemson graduate students Jared Evatt, Anne Hawkes, Jennifer Holloway, Charles Mitchell Lee, and Lewe Woodham; to Judy Payne and Pearl Parker of the secretarial staff of Clemson University's English Department; to Jacques Macy, Leonard Perry, and Ludmila Savitsky of Clemson's Modern Language Department; to George William Koon and Robert Waller for release time; to Richard Fyffe and the staff at the Essex Institute; to Edith Harman and Edward Stevenson of The House of the Seven Gables; to Joseph Flibbert, Salem State College; Buford Jones, Duke University; David B. Kesterson, University of North Texas; Melinda Mowry Ponder, Pine Manor College; James L. Skinner III, Presbyterian College; Patricia Valenti, Pembroke State University; Thomas Woodson, Ohio State

University; Marian Withington, the Robert Muldrow Library, Clemson University; Blair Rouse, deceased, University of Arkansas; Norman Olsen, College of Charleston; and Randolph Hawthorne.

Sterling K. Eisiminger and John L. Idol express thanks to the staff of the library of Clemson's School of Architecture.

Introduction

Only in recent years has the full range of Nathaniel Hawthorne's knowledge of the visual arts and his attitudes toward artists and their work begun to emerge. Earlier statements about Hawthorne and the visual arts had not always been judicious, even though they often came from widely respected critics. To fairminded students of Hawthorne's life and works, the words of Van Wyck Brooks (1958) and Henry James (1879), for example, grossly misrepresented Hawthorne's stock of information and attitudes. First Brooks:

> Hawthorne had little feeling for art, and it was largely to please his wife that he dragged himself through miles of picture galleries. (136)

Next James:

> The plastic sense was not strong in Hawthorne; there can be no better proof of it than his curious aversion to the representation of the nude in sculpture. This aversion was deep-seated; he constantly returns to it, exclaiming upon the incongruity of modern artists making naked figures. He apparently quite failed to see that nudity is not an incident, or accident, of sculpture, but its very essence and principle; and his jealousy of undressed images strikes the reader as a strange, vague, long-dormant heritage of his straight-laced Puritan ancestry. Whenever he talks of statues he makes a great point of the smoothness and whiteness of the marble—speaks of the surface of the marble as if it were half of the beauty of the image; and when he discourses on pictures, one feels that the brightness or dinginess

of the frame is an essential part of his impression of the work—as he, indeed, somewhere distinctly affirms. Like a good American, he took more pleasure in the productions of Mr. Thompson and Mr. Brown, Mr. Powers and Mr. Hart, American artists who were plying their trade in Italy, than in the works which adorned the ancient museums of the country. (161)

If called upon to support their contentions, James and Brooks could have cited numerous passages in Hawthorne's notebooks, passages admitting that his wife easily outstripped him in exploring the art treasures in European galleries and churches, passages lambasting an artist for producing yet another nude statue or painting, passages confessing his wish that some paintings could be whitewashed or that many statues could be tossed into a lime kiln. Hawthorne could sound like a monstrous cross between a Puritan and a Vandal. He would have frankly said that he was no John Ruskin, nor even an Anna Jameson or George Hillard, two nineteenth-century travelers and critics to whom he looked for suggestions on what to see and what to think about the art objects he took time to contemplate. He lacked Ruskin's interest in aesthetic theories, Jameson's fervid zeal to share her interpretations of religious art, and Hillard's rigor and zest. But if James and Brooks had been able or willing to read the notebooks more closely, they would have found passage after passage revealing not only sensitive appreciation of paintings and statues but also an eagerness to discover the deepest truths and insights embodied in great works of art. Surprisingly, the scholarly Eugene Schuyler read no more attentively than James and Brooks when he prepared his chapter on Hawthorne for *Italian Influences*. For Schuyler, Hawthorne remained largely ignorant of and insensitive to art.

Picking up where George Hillard (1870), Samuel Carter Hall (1860), and William Dean Howells (1872) started when they considered Hawthorne's comments on art and artists in the notebooks and *The Marble Faun* (in *The Centenary Edition of the Works of Nathaniel Hawthorne*), recent students of Hawthorne's work have weighed his words about art, including comments by his wife, and have concluded that he was often a keen yet diffident student of the visual arts. Foremost among them is James Mellow (1980), who offered more information on Hawthorne's knowledge of the visual arts than any other biographer except Julian Hawthorne. Though others had been in the field before Mellow, most of them doctoral candidates eager to show that Hawthorne was more sophisticated and less puritanic than James and Brooks had contended, but a few corrective steps had been taken by Millicent Bell (1962), Marjorie Elder (1972), Richard Harter Fogle (1952), Nathalia Wright

(1965), Leland Schubert (1944), Richard Jacobson (1965), Nina Baym (1967), and Rudolph Von Abele (1955). Partly because they only knew Hawthorne's notebooks in their pre-Centenary edition state, they paid little if any attention to Hawthorne's encounters with the visual arts in his native Salem, Massachusetts, at Bowdoin College, or in Boston, and little attention to his attempt to acquire an informed taste for the visual arts during his consular years. Their comments were largely limited to *The Marble Faun* and related passages in the Italian notebooks. That practice continued as late as Agnes McNeill Donohue's *Hawthorne: Calvin's Ironic Stepchild* (1985), despite the pioneering work of such younger scholars as Judith Budz, whose dissertation on Hawthorne and the visual arts, directed by Jean Hagstrum, author of *The Sister Arts: The Tradition of Literary Pictorialism and English Poetry from Dryden to Gray*, moved beyond Hawthorne's words and into his cultural milieu. Budz recognized the importance of examining his responses to the visual arts available to him in Salem and Boston. She knew that Bostonian life afforded him many opportunities to see the work of American and European artists, though she failed to document all his opportunities (perhaps because she did not examine his early letters). But she was aware of Hawthorne's involvement in the pictorialist tradition and traced many of his aesthetic principles to their sources in his reading: Archibald Alison, Edmund Burke, Francis Hutcheson, and Lord Kames. Though she did not read far beyond the major texts, her dissertation and the one article drawn from it were a major step toward understanding Hawthorne's knowledge and uses of the visual arts in the context of his own creative achievements.

Like many Americans of his time who were directly concerned with issues of aesthetics, taste, and creativity, Hawthorne deliberately took steps to learn more about the visual arts. His longing to know more about them was heightened when he met Sophia Peabody, whose talents as a copyist and original artist had won praise in Boston's artistic circles. He soon shared her dream of one day going to Italy to see the works of the Italian masters. The steps he took were often small and stumbling, but they do reveal much about him both as man and artist, for his involvement with the visual arts directly fed his own work, both his notebooks and his fiction. Without claiming that his path to enrich himself is representative of the nation's efforts to assimilate European artistic traditions, we do see Hawthorne's efforts to acquire an informed taste as an instance of how a sensitive and creative American sought to understand how sketches, paintings, and statues were created and how to judge them correctly. The experiences of William Cullen Bryant, James Fenimore Cooper, Herman Melville, Harriet Beecher Stowe, William Dean Howells, Mark Twain, and other American authors who struggled to absorb European art suggest that Hawthorne's struggling was representative of a peculiarly American search for cultural roots as well as a writer's yearning to explore the relationship of the sister arts.

Steadily though often unsurely, Hawthorne climbed a ladder of taste, one ranging from realistic representations of the mundane and secular to allegorical depictions of the sacred and divine. He was willing to go rung by rung even though he would have been content to stop at the Dutch realists. Despite the prevailing assumption that the Italian idealists were at the top of the ladder, Hawthorne preferred realistic representation that nonetheless suggested spirituality. Like Samuel Johnson on matters of good prose, Hawthorne responded most favorably to those paintings and statues done in a style neither too high nor too low, pieces pleasing both the outward eye (the one used to observe physical data) and the inward eye (the one seeking to "see" or share the creative impulse behind a work of art). Using both "eyes" Hawthorne meant to climb the ladder as far as he could, to meditate on the creative links between writing and painting and sculpting.

Our book examines Hawthorne's exposure and response to the visual arts from the earliest instance to his final recorded visit to an artist's studio and shows how he used them in letters, tales, and romances. The study is illuminated by photographs of many of the works of art that Hawthorne saw and wrote about so that readers can understand and judge Hawthorne's response to each of them by looking at what he saw and reading his words about them. His biases, insights, sensitivity, fretfulness, enjoyment, disgust, exhaustion, eagerness to share his views or argue his principles, and his lifelong habit of ambivalence can best be demonstrated by bringing together a representative collection of art objects and his own words about them.

Perhaps because Hawthorne never swerved from his early admiration of Spenser, Bunyan, and Scott and never put aside the theories of such Scottish Common Sense aestheticians as Dugald Stewart and Archibald Alison, the one continuous thread running through Hawthorne's responses to art (whether verbal or plastic) is his commitment to pictorialism (the use or creation of pictures or visual images). A basic concern for him was how the hearts and minds of viewers or readers could be reached or swayed through visual images. A related and even nagging concern was an individual's capacity to absorb and retain visual images and the duration and intensity of their effect on that individual's life. That concern became a consuming interest as he tried to hone his taste for art in England, France, and Italy. It was a kind of uncertainty principle linked to Hawthorne's recognition that appreciation of art could not escape some element of subjectivity. Hawthorne was sometimes left with the uneasy feeling that he had not seen what the artist attempted to show.

Working up a taste meant making stiff demands on himself, chiefly his determination to be a sympathetic perceiver. As one artist responding to another, he tried to put himself in the shoes of a painter or sculptor and imagine the work emerging from the first flash of inspiration to the finishing touches. Viewing a sketch was especially satisfying since it was close to the initial moment of inspiration. The further removed an artwork was from that first burst of creative energy, the less likely was Hawthorne to appreciate it fully. He came to detest peering through accumulations of grime and smoke or tracing faded outlines and colors of frescos as he wandered through the churches and galleries of Italy. But on occasion even these dirty or pale masterpieces spoke to him and thereby became a part of his cultural inheritance. They became wondrous because Hawthorne regarded the artist as a perceiver, even a guide, one who must see and speak about the human condition. The task of the perceiver was to read or interpret works of art correctly. That credo finds its most obvious expression in Hawthorne's belief that works of art owing their origin to some moral imperative were most deserving of praise and preservation. But to follow that credo was not always easy and was subject to such accidentals as lighting conditions, the state of the artwork and its mode of display, the freshness or weariness of the beholder, and the distracting words or movements of other beholders.

Only in rare moments did Hawthorne fully appreciate a work while patiently gazing at it and musing on the artist's inspiration or intent. More often appreciation came when Hawthorne gave a particular work of art a sidelong glance, when he was not forcing it to yield up its meaning. If a work would speak to him, would become what he called a "spiritual possession," it must (as he said) unveil itself when the perceiver was not intent on discovering its aesthetic or moral significance. Admittedly, however, a work had a better chance of speaking or unveiling itself if it contained more than a small portion of the moral picturesque, the fashion of expressing "meanings through figures rather than in explicit statement," to take Darrel Abel's definition (2). But interesting exceptions to this principle can be found, such as Hawthorne's pleasure in Rubens's jolly, intoxicated Bacchus at the Uffizi Gallery in Florence. And because, like most of his country-men, Hawthorne placed high value on representational art, he was troubled by J.M.W. Turner's paintings, in which tangible reality seemed to dissolve into mist.

Our overarching conclusion is that Hawthorne repeatedly tried to acquire a taste for the visual arts, an effort frustrated by the limited scope of his receptive faculty and his desire to take spiritual possession of the works he truly admired. Trying to digest too much too fast during his European sojourn overwhelmed him at times and provoked peevishness. He did not have his wife's aesthetic background or her patience, and he was more curious about the artistic process and what it revealed of the human psyche than he was about any art object, however celebrated. As a corollary to this curiosity, he repeatedly tried to present the workings of the artistic mind in his fiction. His record of himself as perceiver, a record kept in his notebooks, contributes both directly and indirectly to his fiction. To trace his efforts to acquire a taste for art, to look over his shoulders or see through his eyes, to discover how insightful or blind he could be, to recognize the range and depth of his ambivalence, we found it essential to pay close attention to what he termed his "journalizing." Consequently, we had to give greater scope to biography than we had originally intended, with the ultimate purpose of illuminating the readers' understanding and appreciation of Hawthorne's own art.

Our second discovery is that his preference for Dutch painting, like that of George Eliot, reflects his abiding admiration for artists who could treat life realistically without succumbing to a "worldly" view of life. Emblematic, symbolic, idealistic though he was in his tales and romances, struggling like Italian and French artists to transform the mundane into the ideal and symbolic, Hawthorne was often uncomfortable with the idealizations of the Italian Renaissance artists, especially if he learned that an artist's mistress served as a model for an idealized saint or the Virgin Mary. Like Howells in *Venetian Life*, Hawthorne found himself thinking of the hypocrisy of Italian artists while he looked at paintings with sacred subjects. Where Dutch artists appeared honest in their attempts to catch life as they saw it, too many Italian artists seemed to be shrewd manipulators of seductive surfaces. Something was wrong if an amoral or lascivious artist painted or sculpted works designed to provide ethical, moral, or religious instruction. However, Hawthorne was not rigid in applying this principle. Had he been, he never could have responded with such sympathy and insight to Sodoma's *Christ Bound to the Pillar*. In short, his sympathetic responses ranged far beyond those of his prudish Hilda, often considered his mouthpiece in *The Marble Faun*. Yet Hawthorne's preference for Dutch realists reveals something basic to his nature, which—despite his predilection for allegorical tales, symbolic romances, and the moral picturesque—explains his admiration for the "beef and ale" of Anthony Trollope and other writers notable for their realism.

Still, he and his prim New England maiden, Hilda, owe an aesthetic debt to the conservative theoreticians whose views were expressed in 1830 on the occasion of the Boston Athenaeum's fourth exhibition:

> The taste for Beauty in art and nature is nearly allied to the
> love of Good—so nearly indeed, that it has often been doubted
> whether Beauty be any thing more than a visible manifestation

of those amiable moral qualities of which the mere idea fills the heart with delightful emotions, and confers a charm on every person or thing with which they appear to be associated. . . . [O]bservation of the beautiful forms of nature and the imitations or expressions of them in works of art, has the effect of cherishing the benevolent affections, repressing evil passions, and improving the general tone of moral feeling. In a community like ours, where the disposition to active pursuits, and the selfish views and angry controversies that are naturally connected with them, is perhaps too strong—where the form of government keeps up an almost uninterrupted war of political parties—it is highly important that every principle of a soothing and civilising tendency should be brought as much as possible into vigorous action. The cultivation of the arts [aids] the great and essential elements of civilization, which are found in a judicious system of political and religious institutions, and gives the last polish to the character of men and nations. (*North American Review*, October 1830: 309-10)

He heard similar views from George Hillard, Washington Allston, Margaret Fuller, and his future sister-in-law, Elizabeth Palmer Peabody, and probably from his future wife, though in Florence, Hiram Powers would argue that scoundrels often had good taste.

Our third discovery is that Hawthorne was deeply ambivalent in his judgment of art and artists. Catch him on a good day and he is sensitive, understanding, sympathetic. Listen to him on a bad day and find that he would not hesitate to consign every painting and statue to fiery destruction. (One of the problems with Agnes Donohue's assessment of Hawthorne's attitudes about Italian art is that she overweighted what Hawthorne said on his bad rather than his good days. Another problem is her assumption, like James's, that Hawthorne's religious background rather than his aesthetic principles governed his aesthetic responses.) Read him in his early work and conclude, correctly enough, that his artists and *objets d'art* represent allegorical forces or ideas. Consider his most mature statement on artists in *The Marble Faun* and admire his probing analyses of the artistic temperament and his insightful commentaries on many of the world's masterpieces. Slowly, painfully, he did develop something of a taste for pictures and statues, though, characteristically, he was more modest about his achievement than he should have been. In short, his efforts to enrich himself in the visual arts yielded an unusually high dividend, *The Marble Faun*, which on a good day he thought to be his best work. On a bad day, he had his doubts.

Developing that taste for the visual arts required generous reciprocity, a willingness to invest emotional and intellectual energies in an art object in an effort to understand with the artist the creativity that enabled mind, heart, and hand to give physical expression to the conception. Not to reciprocate was to be a mere dilettante, a receptacle for images, an onlooker. Unless Hawthorne could get inside a work, could hear it speak to him, and could feel it demanding something from him, he had doubts about its worth, even though it might have earned high praise from others. In short, Hawthorne expected art to stretch his mind and emotions, but he was aware that artists could create something he would be unable to understand fully.

Our final discovery is that Hawthorne posed many arresting questions about artists and the visual arts:

- How far should, or can, artists probe into and reveal the workings of the human heart?
- Should artists remain detached observers, simply reporting what they see?
- Can artists ever be sure they have found the truth of the heart or spirit?
- Might artists harm themselves by withholding themselves from ordinary human intercourse?
- Is it true that great artists kept strong ties to humanity?
- How can artists use emblems or symbols and avoid the risk of being appreciated and understood only by the knowing few?
- How much weight should be assigned to the talent, inspiration, and originality of artists, how much to their training and the tastes of the age?
- What constitutes a worthy subject for artists?
- Can the achievements of artists ever be fully understood?
- What roles should, or do, the emotions and intellect play in a viewer's appreciation of an artwork?
- How important is the spectator's ''collaboration'' in assigning value to works of art?
- How important to a viewer's response is distance in time from the artwork?
- Is the aesthetic value of a sketch or unfinished work greater than that of a finished work?
- Does an artwork lack value if it has no perceptible inspiration?
- How important is the physical condition of an art object or its mode of display?
- Can portraits reveal profound truths about a sitter's character?

Not listed as a discovery, but rather taken as a given, is Hawthorne's conviction, shared with most cultivated people of his age, that pictorial qualities govern the mimetic arts and that art objects could be valued according to a scale that placed works depicting sacred and heroic subjects at the top and landscapes and still lifes near the bottom.

These discoveries, and the questions that came into focus as they were made, provide new ways of understanding Hawthorne's life and art.

The American Experience

THE VISUAL ARTS IN HAWTHORNE'S LIFE UNTIL 1853

Awaiting paintings by his fiancée, Sophia Peabody, for his bachelor's quarters, Hawthorne confided to his beloved, his "Dove,"

> I never owned a picture in my life; yet pictures have always been among the earthly possessions (and they are spiritual possessions too) which I most coveted. I know not what value my Dove's pictures might bear at an auction-room; but to me, certainly, they will be incomparably more precious than all the productions of all the painters since Apelles. When we live together in our own house, belovedest, we will paint pictures together—that is, our minds and hearts shall unite to form the conception, to which your hand shall give material existence. I have often felt as if I could be a painter, only I am sure that I could never handle a brush;—now my Dove will show me the images of my inward eye, beautified and etherealized by the mixture of her own spirit. (XV: 397-98. Unless otherwise stated, Hawthorne quotes are taken from *The Centenary Edition of the Works of Nathaniel Hawthorne*, edited by William Charvat et al. 19 vols. Columbus: Ohio State University Press, 1962. References are to volume and page number.)

This letter of 3 January 1840 points back to Hawthorne's long-held interest in painting and anticipates adventures he would share with Sophia and their children as he learned more about the visual arts. Hawthorne had moved far enough beyond his "straight-laced Puritan ancestry" (James 161) to covet paintings, to want them in his life, to envy the talents of people who could express themselves with a brush.

This confidence shows that he knew some art history even as he indulged in a lover's hyperbole. More than that, the letter sets forth a plan: "When we live together in our own house . . . we will paint pictures together—that is, our minds and hearts shall unite to form the conception, to which your hand shall give material existence." That they would indeed do, but they would do more. Sophia was to be his mentor, showing him how to use his inward eye, helping him to under-stand the workings of minds and talents practicing the visual arts, sharing his experiences with artists and their works, which resulted in a masterwork, *The Marble Faun*. But Hawthorne did not come under Sophia's tutelage without some prior study. To appreciate more fully what Hawthorne's own art owes to his knowledge of artworks and artists, we must follow him through Salem's streets and houses and beyond to see some of the art objects and to meet some of the artists who helped shape Hawthorne's aesthetic standards and practices. His cultural milieu and his artistic output cannot be separated.

Like many Salem families of their own time, in a tradition dating back to a much earlier time, the Hathornes (spelled as such until Nathaniel changed the name to "Hawthorne") had sat for portraits, a circumstance that enabled the orphan Nathaniel to see the countenances of his father and paternal grandfather. These miniatures (later to be engraved by Stephen Alonzo Schoff [1818-1905]) were at once a link to the past and a means of identifying with his father's side of the family. But they were not the only works of art in the household. Surprisingly, there was also a bust of John Wesley, given to Hawthorne during his childhood by his sister Elizabeth.

If the Hathorne family had had the means, or inclination, to buy art objects in this once prosperous seaport, many art objects besides the bust of John Wesley could have been found. Salem had a rich heritage in naval and domestic arts (evident in present-day Salem's Peabody Museum). Owners and captains of trading ships built in Salem and sailing from its once bustling wharves regularly commissioned such local artists as Antoine Roux and George Ropes to depict their newly constructed ships and then hung these drawings, many of them crude but a few of them nicely done, in their parlors, counting houses, or ship's cabins. Wealthier owners and captains might commission Cantonese artists to depict not only their ships but also themselves and relatives back home if the doting father or husband provided a sketch from which to work. Cantonese seascapes and portraits (many of them presently displayed in Salem's Peabody Museum) joined a host of other Oriental art objects in Salem households: figurines, china and silver service, fans, picture books, fire screens, bronze vessels and wall decorations, furniture, and wallpaper.

Salem's wealthier citizens, its merchants and traders, also hired architects to design houses, the most renowned of whom were Charles

Bulfinch (1763-1844) and Salem's own Samuel McIntire (1757-1811). As a result, stately houses in the new federal style began to line Salem's streets and to serve as showplaces for Oriental, European, or African wares. In McIntire the town discovered more than an architect and turned to him for figureheads for its clippers and a carving of an American eagle for its custom house. If the Hathornes were socially below Salem's merchant kings, through Nathaniel's aunt Sarah's marriage to a Crowninshield, they witnessed the bond between prosperity and the arts that Salem forged during its heyday. But even without the Crowninshield connection, Hawthorne had ready access to the collection of man-made and natural curiosities at the East India Marine Society to capture his ready attention. This forerunner of Salem's Peabody Museum housed paintings and scrimshaw, figureheads and shrunken heads, and a host of other objects. Whether he pored over these as a boy and youth as he did over the portraits of military and civic leaders in his manhood at the Essex Institute, we have no way of knowing, but the future author of "A Virtuoso's Collection" (1842) surely must have been delighted with the wide variety of artifacts and natural wonders gathered by members of the East India Marine Society. (See Charles Goodspeed's *Nathaniel Hawthorne and the Museum of the Salem East India Society: or the Gathering of a Virtuoso's Collection* for a richly detailed account of this museum's holdings.)

Visits to the homes of kinsmen and neighbors enabled Hawthorne to see numerous portraits. John Neal's comments about portraits in New England homes might aptly describe Hawthorne's uncle Robert Manning's well-furnished house in Raymond, Maine, as well as other homes of Hawthorne's kinsmen and neighbors: "You could hardly open the door of a best-room anywhere [without seeing portraits] staring at you with both eyes." In the home of his Salem tutor, Benjamin Lynde Oliver, Hawthorne could see thirteen family portraits, done by such artists as John Smibert and John Singleton Copley (Grayson 7). And at the Essex Institute Hawthorne examined dozens of portraits of colonial leaders, including Governor Leverett, Sir William Pepperell, and Peter Oliver. The knowledge that families lived with portraits, that these paintings were once a felt presence in New England households, conveying a sense of a past that might anticipate the future, would be incorporated into his fiction, for example in "Edward Randolph's Portrait" (1838) and *The House of the Seven Gables* (1851). He did not need Gothic conventions to show him how a portrait could still continue to speak to descendants. But, of course, they helped.

When he left Salem to attend college at Bowdoin, he could view at his leisure a small collection of paintings and drawings. Some 180 works of art, most gifts of the Bowdoin family, awaited Hawthorne's attentive if uninstructed eye, among them drawings and paintings by Salvator Rosa, Guido Reni, Jan Fyt, Pietroda Petri, Frans Francken, Nicholas

Poussin, and Caravaggio, and copies of paintings by Titian, Rubens, Teniers, and Raphael.[1] If the collection was not distinguished, it was nonetheless rich enough to feed the pictorial hunger of someone nurtured on the splendid descriptive passages of Spenser, Bunyan, and Scott. Hawthorne could linger at a biblical or mythological scene, pause before a landscape, anatomize portraits, or study a Dutch still life.

But Hawthorne is strangely silent about Bowdoin's attempt to provide its students with a sampling of the visual arts. Perhaps at Bowdoin he first began to enjoy the realism of the Dutch painters; their renderings of hares, birds, fish, and fruits would have appealed to someone who had relished the woodlands and wildlife in nearby Raymond. Since the taste of the time stressed the ideal, his preference for the materiality of Dutch artists might have put him at odds with many of his fellow students and teachers. Whatever the idealists in his circle might have thought of his developing tastes, Hawthorne was obviously acquiring an under- standing of how realism helped lend both authenticity and fidelity to a scene or setting.

But in many ways, Hawthorne was already a nonconformist. He and his friend Horatio Bridge decided not to have silhouettes cut for the senior yearbook. Apparently he relented afterward, for a profile of him does appear in the collection of his classmate, George Snell (Gollin, *Portraits,* 16-17). And he sent a copy of the silhouette to his sister Louisa, remarking (4 May 1823), "I do not believe you can tell whose profile the inclosed is" (XV: 178). This remark pointedly suggests his predilection for verisimilitude.

Bowdoin, however, required him to deal with more important aesthetic questions than whether silhouettes were realistic. Hawthorne found them in Thomas C. Upham's course in moral and mental philosophy (Gollin, *Truth of Dreams,* 26). Like most moral and mental philosophers of his age in American colleges, Upham drew heavily upon Scottish Common Sense philosophers, particularly Dugald Stewart. Stewart's thoughts on the function of the imagination as presented by Upham should have given Hawthorne something to ponder deeply, not so much because they could help him understand the act of creativity as empowered by the imagination but because they shed light on the role of the imagination in developing the mind's receptive faculty, the apprehensive power needed for appreciating invention and new combinations, the very essence of imagination according to Stewart. Acquiring taste requires nurturing the imagination and a continual cultivation of it to avoid becoming an incomplete and crippled human (Stewart, *Collected Works,* 2: 368-79). Of course, cultivation of the imagination must be governed by reason and good sense. As Terence Martin observes in *The Instructed Vision,* imagination thus conceived and regulated is better suited to the appreciation than to the creation of art (122). The force of Stewart's and Upham's arguments would show itself later in Hawthorne's efforts to acquire taste by reading books on aesthetics, by attending exhibitions of paintings and statues in Boston, and by concertedly seeking to develop a taste for art in England, France, and Italy.

If Hawthorne did not return home from Bowdoin in "spiritual possession" of any of its paintings and prints, he did carry away a deep curiosity about aesthetic principles, a hunger that eventually led him to Lord Kames's *Elements of Criticism,* which he read in June 1827. He continued to explore aesthetic theory in the following months by reading Archibald Alison's *Essays on the Nature and Principles of Taste,* Francis Hutcheson's *An Inquiry into the Original of Our Ideas of Beauty and Virtue,* and Edmund Burke's *Enquiry into the Sublime and Beautiful,* the first two of which he read in August 1827, the last in November 1828 (Kesselring 43, 45, 53, 54).

A passage encountered early in Kames's introduction could easily explain Hawthorne's continued reading in aesthetic theory and could be used as a factor encouraging his quest to develop his taste for the visual arts:

> The fine arts are contrived to give pleasure to the eye and the ear, disregarding the inferior senses. A taste for these arts is a plant that grows naturally in many soils; but, with culture, scarce to perfection in any soil. It is susceptible of much refinement; and is, by proper care, greatly improved. (I: 6-7)

Before moving on to Alison or Hutcheson, Hawthorne read that good taste and the moral sense are nearly allied; that passions and emotions of various kinds affect man's responses to nature and the fine arts; that beauty can be intrinsic or relative and depends "for its existence upon the percipient as much as upon the object perceived" (I: 261); that great and elevated objects are considered sublime; that motion, force, and novelty can be agreeable; that laughter can be an expression of amusement or of scorn; that in judging persons or objects man engages in comparison ("resemblance") and contrast; and that "works of nature are remarkable in their uniformity not less than in their variety; and the mind of man is fitted to receive pleasure equally from both" (I: 415). Perhaps the key thought Hawthorne carried away from Lord Kames relates to that Scottish rationalist's argument that apprehension of beauty demands a sympathetic relation between the perceiver and the "object perceived."

Alison's closely argued essays raised important issues: how emotions are related to the imagination, how predispositions of viewers and readers direct their recognition of the beautiful or sublime, how studying nature helps to develop sensibilities in both the artist and the beholder of his work, how the sounds and colors of nature serve to convey a sense of the beautiful and the sublime, and the roles of technique and genius in the creation of art. Alison even offered comments on "the two great varieties of complexion, the fair and the dark" (342) and connected dark ones with melancholy dispositions, fair ones with cheerful outlooks, supporting his observation with the remark that "professors of medical science" had ascertained the connection.

Although we cannot document Hawthorne's response to any particular passage, it seems likely that Alison's remarks about colors, light, shade, and their effects on the emotions confirmed Hawthorne's conviction that Spenser, Milton, Bunyan, and Scott knew precisely what they were doing when they made literary use of color and light and shade to stir the emotions. As Hawthorne's own writing suggests, he must have taken to heart such words as these:

> I must satisfy myself . . . with observing in general, that in all the fine arts, that composition is most excellent in which the different parts most fully unite in the production of one unmingled emotion, and that taste is most perfect where the perception of this relation of objects, in point of expression, is most delicate and precise. (Alison: 106)

Hawthorne's commitment to this ideal of aesthetic unity is evident throughout his work but nowhere more poignantly than in his struggle to impose coherence on his unfinished romances.

Hutcheson's inquiry (much shorter than Alison's) had tighter philosophical knots to unravel: Is beauty an idea occupying a realm of pure form? Is beauty absolute or relative and comparative? Does beauty depend on the mind of the perceiver? What is the relation between beauty and moral goodness? How does the perception of beauty give pleasure to the beholder? What is the role of the senses in apprehending beauty? Reluctant as he was to enter into theological discussions, Hawthorne probably felt uneasy about Hutcheson's attempts to ascribe man's sense of beauty to general laws given by a deity, though he no doubt was pleased to find that Hutcheson confirmed his belief that beauty and moral goodness are linked. Potentially more useful to Hawthorne were Hutcheson's occasional ventures into practical criticism, especially his remark about the superiority of well-written history to a dull collection of gazettes:

> The superior pleasure of history . . . must arise . . . when we see a character well drawn wherein we find the secret causes of a great diversity of seemingly inconsistent actions, or an interest

of state laid open, or an artful view nicely unfolded. . . . Now
this reduces the whole to an unity of design at least; and this
may be observed in the very fables which entertain children,
otherwise we cannot make them relish them. (Hutcheson: 78)

But whether or not that observation about unity of design provided a
hint for the unifying devices Hawthorne later developed for *Biographical
Stories for Children* and *Grandfather's Chair,* one such device—his use of a
chair with a carved lion's head as its outstanding feature—enables
Grandfather to engage and hold the attention of children as he tells
stories about colonial America.

Hawthorne also read Edmund Burke and Washington Allston on the
nature of the sublime. But he cared less for Burke's conception than he
did those of Allston and Alison, feeling obviously uncomfortable with
Burke's emphasis on the infinite, the grand, the terrible, the high and
lofty. Hawthorne's "distrust of emotion uncritically experienced" and
skepticism about theories in general help to explain his stance (Levy,
"The Landscape Modes of *The Scarlet Letter,*" 392). Given a choice,
Hawthorne probably would have much preferred Niagara Falls to rock
slides in the White Mountains, if "My Visit to Niagara" can be taken as
more representative of the tenor of his tastes than "The Ambitious
Guest," a tale set in the White Mountains.

As Hawthorne read and weighed these philosophical treatises, he also
continued to glean theories about art and facts about artists from the
many magazines, travel accounts, and encyclopedias he checked out
from the Salem Athenaeum. Those gleanings are relatively easy to trace.
For example, William Dunlap's *A History of the Rise and Progress of the
Arts of Design in the United States* contained the germ of "The Prophetic
Pictures" and supplied him with facts about Benjamin West and
hundreds of other American artists. Hawthorne evidently learned about
Dunlap's book from a review of it in the *North American Review* (vol. 41),
charged from the Salem Athenaeum on 9 March 1836. On that same day
and again on 21 May, he borrowed Dunlap's history (Kesselring 43, 58).
And a review of Alison's essays in volume 12 of *Blackwood's* (charged on
9 May 1827) led Hawthorne to Alison's book a few months later (7
August 1827).

What cannot be fully ascertained is how much information he stored
away or what impressions he might have formed about artists, critics,
and art theory. If he had read everything on the visual arts in the books
and journals charged on his aunt Mary Manning's card, he could have
acquired a wealth of facts, lore, ideas, and opinions, ranging from the
bare statement that the Parisian dyemaker Giles Gobelin had discovered
"the secret of dyeing that beautiful scarlet color that is named after him"
to a hundred-and-two page article on engravers in the Low Countries.

Perhaps the Gobelin entry in Abraham Rees's *Cyclopaedia; or Universal Dictionary of Arts, Sciences, and Literature* (1810-42) paid dividends when Hawthorne identified the tapestry of David and Bathsheba in Dimmesdale's room as a Gobelin (I: 126). Although he said nothing about the colors of that tapestry, it is tempting to imagine Bathsheba garbed in Gobelin scarlet, and perhaps David as well.

But almost certainly one seed for "The Artist of the Beautiful" (1844) came from the life of David Rittenhouse as recorded in Jared Sparks's *The Library of American Biography*, checked out in 1837. Here Hawthorne read that Rittenhouse, eventually much celebrated for his achievements in mathematics and astronomy, had worked as a clockmaker, applying himself so unremittingly to his trade that his health failed, and, for a time, he had to abandon his work. But once he returned to his shop, he began to perfect his mechanical skills, despite discouragement from his family, ultimately acquiring fame for his craftsmanship. "This reputation was spread abroad by the numerous highly-finished pieces of mechanism which issued from his workshop, bearing the maker's name inscribed upon their dials" (Sparks 322). It seems likely that Rittenhouse's role as a clockmaker, his decision to oppose his family's wishes, his assiduous dedication to his craft, his illness, and his return to his shop after his recovery lingered in Hawthorne's mind and helped him conceive a few of the traits and activities of Owen Warland when he wrote "The Artist of the Beautiful."

More broadly, Hawthorne's allusions to artists, anecdotes about them, and his references to specific artworks suggest a fairly wide and attentive perusal of information on the visual arts in the books and journals he read. Considerable reading underlies such a sketch as "A Virtuoso's Collection," in which he mentions Lyssipus, Apelles, Claude, Horatio Greenough, Thomas Crawford, Hiram Powers, and Washington Allston. Although Plutarch and Pliny surely provided information about the first two artists and he learned of the others from modern books, journals, and newspapers, as well as conversations with friends, he encountered a wide range of information as he turned the pages of books and journals borrowed from the Salem Athenaeum. In the more than one hundred volumes of *The Gentleman's Magazine* that he had an opportunity to peruse, he could have read everything from notes on mathematical rules for drawing in perspective to reviews of histories of art and new painting exhibitions in London. Volume 20 of *The Gentleman's Magazine* offered "a chronological list of eminent painters" under five headings—"Masters, Disciples of, Liv'd at. Excell'd at, Died," just the sort of thing either a dilettante or a serious beginning student of art would find useful. Other volumes included a series of engravings based on curiosities found in the ruins of Herculaneum, among them Greek paintings depicting winged boys, bare-breasted women, and mythological figures (vols. 44, 45, 47), and an engraving of Niagara Falls in volume 21, probably one of the images he tried to suppress when trying to apprehend Niagara as though he had not been exposed to artistic renderings of it (XI: 284).

For all of its variety, *The Gentleman's Magazine* was not as thoroughgoing in its attention to the visual arts as other British periodicals Hawthorne read—the *Edinburgh Review,* the *Westminster Review,* and especially the *Modern Monthly.* *Blackwood's* included technical discussions of lithography and fresco painting, lively exchanges on theories of the picturesque, lectures on George Cruickshank's art and the state of the arts in America, and remarks on Francis Chantrey's statue of General Washington, a work Hawthorne later described in the pages of the *American Magazine of Useful and Entertaining Knowledge* (Turner, *Hawthorne as Editor,* 137-38). *Blackwood's* also carried a review of Moritz Retzsch's *Eight Outlines to Schiller's Fridolin; or, An Errand to the Iron Foundry.* If Hawthorne read the piece, he knew of Retzsch's work before he met and married one of Retzsch's most ardent admirers and imitators, Sophia Peabody. Perhaps he saw Retzsch's drawings for the first time during his courtship of Sophia. However he came to know them, he alluded to them graphically when he was working as a coal measurer at the Boston Custom House and described for Sophia "the blackfaced demons in the vessel's hold, (they look like the forgemen in Retsch's Fridolin)" (XV: 296).

Among the long essays that Hawthorne might have read in the *Edinburgh Review* were discourses on Sir Charles Bell's *Essays on the Anatomy of Expression in Painting* and Alison's *Essays on the Nature and Principles of Taste.* As a physiologist, Bell explained how muscle movement helped to express such passions as grief and joy,[2] drawing on LeBrun's personification of the passions to demonstrate how painters must pay heed to muscular behavior to depict human passions accurately and perhaps influencing him to make literary uses of gestures and other forms of body language in an early masterpiece like "My Kinsman, Major Molineux" (1828) or in a late one like *The Marble Faun* (1860). In these and many other works Hawthorne depended on gestures, gazes, facial expressions, and the willingness or unwillingness to touch to express attitudes and feelings that words alone could not convey. And the *Edinburgh* reviewer's praise of Alison's book as "the best and most pleasing work which has yet been produced on the subject of Taste and Beauty" (vol. 18, 1) probably caught Hawthorne's eye, especially since he had sought out the book after reading a *Blackwood's* review of it (9 May 1827). But all twenty-eight volumes of the *Edinburgh Review* provided rich fare on the visual arts: reviews of John Knowles's *The Life and Works of Henry Fuseli,* D. E. Williams's *The Life and Correspondence of Sir Thomas Lawrence,* and Allen Cunningham's *The Lives of the Most Eminent British Painters, Sculptors, and Architects;* essays on England's need for a public gallery worthy of the name of a national museum; and pieces on the state of contemporary English galleries.

Rich and varied as *Blackwood's,* the *Westminster Review,* and the *Edinburgh Review* were in items on the visual arts, those in the *Monthly Magazine* were livelier. From February 1831 to July 1838, Hawthorne evidently perused twenty volumes of this readable miscellany. Here appeared critical coverage of exhibitions of new paintings as well as dioramas and cosmoramas, the latter an exhibition of various views of the world made to appear realistic by the use of mirrors, lenses, and lights. Here were letters from a correspondent identified as A.B.C., who offered remarks on North American painters and paintings, including the work of Allston and Thomas Doughty, both mentors of Sophia. The *Monthly Magazine* also published reviews of keepsakes and annuals and commented on their engravings (or "embellishments," as Victorians called them). Its pages also included clear and forceful espousals of contemporary aesthetic standards, standards Hawthorne himself would endorse:

> The common *dictum* of the modern artist is, that the utmost development of the human figure is not indelicate; or that those to whom it is such, have the indelicacy in their own minds. But we know the fact is quite on the opposite side; that a totally undraped statue, whose purpose is to resemble as closely as possible a totally undraped male or female, is offensive in the degree of innocence and modesty of the looker-on; that the young and pure-minded must feel the unfitness of the display. . . . The unquestionable fact is, that by our habits and style of education . . . nudity is indecency whether in the living form, the picture, or the statue. (vol. V, n.s. 646)

Hawthorne also encountered comments on the visual arts in several of the travel books he read, among them Zachariah Allen's *The Practical Tourist; or Sketches of the State of the Useful Arts, and of Society, Scenery, etc. in Great Britain, France and Holland* (a work charged to Hawthorne twice in 1834 and twice again in 1836), and Joseph Forsyth's *Remarks on the Antiquities, Arts and Letters, During an Excursion to Italy in the Years 1802 and 1803* (charged 27 March 1827). Allen described cathedrals, college buildings, dioramas, and ruins, and explained the techniques of glassmaking, lithography, and painting on porcelain. Forsyth, who had rambled across much of Italy and stopped at cathedrals, palaces, and famous buildings, energetically voiced his likes and dislikes and shared his critical theories. For example, he derided Italian artists' display of their mistresses, "who impudently court your remark" (28), and he criticized colored statues, proclaiming that "a statue should be of one colour. That colour, too seems the best, which least suggests any idea of colour, and is freest from any gloss or radiance that may tend to shed false light, and confuse vision" (5). Hawthorne was to voice a similar opinion when he saw the colored statues of John Gibson in Rome in 1858 (XIV: 157). Forsyth's confession of fatigue and satiety sound prophetically like Hawthorne's responses to the numerous churches and galleries Sophia wanted him to see during their tour of Italy:

> We make the tour of Italy, as we make the circuit of a gallery. We set out determined to let nothing escape us unexamined, and thus we waste our attention, while it is fresh, on the first objects, which are not generally the best. On advancing we are dazzled with excellence, and fatigued with admiration. We can take, however, but a certain dose of this pleasure at a time, and at length, when the eye is saturated with pictures, we begin to long for the conclusion, and we run through the last room with a rapid glance. (Forsyth: 319)

On similar occasions, Hawthorne would hasten to the streets of Rome, Florence, or Paris and cry out for whitewash to cover some faded fresco, his receptive faculty "fatigued with admiration."

Allen and Forsyth undoubtedly alerted Hawthorne to the value of travel writing as a guide to paintings, statues, cathedrals, and palaces. They prepared him to read such a travel writer as Anna Brownell Jameson, whose work later gave him "great pleasure and profit" (XIV: 200). They also helped him to appreciate the travel books of friends and fellow countrymen, particularly George Hillard's *Six Months in Italy* (1853) and William Ellery Channing's *Conversations in Rome, Between an Artist, a Catholic, and a Critic* (1847).

Even a cursory survey of Hawthorne's reading of books and journals suggests how broadly and deeply Hawthorne could have educated himself in the visual arts had he read everything available to him. Apparently, he followed no concerted plan for such self-education, reading, instead, as his interests or needs led him. A programmatic approach surely would have led him to work his way through available volumes of Rees's *The Cyclopaedia*, where a comprehensive coverage of painters, sculptors, engravers, and architects could have served as a makeshift textbook.

Yet he did not have to rely solely on the resources of the Athenaeum for such knowledge. Information on art and artists appeared regularly in the giftbooks and magazines to which he contributed in the 1830s and 1840s. Giftbooks sometimes featured brief biographies of artists and appreciations of paintings and statues, and most of them took pride in their ten or more illustrations or "embellishments." In the issues of *The Token* or the combined *The Token and Atlantic Souvenir* where his tales appeared, Hawthorne could see dozens of postcard-size engravings of paintings by English and American artists, including Sir Joshua Reynolds, Sir Thomas Lawrence, Sir Edwin Landseer, Washington Allston, George Loring Brown, and Thomas Cole. The quality of the engravings was often good, especially those by John Neagle, John Cheney, and Joseph Andrews. But as their titles suggest, most of the embellishments were dreary hackwork designed to illustrate some sentimental poem or to portray some domestic scene typical of Victorian family life: "The Cottage Girl," "The Lost Boy," "Just Seventeen," "The Toilet," "The Dead Soldier," "The Bridesmaid," "I Went to Gather Flowers," and "The Only Daughter." The occasional land-scapes and urban scenes were drab and poor cousins to Currier and Ives prints. In short, few of these embellishments would have helped develop a sophisticated taste for art, though some were minor master-pieces, such as John Neagle's engraving of his own *Pat Lyon at the Forge*, which appeared in the *Atlantic Souvenir* in 1832.

Occasionally an American magazine might include a provocative statement about art by a contemporary artist, such as when Thomas Cole's "Essay on American Scenery" appeared in *The American Monthly Magazine* in January 1836, a month before the same magazine published Hawthorne's "Old Ticonderoga." Emphasizing a dictum that Haw-thorne had already encountered in his readings of the Scottish aestheti-cians, Cole proclaimed that sublime painting and poetry afford fore-tastes of immortality and that the human mind perceives clear and lasting bonds between the good and the beautiful.

When in 1836 Hawthorne left his solitary life as a storyteller for magazines and giftbooks to spend almost eight months as editor of the *American Magazine of Useful and Entertaining Knowledge*, he became directly connected with the period's commercial engraving of high and low art. His chief function for the Bewick Company, a publishing and engraving firm, was writing copy to accompany engravings done for Bewick by various artists, a task that required access to a good library. But his employers refused to buy him the membership in the Boston Athenaeum that would facilitate finding information for commentaries on the illustrations he was instructed to use. Because of their tight-handedness, Hawthorne considered his employers "a damned sneaking set" (XV: 234). When, in disgust, he resigned his post, he expressed his regret that he lacked a veto over some of the engravings he had been forced to use, arguing that "his taste and judgment would inevitably be held responsible" (Turner, *Hawthorne as Editor*, 224). Such a statement pointedly suggests a conviction that he had made some progress in developing aesthetic standards.

But both that "taste and judgment" continued to expand as he saw paintings, sketches, and statues by European and American artists in the Athenaeum and read reviews of the annual Athenaeum exhibits in *The North American Review*. In the exhibit of 1836, the year Hawthorne moved to Boston to begin his editorial hackwork, 169 paintings and 13 miniatures awaited his "spiritual possession," many of them by American artists: Thomas Birch, Washington Blanchard, George Loring Brown, John Singleton Copley, Thomas Doughty, G.P.A. Healy, John Neagle, Robert Salmon, Cephas Thompson, and John Trumbull. Among the foreign artists whose works were on exhibit were Nicholas Berchim, Annibale Carracci, Pannini, Rembrandt, Ribera, Romanelli, Rubens, Snyders, and Watteau (Perkins and Gavin 3). This exhibit, like the ones before and after it, also included statues (most of them copies of renowned pieces), as well as prints and sketches, and the exhibition catalogues contained not only descriptions of displayed works but biographical notes. Evidently nothing in the 1836 exhibition oppressed him as heavily as a work shown the following year, an etching by Giovanni Vendramini of Guido Reni's *Judith with the Head of Holofernes*. When he saw the original in Italy more than twenty years later, Hawthorne confided that the copy "used to weary me to death, year after year, in the Boston Athenaeum" (XIV: 218).

If his duties as co-compiler of a geography for the Peter Parley series imposed upon him the task of finding suitable engravings for the text, his editorial duties for Bewick forced him not only to rummage among books, newspapers, and magazines for copy but also to look at scores of illustrations he would then describe as he passed judgment on the artist and his work. His comments on an engraving of Sir Francis Chantrey's statue of George Washington reveal Hawthorne's working methods. He scouted out facts about the work, briefly described it, and reported where it could be seen. In this case, he went beyond a description of Chantrey's drapery to remark on Antonio Canova's presentation of Washington in Roman garb for a statue recently destroyed in a fire at the capitol building in Raleigh, North Carolina. Foreshadowing a stand he would take in Italy, Hawthorne argued that, instead of Roman military dress, Canova might have given Washington "the garb of an Indian Chief" because that "would have been quite as graceful, and more appropriate to the American warrior." Chantrey, however, "while clothing the statue in the Revolutionary uniform, has taken advantage of the voluminous folds of the cloak, to give the figure of Washington a classic grace and dignity, and to hide all those details which, as belonging to a fashion so recently passed away, might excite ludicrous emotions in the spectator" (Turner, *Hawthorne as Editor*, 138).

Working as a commentator and critic for an engraving company brought Hawthorne into one of the outer circles of art and drew his attention to the ways in which artists and publishers were feeding an

American hunger for images to display in homes and schools. Like a hack poet hired to write a poem to accompany an engraving in an annual or giftbook, Hawthorne provided commentary for the portrait of Washington done by Alonzo Hartwell, an engraver at the Boston Bewick Company. Hawthorne was not content merely to describe the engraving, which showed Washington among a cluster of military emblems, but plunged ahead and proved himself a true son of his emblem-loving forebears:

> If, therefore, they could have been visible amid the war-smoke and the thunder-cloud, the artist would have mingled tokens of the peaceful virtues, and the statesman's calmer wisdom, with those heroic emblems. A canopy of state, to represent his civil sway—a horn of plenty , scattering its abundance on the soil—a written scroll, to denote the power of his pen—a Bible, to point out his trust, in doubt and danger—a bounteous harvest-field, instead of warriors and steeds, and a wintry river—all these might have been seen around the bust of Washington. In our pride of country, let it be the proudest thought, that America, in the very struggle that brought her into existence as a nation, gave to history the purest and loftiest name that ever shone among its pages. (In Turner, *Hawthorne as Editor*, 20)

These remarks foreshadow Hawthorne's later cooperative efforts with his wife and the engraver Hammatt Billing to choose illustrations for his tales and children's stories.[3] That short tenure as editor of a magazine, disappointing as it was on financial and other scores, provided worthwhile experiences for a developing writer. Writing verbal complements to engravings forced Hawthorne to study them closely and to learn something about artistic conventions. Frustrating as the editorship proved to be, it nonetheless marks a significant phase in Hawhorne's ability to understand and use the visual arts. From this point on, creating an emblematic scene, suggesting the iconicity of an art object, or presenting a tableau would be less of a challenge than before.

Closer ties to Boston's and Salem's advocates of art lay ahead for Hawthorne. One evening in the fall of 1837, in response to Elizabeth Peabody's invitation, the two Hawthorne sisters appeared at the Peabody house on Salem's Charter Street, their brother squiring them. Elizabeth later recalled that night (11 November 1837) for her nephew Julian Hawthorne:

> A great ring came at the front door. I opened it, and there stood your father in all the splendor of his young beauty, and a hooded figure hanging on each arm. . . . I greeted them, [and] hurried to explain the pile of books. They had not seen them before, and expressed interest. "You do not say, I am going to

have the pleasure of introducing you to Flaxman, the modern ancient! and on this I opened the Illustrations of the Iliad, and they all drew up their chairs to the table, and we were all at ease at once, and we looked over the whole five volumes, and talked of Homer and Hesiod, Aeschylus and Dante, with all of whom they were perfectly at home." (In Pearson, 262-63)

But Elizabeth did more than turn the pages of the Flaxman volumes with the Hawthornes. She spoke of her younger sister, Sophia, whose headache had kept her in her room, and told her guests that Sophia was busy copying Flaxman's outlines as part of her program of developing her own artistic talents, nurtured over the years by lessons from Thomas Doughty and by copying the work of such artists as Washington Allston and Robert Salmon (a British artist then gaining respect in Boston for his seascapes).

Hawthorne was soon to meet Sophia, quick to fall in love with her, and perhaps flattered that Sophia passed along Emerson's compliment of his "inspired criticism" of Washington Allston's *Dead Man Restored to Life:* "'the sentence of a Seer,'" Emerson had said when they had discussed Hawthorne's response to Allston's painting, a remark Sophia considered "'immense praise.'" Hawthorne in turn was to praise her work when, soon after, she presented him with an illustration of the Quaker lad in "The Gentle Boy" and asked, "'I want to know if this looks like your Ilbrahim?' He sat down and looked at it and then looked up and said, 'He will never look otherwise to me'" (In Pearson, 267).

Nothing short of a separate publication of the tale with Sophia's Flaxmanesque and Retzschian drawing would satisfy Hawthorne, who arranged with Weeks, Jordan and Company in Boston and Wiley and Putnam in New York to publish it. The tale was advertised as in press in late December 1838 by the Boston *Daily Evening Transcript*, which also reported its appearance on 2 January 1839. But there had been problems getting an acceptable engraving from the Hingham-born engraver Joseph Andrews, and a few review copies with Andrews's "distorted" engraving had been sent out, to Sophia's chagrin. Washington Allston and Hawthorne stepped in. A review published 19 January 1839 in the *Christian Register and Boston Observer* by A, presumably Allston, identified the main problems: "We have left ourselves hardly room to speak of the engraving: in which Andrews has done beautiful justice to the original drawing, except [to] the face of the boy, which in the drawing was so pathetic and beautiful, we did not believe we could ever see it again. We are glad to learn however that this portion is to be retouched." The engraving was retouched and a new plate printed after Sophia told Andrews what changes she required. A letter to her father (Wednesday January 1839, MS, Berg Collection, NYPL) spells out Andrews's "unwarrantable liberties": the position of the eyes changed, the brow darkened, the corners of the mouth turned down and not curved, the under lip enlarged, the chin indicated. But even after the second engraving was completed, Hawthorne struck a defensive attitude in his preface. Speaking of Sophia's drawing, Hawthorne wrote: "The original sketch of the Puritan and the Gentle Boy, an engraving of which now accompanies the Tale, has received—what the artist may well deem her utmost attainable recompense—the warm recommendation of the first painter in the world." Not content to defend Sophia's talents by citing Allston's endorsement, Hawthorne gave his own opinion: "If, after so high a meed, the Author might add his own humble praise, he would say, that whatever of beauty and pathos he had conceived, but could not shadow forth in language, have been caught and embodied in the few and simple lines of this sketch (IX: 568). Obviously still smarting for Sophia and wishing to protect her artistic reputation, Hawthorne did not send copies of the tale to his closest friends, at least not to J. L. O'Sullivan: "I did not send you The Gentle Boy, because the engraving did no sort of justice to the original sketch" (XV: 314).

Even as Hawthorne cited Allston's words of praise for Sophia, Boston was preparing to honor Allston by mounting an exhibit of dozens of his paintings. Because Boston had an active artistic tradition, dating back to John Smibert's studio in the 1730s and John Singleton Copley's career in the 1760s and 1770s, the exhibition of Allston's celebrated works was an event that few cultured Bostonians would miss. Among the literati who attended the show were Margaret Fuller, Oliver Wendell Holmes, and Elizabeth Peabody, all of whom wrote descriptions and sensitive criticism of the paintings.[4] Hawthorne went too, both with Sophia and alone. But unlike Holmes, Margaret Fuller, or his future sister-in-law, he recorded no responses to the paintings he saw there, among them *Beatrice, Florimel, Jessica and Lorenzo Listening, Moonlight Landscape, The Dead Man Restored to Life, The Head of Peter*, and *The Massacre of the Innocents*. Perhaps he remained silent because he was struggling to assimilate the more developed tastes of the Peabodys and their artistic friends. Just how far he had cast Sophia in the role of mentor can be seen in his remark about a later visit (11 June 1840) to the Athenaeum Gallery: "I cannot see pictures without thee; so thou must not expect me to criticize this exhibition. There are two pictures there by our friend (thy friend—and is it not the same thing?) Sarah Clark—scenes in Kentucky. Doubtless I shall find them very admirable, when we have looked at them together" (XV: 472-73).[5]

Though a lover's compliment lies behind these words, Hawthorne was willing to learn about painting and sculpture from Sophia and eager to hang her work in the bachelor's quarters he rented from the Hillards while working in the Boston Custom House. "You cannot think how much delight those pictures are going to give me" he said. "I shall sit and gaze at them whole hours together—and these will be my happiest hours" (XV: 397). He kept his promise: when the paintings arrived on 24 January 1840, he "sat a long time before them with clasped hands, gazing, and gazing, and gazing, and painting a facsimile of them in [his] heart, in whose most sacred chamber they shall keep a place forever and ever" (XV: 401).

The source of his joy and pride was a pair of paintings done in the manner of Thomas Doughty and named the *Isola* and the *Menaggio*, apparently for Isola Bella in Lake Maggiore, near Como, and the resort of Menaggio. The *Isola* shows a solitary female figure in the foreground, her back to the viewer, leading Hawthorne to sigh, "How I wish that naughty Sophie Hawthorne could be induced to turn her face towards me! Nevertheless, the figure is her veritable self" (XV: 414). The *Menaggio* depicted both Sophia and Hawthorne standing on a bridge. Of himself as a figure in his beloved's landscape, Hawthorne said, "It is not my picture, but the very I; and as my inner self belongs to you, there is no doubt that you have caused my soul to pervade the figure." His comments on the two of them as caught by her hand end in a Keatsian reflection: "There we are, unchangeable. Years cannot alter us, nor our relation to each other" (XV: 402).

These words came from a lover, not an art critic, but they do reveal an aesthetic standard dear to Hawthorne's heart: art should enable the artist to open an intercourse with humanity, and that meant finding an art expressive of the spirit, not merely designed to capture surfaces. These words also show that Hawthorne and Sophia had formed a bond of spirit and heart that justified them, more than thirty months before they exchanged marriage vows, in considering themselves husband and wife. Gazing at these pictures, the first two he ever owned, and viewing them under different conditions of light and from behind veils (to protect them from coal smoke), Hawthorne revealed himself to be a man who sought more from art than mere decoration.[6] He wanted to display only works of art that expressed ideas, emotions, and values important to him and Sophia, a point made in a letter to her a few months later (2 June 1840): "Dearest, I have bought some lithographic prints at auction. . . . Thou art not to expect anything very splendid. . . . Perhaps there are one or two not altogether unworthy to be put on the walls of our sanctuary; but this I leave to thy finer judgment" (XV: 470). More than the display of good taste was on Hawthorne's mind. He shared with Sophia the belief that artworks displayed in a home expressed spiritual and philosophic values as well as aesthetic ones, a principle he would carry into his fiction, notably *The House of the Seven Gables*.

Even as he deferred to her "finer judgment," Hawthorne continued to prove himself an apt student, drawing upon their common stock of knowledge to help Sophia visualize his job as a coal measurer: "[Y]our image will flit around me while I am measuring coal, and will peep over my shoulder to see whether I keep a correct account, and will smile to hear my bickerings with the black-faced demons in the vessel's hold, (they look like the forgemen in Retsch's Fridolin) and will soothe and mollify me amid all the pester and plague that is in store for me tomorrow" (XV: 296).

As a writer wanting to put something of his before the public, he had practical needs of Sophia's skill in art and requested from her some caricatures for an edition of *Grandfather's Chair* being readied for the press as he prepared to settle among the utopians at Brook Farm. He wrote her to ask "whether thou hast drawn those caricatures—especially the one of thy husband, staggering, and puffing, and toiling onward to the gate of the farm, burthened with the unsaleable remnant of Grandfather's Chair. Dear us, what a ponderous, leaden load it will be!" (XV: 505). Unhappily, Sophia seems not to have rendered this updated version of Christian trudging off to another version of Vanity Fair. Instead of caricatures, she evidently did only an illustration of Lady Arabella sinking into the great chair after looking from a window at Boston's wilderness.

Meanwhile, during their long courtship, while Hawthorne completed a sketch of Benjamin West for his *Biographical Stories for Children*, they continued to visit art exhibits together, they wondered about a new way of catching glimpses of the soul through sunlight—the daguerreotype (see XV: 354)—, they received prints from Emerson for their future home,[7] and they planned what sketches Sophia would do as illustrations for *Grandfather's Chair*.

The most detailed instruction to his beloved collaborator concerns his suggestion for the sketch of Master Cheever, the schoolteacher who comes into possession of grandfather's chair for a time. Hawthorne's notions for the sketch closely resemble the sentimental engravings that appeared in books and magazines of the time, especially the giftbooks:

> Belovedest, Master Cheever is a very good subject for a sketch—especially if thou doest portray him in the very act of executing judgment on an evil-doer. The little urchin may be laid across his knee, and his arms and legs (and whole person, indeed) should be flying all abroad, in an agony of nervous excitement and corporeal smart. The Master, on the other hand, must be calm, rigid, without anger or pity, the very personification of that unmitigable law, whereby suffering follows sin. Meantime, the lion's head [on the chair] should have a sort of sly twist of one side of its mouth, and wink of one eye, in order to give the impression, that, after all, the crime and the punishment are neither of them the most serious things in the world. I would draw this sketch myself, if I had but the use of thy magic

fingers. Why dost thou—being one and the same person with thy husband—unjustly keep those delicate little instruments (thy fingers, to wit) all to thyself? (XV: 569-70)

His other suggestions, given with fewer details for composition, nonetheless emphasize a preference for pictorial richness and detailed historical accuracy rather than the spare lines of Sophia's favorite models, Retzsch and Flaxman. He wanted a scene of the Acadians landing, one of Cotton Mather walking the streets of Boston, one of a military council held by the Earl of Loudon in Boston, and, finally, one of the Liberty Tree. To help her render those last two scenes, he advised her to look at the military customs of Louis XV's time and to consult Caleb Snow's *History of Boston*.

Though she did complete a sketch of Master Cheever's schoolroom, Sophia chose other subjects for the few other sketches she found time to do: grandfather's chair and Lady Arabella seated in that chair and surrounded by children. These three sketches appeared in the volume entitled *Historical Tales for Youth*, a reissue of earlier works containing *Grandfather's Chair*, *Famous Old People*, *Liberty Tree*, and *Biographical Stories*, and published in April or May 1842, shortly before Hawthorne and Sophia became partners for life and moved to the Old Manse. In his requests for illustrations drawing upon New England's history, we once again see Hawthorne's desire to be accurate and densely realistic, to be more like Gerard Dou than John Flaxman.

In decorating Hawthorne's study at the Old Manse, Sophia sought to please her husband. She reported to her mother, "I have hung on his walls the two Lake Como and the Loch Lomond pictures, all of which I painted expressly for him. . . . On one of the secretaries stands the lovely Ceres, and opposite it Margaret Fuller's bronze vase" (Lathrop 185). Other rooms also received a special touch from Sophia's artistic hand, notably the bedroom, which Mrs. Julia Howe and F. B. Sanborn saw during a social call at the Old Manse: "Mrs. Hawthorne kindly showed us the bedroom furniture which she had adorned with pen and ink drawings. At the foot of her bed were Thorwaldsen's Night and Morning. On the washstand was outlined Venus rising from the sea, from Flaxman's illustrations of Homer" (Sanborn 41). This witty transfer of a classic scene to the marital lavatory shows that Hawthorne's bride had her share of quiet humor.

But art was to be taken seriously, too, not only because it was a rewarding intellectual and creative outlet for both Hawthornes but also because the sale of one of Sophia's original pieces or a copy of a famous painter's work could bring in much needed cash. One of the original pieces she hoped to place on the market for "one hundred dollars independently of the frame" was *Endymion* (1844), "a picture in pale brown monochromes." Sophia did not want to part with it: "I shall be glad some day to redeem it, for it has come out of my soul." *Endymion* symbolized her blissful life with Hawthorne; she therefore felt a terrible wrenching when she wrote her mother about selling it: "For Endymion, I must look upon a small bit of gold" (Lathrop 72); but she could have spared herself the anguish, for when Elizabeth Peabody tried to find a buyer for it, Hawthorne intervened and refused to let the painting go. *Endymion* eventually was accorded a proud place over the center table in the drawing room of the Little Red House in Lenox (Julian Hawthorne, *Hawthorne and His Wife,* I: 369). Hawthorne had clearly taken "spiritual possession" of it and was discovering in Sophia's devotion to her art some of the traits he would later give Hilda in *The Marble Faun.* Through her Endymion, a figure of eternal youth, Sophia paid tribute to the masters of art that she so deeply admired. But in the Old Manse where Hawthorne had created "The New Adam and Eve," Sophia was also celebrating her own Adam.

When lack of money and loss of their lease finally forced them to give up their (essentially) Edenic life at the Old Manse, Hawthorne accepted the post as custom house surveyor in Salem. Caring for two small children and trying to brighten the lives of Hawthorne's mother and sisters, who occupied a separate apartment in their Mall Street home, left Sophia little time for her easel and brushes, but she and her husband were intent on giving both Una and Julian a chance to appreciate art. Una had already progressed so far that she seemed to recognize most of the numerous prints, statues, and original works in the Hawthorne household. To encourage further development, the Hawthornes acquired a copy of Flaxman's drawings and prints by other artists, and one January afternoon, free of his duties at the Custom House, Hawthorne sat looking at artworks with Una and Julian and recorded this little cultural enrichment scene in his notebook:

> Julian and Una are looking at drawings and engravings. . . . He criticizes them to his mother: one is too sad for his taste; "but dis booful little picture is not sad." "Oh, I see a horse running so fast!" "That is a 'teeple, and that a house." . . . "What's that crying for his father?," asks he, looking at a picture of a widow and her son. "Oh, see de booful little boy!" cries he, of the picture of a boy by Sir Thomas Lawrence. . . . Nothing escapes him in the picture. He brings me Flaxman's drawing of Juno and Minerva going to assist the Greeks, in a car, drawn through the celestial regions by two horses; and calls it "Horses running so hard to get to the barn." . . . This scene ends with a squabble between the two children for the possession of a book. (VIII: 416)

Obviously the Hawthornes thought that looking at art books as well as art objects on the walls or pieces of furniture would help the children appreciate art. But books alone would not do: they had them begin sketching lessons as they grew older and took them later to the Manchester Exhibition and to dozens of places in Italy to see both celebrated and uncelebrated pieces of art.

Even as Hawthorne enjoyed helping to collect and display a small personal collection of art, including original pieces by Sophia, he was reading about art and artists. His reading involved an act of friendship and a return to the subject of art history. In the winter of 1847, one of the works he read in manuscript was his friend William Ellery Channing's *Conversations in Rome, Between an Artist, a Catholic, and a Critic,* hoping to help Channing find a publisher. Hawthorne wrote Evert A. Duyckinck that the work seemed "to contain higher and better criticism than I have before met with, on the same subjects" (XVI: 204). Since Channing's numerous subjects include church architecture, statuary, celebrated paintings and painters, galleries and museums, and theories of appreciating art and architecture, Hawthorne was laying claim to a fair amount of knowledge about the visual arts in praising the manuscript, which the Boston firm of William Crosby and H. P. Nichols published later that same year. Channing's conversational technique enabled Hawthorne to weigh varied opinions about such old masters as Claude, Guido, Raphael, Guercino, Leonardo da Vinci, Titian, Salvator Rosa, Veronese, and Michelangelo. And urging the value of viewing ancient sculpture, Channing said, "If we study the Venus, the Fawn, and Antinous, we add to our learning; let those who will include that hymn of pain, the Niobe, and Laocoon" (Channing 90). Years later Hawthorne would stand thoughtfully before these statues in Rome. But while he still waited for some spark to set him going creatively, in the late spring and summer of 1848 he read John Ruskin's *Modern Painters* and Charles Lester's *The Artists of America,* and soon after completing *The Scarlet Letter* he took up Henry Lodge's translation of Johann Joachim Winckelmann's *The History of Ancient Art* (Kesselring 55, 60, 64). Perhaps he was preparing to help Sophia educate their children or anticipating the time they could all go to Europe and see great masterworks together. Or perhaps he was stocking his imagination while awaiting the time his writing career would resume. In any case, his willingness to evaluate Channing's manuscript and his conclusion that it contained "higher and better criticism" than he had encountered before show more than a little confidence in his progress toward cultural enrichment.

His return to fiction came unexpectedly when he was "turned out of office" at the Salem Custom House (early June 1849). He took up his pen, wrote *The Scarlet Letter,* and became a famous man, one whose portrait was in demand not only by the publisher, Ticknor and Fields, but also by editors of magazines and newspapers. Therefore his publisher commissioned Cephas Giovanni Thompson, whose many successful portraits included one of William Cullen Bryant (VIII: 491). This was to be Hawthorne's fourth portrait, earlier ones having been completed by Charles Osgood in 1840, by Eastman Johnson in 1846, and an unknown miniaturist before Hawthorne left for Brook Farm (VIII: 661-62; Gollin, *Portraits*, 19-24, 29-35).

In Thompson's studio, Hawthorne enjoyed the company and work of another creative person:

> An artist's apartment is always very interesting to me, with its pictures, finished and unfinished; its little fancies in the pictorial way, as here two pictures of children, among flowers and foliage, representing Spring and Summer—Winter and Autumn being yet to come out of the artist's mind; the portraits, of his wife and children, not beautiful subjects, but perhaps appearing so to him; here a clergyman, there a poet; here a woman, with the stamp of reality upon her; there a feminine conception, which we feel not to have existed. There was an infant Christ, or rather a child-Christ, not unbeautiful, but scarcely divine. I love the odor of paint in an artist's room; his palette and all his other tools have a mysterious charm for me. The pursuit has always interested my imagination more than any other; and I remember, before having my first portrait taken, there was a great bewitchery in the idea, as if it were a magic process. Even now, it is not without interest for me. (VIII: 492-93)

During Hawthorne's second sitting, he and Thompson talked about paintings of Christ, agreeing that they were inadequate and untrue because human powers were unequal "to the task of painting such purity and holiness in a manly development" (VIII: 498). Here Hawthorne began to explore some questions he would probe further with artists in Italy: the narrative element in art and the ideal versus the real rendition.

This conversation was interrupted several times by visitors to the studio but progressed by stages to Thompson's plan to depict the casting of lots for Christ's garments. Thompson hoped to show how the soldier who won the garment would sense "the former wearer's holiness" as he examined the garment at home, and Hawthorne wondered how Thompson could "make such a picture tell its own story." Hawthorne found the idea suggestive and thought he himself "could make something of it" (VIII: 498). Meanwhile, Hawthorne intently watched Thompson, who was "painting with more and more eagerness; casting quick, keen glances at me, and then making hasty touches on the picture, as if to secure with his brush what he had caught with his eye. He observed that he was just getting interested in the picture; and I could recognize the feeling that was in him, as akin to what I have experienced myself, in the glow of composition" (VIII: 498-99).

At the time of these sittings (5-7 May 1850) Hawthorne's eyes were sharply alert to art objects in his surroundings, as when he closely inspected the pictures and prints in Parker's Saloon, one of Boston's favorite restaurants. Recording a scene he would later incorporate into *The Blithedale Romance*, he noted "a painting of a premium ox, a lithograph of a Turk and of a Turkish lady, . . . a small painting of a drunken toper, sleeping on a bench beside the grog-shop,—a ragged, half hatless, bloated, red-nosed, jolly, miserable-looking devil, very well done, and strangely suitable to the room in which it hangs" (VIII: 495). Not content merely to describe this toper, evidently conceived by some follower of Teniers or Hals, Hawthorne rendered his notes on the "choice specimens of dainties exhibited in the windows" at Parker's Saloon as though he were preparing himself to do a still life in the Dutch manner: "a pair of canvas-back ducks, distinguishable by their delicately mottled feathers; an admirable cut of raw beefsteak; a ham, ready boiled, and with curious figures traced in spices on its outward fat; a half, or perchance the whole, of a large salmon" (VIII: 494). This was one of Hawthorne's good days, a time when his receptive faculty stood ready to serve him to its fullest, a time when he could momentarily forget the religious, allegorical, and landscape paintings on his own walls and relish art by painters content to present life as they saw it.

The work he was about to launch at this time, *The House of the Seven Gables*, stood to profit from attention to detail. Telling his publisher James T. Fields about the nearly completed romance that November, Hawthorne said, "Many passages of this book ought to be finished with the minuteness of a Dutch picture, in order to give them their proper effect" (XVI: 371).

Now that he had entered upon the busiest time of his creative life and was once more writing a book for children, *A Wonder-Book for Girls and Boys*, Hawthorne decided to have his retelling of classic myths illustrated and agreed with his publisher that Hammatt Billings, who had previously illustrated for Ticknor and Fields, might be the right choice. As Hawthorne told Fields, an artist would have "good scope" for some "fanciful designs," adding, "my stories will bear out the artist in any liberties he may be inclined to take" (XVI: 436-37), words he might have rued when "the erudite Mr. Billings" converted Bacchus into Mercury (XVI: 652). As plans for the book moved ahead, Hawthorne wanted Sophia to sketch "the veritable porch of Tanglewood, so that Billings might have pictured the student [Eustace

Bright] and the children sitting on the steps'' (XVI: 459). But because
Sophia did not feel well enough to do the sketch, the job eventually fell
to Burrill Curtis, a minor artist living in the Lenox area. Hawthorne
told Fields that Billings could ''alter it to suit his own taste, as accuracy is
of no consequence; and I would advise that he overgrow it with a good
deal of shrubbery. Moreover he will hardly find room for so many
children, without multiplying the steps'' (XVI: 475). The combined
attention to artistic independence and the artist's practical needs while
doing a sketch reveals Hawthorne's sense of what effective collaboration
requires, something perhaps developed earlier when he worked with
Sophia on *Grandfather's Chair*. But despite Hawthorne's hints and the
latitude accorded him, Billings did not go about his task as quickly as
Fields wished. On 21 August 1851 Fields told Hawthorne, ''Billings is so
uncertain that up to this hour I have not been able to get from him the
Mss. of the Wonder Book to put into the Printer's hands. I have given
him the Porch drawing which he promises with the rest tomorrow''
(Berg). Billings eventually got his sketches to Fields, and except for
Hawthorne's disclaimer about the metamorphosis of Bacchus into
Mercury, no word has come down to us about his impressions of
Billings's contribution to *A Wonder-Book*. But had he been displeased, he
surely would not have agreed to let Billings illustrate its sequel,
Tanglewood Tales.

SOME CHERISHED AESTHETIC PRINCIPLES

For a cultured man nearing fifty, Hawthorne could not justly be
described as having a deep and rich knowledge of the visual arts, but an
objective survey of his encounters with the plastic arts and with artists
reveals his continuing effort to learn something about them and to
develop his receptive faculty by reading about artists, by visiting
museums and exhibits, by talking about paintings and prints with his
family and friends, and by learning from Sophia how she judged a work
of art or an artist. To be sure, his experiences in Salem, Brunswick, and
Boston were not nearly so full as those of international travelers who
had already gone to Europe: Irving, Cooper, and others. Yet his circle of
friends drew him within the orbit of one of the nation's acknowledged
masters, Allston, and enabled him to see the minds and techniques of
artists from the inside. He had acquired enough of a taste for the visual
arts to want more leisure to gaze at them, absorb them, and possess
them spiritually. Ahead of him and his family lay the Manchester
Exhibition of 1857 and scores of galleries and churches in England,
France, and Italy as they all tried to enlarge their knowledge of the visual
arts.

Conclusions about what taste he formed before embarking for Europe must be largely conjectural because Hawthorne's recorded comments on specific art pieces are so few. Even assuming that his taste was partly formed by sympathy with Sophia's more informed preferences and by his milieu's emphasis on the ideal, the picturesque, and the transcendental, we must notice his predilection for tangible reality. He apparently preferred sculpture to painting to the extent that it kept touch with reality: "Sculpture, in its highest excellence, is more genuine than painting, and might seem to be evolved from a natural germ, by the same law as a leaf or flower" (X: 257). He sometimes distrusted the sensuous veil of painting with its potentially distracting colors; statues had fewer sensuous veils and were not so easily ravished by time and climate. Sculptors should not, he thought, aim for classical ideals by treating contemporary figures as though they were Greeks or Romans. They should strive for realism but not become so caught up in minute details that they put distracting drapery between their subject and the viewer. Sculptors debased marble if they carved buttons or other accoutrements of modern dress. Their aim should be to render the spirit or character of their subject expressively. One means of doing that was to bring the form lying within the block of marble or wood to its fullest expressiveness by chipping away everything not inherent to the form the artist was seeking to realize. Of course, this was a hoary aesthetic cliché, but one enjoying renewed support by Romantic idealists. The true artist through sympathy and love, and certainly not through mere technical adroitness, knows what must be done to give shape to the ideal he labors to express. And if nudity is essential to the expression of that ideal, so be it. Hawthorne had qualms about nudity, to be sure, but most of his attacks on nude statues stemmed from what he took to be prurient interest or servile classicizing.[8]

Primarily because of the sensuous veil that color cast upon the painter's subject, painting seemed harder to possess. Painting oftentimes was too rich for Hawthorne to absorb readily. He thought absorption should begin, but not ultimately end, by demanding of the artist that he be both realistically representational and consciously idealistic in his treatment of a subject. Consequently, Hawthorne admired the lifelikeness and attention to expressive detail in Dutch painting. Filled as they were with illusions of the real, Dutch paintings at their best nonetheless offered glimpses of the ideal. These glimpses revealed the artist's intuitive or imaginative perception of the link between the outward world of mundane fact and the inward sphere of spiritual or transcendental truth or form. Like Sir Thomas Browne, Hawthorne believed that man was a true amphibian, a creature of spirit and dust. Art should capture, interpret, and try to show the problems inherent in such amphibiousness. To idealize humanity so much that traces of dust no longer stained mankind was to fall into the spiritualizing habits of some of the Italian painters. Hawthorne shared with Fra Lippo Lippi the notion that human subjects should be recognizably human.

Any sensuous veil could be faulted if it covered a moral vacuum. On this point, Hawthorne agreed with Archibald Alison, Francis Hutcheson, and other members of the Common Sense school of aesthetics and with most of the Transcendentalists about the moral element of art. As Alison puts it,

> in that system which makes matter sublime or beautiful only as it is significant of mind, we perceive the lofty end which is pursued, and that pleasure is here, as in every other case, made instrumental to the moral purposes of our being. While the objects of the material world are to attract our infant eyes, there are latent ties by which they reach our hearts; and wherever they afford us delight, they are always the signs of expressions of higher qualities, by which our moral sensibilities are called forth. (73)

On these grounds, neither mere fidelity to nature nor skillful handling of artistic illusion satisfied Hawthorne. True artists spoke to the human heart, and only those artists who gave their whole souls to their work could sense and share the highest truths.

Those truths, caught in moments of highest thought or deepest insight, revealed themselves most satisfactorily in an artist's sketch. The sketch did not carry a heavy load of materiality, did not suffer from the obstructions and distractions presented by the sensuous veil of oil. Here the artist and his work could be met intellectually and spiritually as in no other encounter between artist and beholder. Here the viewer, by sympathetic identification with the artist, could join in the process of creativity, could help the artist more fully realize his work.

Similarly, unfinished works like Allston's *Study for Belshazzar's Feast* or some of Michelangelo's statues engage the mind of the viewer more thoroughly than completed pieces do. The viewer, whose imagination draws upon hints from the artist and from inward creative forces, takes pleasure in sharing the experience of bringing a work of art to life. But even shared creativity, rewarding as it is, does not account for Hawthorne's pleasure in unfinished works of art. Underlying his taste for such things was his belief that no work ever hit exactly the mark for which the true artist aimed. The ideal form, the perfect blending of the material and the spiritual, and the morally unambiguous were beyond the reach of mortal artists (Folsom 1-70). A secondary reason, a moral one, is that unfinished pieces remind the beholder of past, present, or future opportunities to do life's work, a belief Hawthorne undoubtedly expressed to Browning in Italy when they discussed the glory of the imperfect.

With unfinished pieces as with completed ones, Hawthorne distinctly liked works with a pronounced narrative element. Prepared by his Puritan background and his reading of Spenser, Bunyan, and others to respond to emblematic *objets d'art* and literature, he enjoyed the pleasures of studying an artist's hieroglyphic use of biblical, mythological, or literary subjects. The most obvious sign of his and Sophia's taste for the emblematic in the visual arts is the collection of prints, paintings, and sculpture they chose for their various homes. His predilection for iconicity keeps readers alert, though some complain with Henry James that Hawthorne larded his pages with symbols.

When he spoke favorably of the copyist's role, Hawthorne was not merely defending Sophia, for he believed that copies done in the right spirit and with good technical skill could help viewers understand faded, smoked, or damaged masterpieces. What a copyist lacked in originality could be recompensed by intuitive penetration and sympathetic re-creation of a piece that untutored eyes might neglect because of the ravages of time.

It was just this bond of sympathy, Hawthorne's knack for putting himself inside someone else's skin, that both enabled Hawthorne to open himself to artworks on a "good day" and to see the world with an artist's eye when he developed such characters as Shem Drowne, Miriam, and Kenyon. Before Hawthorne's European sojourn that bond of sympathy was not often established with either actual or fictional artists, for by his forty-eighth year he had recorded the names of only a handful of artists and referred to few art pieces by name, though he had transmuted a few facts and anecdotes about painters and sculptors into literary capital. He knew something about the tools of painters and sculptors and had declared an absorbing interest in the artist's workplace. He had also learned something about engravers and those unsung craftsmen whose skills in the decorative arts added beauty to the homes, churches, and costumes of Americans. This information would serve him well. Spenser, Shakespeare, Milton, Bunyan, and Scott had taught him that images help a writer express himself emblematically and iconically. That pictorial quality would lead Walter Blair to call Hawthorne's tales and romances "paint-pot narratives" (75). And one type of plastic art helpful in creating pictures was the tableau. Just as he found tableaux useful Hawthorne discovered that the daguerreotype, dioramas, and magic lanterns could serve him well. His

cultural milieu had not indeed been rich, but Hawthorne was not about
to squander what he had learned from it. True enough, Salem, Bowdoin
College, and Boston had no art treasures to match those of Paris,
London, Florence, or Rome, but they were not merely distant outposts
in a desert of the beaux arts.

ENLISTING THE AID OF A SISTER ART

Though Hawthorne often turned to the visual arts before leaving for
Europe, where he would make his most vigorous effort to join the
plastic and verbal arts, appropriately enough, the first tale to treat an
artist extensively was "The Prophetic Pictures," published in *The Token*
in 1836 and based upon a Gilbert Stuart anecdote gleaned from the
pages of William Dunlap's history of American art and artists. Hawthorne next used an art object as an element in the plots of two tales,
"Sylph Etherege," published in *The Token* of 1837, and "Edward
Randolph's Portrait," featured in the July 1838 issue of his friend John
O'Sullivan's *United States Magazine and Democratic Review*. His sketch of
an artisan, "Chippings with Chisel," appeared in the same magazine
two months later. His encyclopedic knowledge of artists and historic
oddities spilled over into "The Virtuoso's Collection," published in *The
Boston Miscellany* in December 1842. Artists appear as characters in
"Egotism; or, The Bosom Serpent," published in 1843 by the *United
States Magazine and Democratic Review*, in "The Artist of the Beautiful,"
which was published in the same magazine the following year, and
"Drowne's Wooden Image," published in Godey's *Magazine and Lady's
Book* in July 1844. Even while working at the Salem Custom House, he
produced sketches and tales that draw heavily upon the visual arts and
examine the minds and hearts of artists: "Main Street," published in
1849 by Elizabeth P. Peabody in *Aesthetic Papers;* "Ethan Brand,"
published 5 January 1850 under the title "The Unpardonable Sin, From
an Unpublished Work" in the *Boston Weekly Museum;* and "The Snow
Image: A Childish Miracle," published in 1851 in a volume called *The
Memorial*. But years before he wrote his bittersweet tale of two gleeful
snow sculptors, Hawthorne had used his knowledge of the visual arts in
two volumes for children: *Grandfather's Chair* (1841) and *Biographical
Stories for Children* (1842), which begins with a brief biography of the
colonial artist Benjamin West. Two subsequent children's books, *A
Wonder-Book for Girls and Boys* (1852) and *Tanglewood Tales* (1853),
continued to reflect his keen interest in the visual arts. But all his
writings from 1849 through 1860 drew with increasing frequency upon
his knowledge of the visual arts.

HOW THE VISUAL ARTS SERVE HAWTHORNE'S FICTION

The question of how Hawthorne used his knowledge of artists and the visual arts leads into the ways he made this knowledge serve his craft. The simplest way, allusion to a particular work or artist, began early and continued throughout his career. For example, the reference to "Dutch tiles of blue-figured China, representing scenes from Scripture" in "Howe's Masquerade" (1838), helps him convey a sense of what life was like in the colonial Province House. But though a lady "may have sat beside this fire-place, and told her children the story of each blue tile" (IX: 240), he does not use the tiles iconically as he would later when he has a tapestry hanging on Dimmesdale's wall.

If the step from a single allusion to a long list of works and artists is not long, it nonetheless allowed for Hawthorne's parade of knowledge, as in "The Virtuoso's Collection." Although the narrator in that tale gazes at the works of ancient painters displayed by the virtuoso, Apelles, Parrhasius, Timanthes, Polygnotus, Apollodorus, Pausias, and Pamphilus, he balks at describing the paintings, refuses to criticize them, and backs away from an "attempt to settle the question of superiority between ancient and modern art" (X: 492). Of course, the narrator is merely a curious townsman determined to observe without passing judgment, but his straightforward catalogue exposes the credulity of the virtuoso collector and the gullibility of a town that would display his hodgepodge of oddities.

Although the virtuoso rushed him to see everything on display, betraying definite Hawthornean signs that his receptive faculty functioned at a slow pace, the narrator says, "The deep simplicity of these [famous sculptures] was not to be comprehended by a mind excited and disturbed as mine was by the various objects that had recently been presented to it. I therefore turned away, with merely a passing glance, resolving, on some future occasion, to brood over each individual statue and picture, until my inmost spirit should feel their excellence" (X: 493). At this point, there was no sidelong glance, nothing that caught the narrator unaware and led him to an inward understanding of the artists' achievements.

To be sure, the catalogue serves the narrative function of completing a list of esoteric oddities, but its chief interest lies in the narrator's response to these wondrous artifacts. Unlike the name-dropping virtuoso, the narrator can only appreciate a work by doing what Hawthorne had done when he first saw Sophia's paintings of Lake Como, brooding over them until he had taken spiritual possession.

Another example of Hawthorne's functional use of cataloguing appears in Liberty Tree (1841). Here Grandfather turns the pages of a book of engraved portraits and as he shows the children crowding around portraits of American Revolutionary War leaders he tells about their deeds and characters, depending on the engravings to provide the children insight into his subjects' personalities, the engraving of Samuel Adams, for example: "a stern, grimlooking man, in plain attire, of much more modern fashion than that of the old Puritans. But the face might well have befitted one of those iron-hearted men" (VI: 173). This observation ties directly to Grandfather's argument in all his stories of colonial America: beneath the Puritans' stern looks lay a joyful hope of freedom and independence. Other engravings in the volume help Hawthorne to establish another point: faces are not easy to read. The portrait of King George III serves as an example: "Little Alice clapped her hands, and seemed pleased with the bluff good nature of his physiognomy. But Laurence thought it strange, that a man with such a face, indicating hardly a share of intellect, should have influence enough on human affairs, to convulse the world with war" (VI: 176).

Just as germane to Hawthorne's craft as cataloguing is his practice of using art objects to give realistic and (sometimes) symbolic touches to his settings. Picture books, prints of an English queen or king or an American political leader, and family portraits like those in Governor Bellingham's home (I: 105) appear throughout Hawthorne's work. Sculpted works are less numerous but their presence sometimes more telling. For example, in the story Holgrave tells Phoebe in *The House of the Seven Gables*, a nude statue stands in the elegantly furnished and decorated room of Gervayse Pyncheon. Holgrave's comments have been overlooked by those who proclaim that Hawthorne was prudish about nudity: "In one corner stood a marble woman, to whom her own beauty was the sole and sufficient garment" (II: 193).

The nude suggests something about the Europeanized taste of the well-traveled Gervayse Pyncheon. It is a part of the setting, an adornment suitable for a house with pretensions to aristocratic tastes. A different purpose is served by the bust of Hippocrates in Dr. Heidegger's office, for the mere mention of this ancient healer's name in the tale (published in 1837) makes the reader question Heidegger's experiment and ask whether he has the right to stage a shattering psychological experience for his old friends. In its unexpected frown and voiced foreboding, "Forbear," the bust comments ironically upon the entire proceedings. A different kind of commentary results from Hawthorne's placement of "a marble copy of Greenough's Angel and Child" in Mr. Pringle's drawingroom in *A Wonder-Book*. In a household swarming with children, the statue suggests that Mr. Pringle, for all his classical loyalties and studious habits, is not merely an isolated, bookish man. Even if they lacked suggestive powers, these pieces of sculpture, like such decorative objects in "Howe's Masquerade" as "Dutch tiles of blue-figured China, representing scenes from Scripture,'' a gilded Indian on the cupola of the Province House, and painted screens and ceilings, lend realism to Hawthorne's settings.

But statues also serve symbolic functions as when Hawthorne gives a fanciful but poignantly meaningful twist to the statue of little Marygold in *A Wonder-Book* when King Midas's greed for gold and his profound love of his little daughter have the dire result of transmuting her into a golden statue: ''Yes, there she was, with the questioning look of love, grief, and pity, hardened into her face. It was the prettiest and most woeful sight that mortal ever saw. All the features and tokens of Marygold were there; even the beloved little dimple remained in her golden chin'' (VII: 53). Here, as often in Hawthorne's fiction, details related to settings figure as plot elements. A minor instance occurs in ''Chippings with a Chisel,'' a sketch in which the sculptor—''[who] may share that title with Greenough, since the dauber of signs is a painter as well as Raphael'' (IX: 408)—stands amidst tombstones and monuments as he wields his chisel. As the stonecutter, Wigglesworth, works on gravestones for his steady stream of clients, both the narrator and the stone-cutter comment on the iconography of death. The iconic tradition restricts both Wigglesworth and his customers to weeping willows, crossbones, hour glasses, death's-heads, roses, scythes, and winged cherubs. The iconography of death is fixed, with meaning instantly and unambiguously expressed.

But a far more potent use of a decorative art object for its iconic value appears in *The Scarlet Letter*. The scene is Dimmesdale's room, where ''the walls were hung round with tapestry, said to be from the Gobelin looms, and, at all events, representing the Scriptural story of David and Bathsheba, and Nathan the Prophet, in colors still unfaded, but which made the fair woman of the scene almost as grimly picturesque as the woe-denouncing seer'' (I: 126). Whether Dimmesdale himself hung the tapestry in this rented room, its presence on his wall must have been a painful daily reminder of his guilt and forced him to recall Nathan's words to adulterous David: ''What you did was done in secret; but I will do this in the light of day for all Israel to see'' (2 Samuel 12:12). In time the New England children of Israel will see Dimmesdale's deed ''in the light of day.'' His confession comes after he had returned from the forest to ''the tapestried comfort of the walls'' (I: 222) to revise his Election Day sermon. Having learned in the forest that Chillingworth was Hester's husband, he seems to recognize that Chillingworth has been divinely appointed to goad him into revealing his secret. As Dimmesdale writes in his tapestried room, the narrator informs us that ''Another man had returned out of the forest; a wiser one; with knowledge of hidden mysteries which the simplicity of the former never could have reached. A bitter kind of knowledge that!'' (I: 223). But this knowledge enables him to deliver his powerful Election Day sermon. Like David he has suffered but he is to know the joy of triumph. His is the kind of wisdom Donatello would also attain after losing his initial simplicity and finding the "knowledge of hidden mysteries . . . bitter."

Hidden mysteries (materialistically rather than theologically based) figure much differently in *The House of the Seven Gables* (1851). A portrait of the builder of the Pyncheon mansion is central to the story's symbolic setting, representing greed in the Pyncheons from the old Colonel straight down to his modern-day counterpart, Jaffrey. Significantly, when the portrait concealing the family secrets tumbles from the wall and falls "face downward on the floor" (II: 316), the Pyncheon mansion does not "come thundering down" (II: 197), as the narrator had intimated it might (II: 197). What that facedown fall signifies is the death and decay of the imperious, aristocratic order, an order that had been strengthened by one of its most Europeanized members, Gervayse.[9]

If the Pyncheon mansion does not have the biblical overtones and linkages of Dimmesdale's tapestried room, the room where the portrait hangs is the scene of a psychological and spiritual struggle nonetheless. With its nude statue, Dutch tiles, ebony cabinet inlaid with ivory, and pictures "that looked old, and had a mellow tinge," the room "was the emblem of a mind" (II: 193), the mind of Gervayse Pyncheon, who in that room contended with Matthew Maule for the control of Alice Pyncheon. After living abroad for years and acquiring aristocratic European tastes, represented by the Claude landscape now proudly displayed in the seven-gabled house, instead of confronting a present danger, the mesmeric carpenter, Gervayse escapes into art. As Alice put her "woman's might against man's might," trying to resist the mesmeric control of Matthew Maule, her father "turned away, and seemed absorbed in the contemplation of a landscape by Claude, where a shadowy and sun-streaked vista penetrated so remotely into an ancient wood, that it would have been no wonder if his fancy had not lost itself in the picture's bewildering depths" (II: 203). As Hawthorne suggests, his head has been turned by the images of aristocratic life that he had learned to associate with Claude. To live in the manner of a European nobleman, Gervayse needs wealth. Since the Maules reputedly have knowledge about a map to the Pyncheons' claim to a large estate, Gervayse wants that information. Once acquired, that lost parchment, and the dowry it could bestow, might enable Alice to "wed an English duke, or a German reigning-prince, instead of some New England clergyman or lawyer!" (II: 204). The Claude landscape, therefore, serves both as a decorative touch reflecting Gervayse's Europeanized tastes and as a partial explanation of his motives (Levy 147-60). So completely is Gervayse absorbed by the Claude and what his work represents that he fails to protect Alice, whose pride prevents her from calling upon him for help. No Claudian paradise awaits Alice and her father because of the curse upon their house and heads. Not until a purer Eve arises will the flower of Eden bloom, though it will not bloom in a Claudian, aristocratic setting. That purer Eve is, of course, Phoebe.

The visual arts also provide realistic touches in *The Blithedale Romance* when a fallen aristocrat, Fauntleroy, finds himself in a heavily decorated saloon. Lifting some paragraphs from his notebook description of Parker's Saloon, Hawthorne provides an appropriate setting for Coverdale's meeting with Fauntleroy, now known as Old Moodie. The pictures as described in the notebook passages suggest Hawthorne's appreciation of a slice of Boston life; in the pages of this romance they create one of his most realistic scenes, for they depicted the pleasures of eating and drinking so much like the objects imitated "that you seemed to have the genuine article before you, and yet with an indescribable, ideal charm; it took away the grossness from what was fleshiest and fattest, and thus helped the life of man, even in its earthiest relations, to appear rich and noble, as well as warm, cheerful and substantial" (III: 176). As comfortable and pleasure giving as the scene is, one picture, one hung "in an obscure corner of the saloon" (III: 176), showed a dark side of drinking, for the toper depicted in it lay in "an apoplectic sleep of drunkenness. The death-in-life was too well portrayed" (III: 176). Here surely is a comment on Old Moodie, described a few pages later as the "wretchedest old ghost in the world" (III: 179), when Coverdale buys him a glass of brandy.

To some degree, all of the visual arts singled out in Hawthorne's settings function within his plots. But several art objects are more central to the plot than the setting, the simplest being the Bunker Hill diorama in *Liberty Tree*. That story moves from one historic event to another, as Grandfather speaks, but when he is asked to recount the battle of Bunker Hill, Grandfather advises the children to visit the diorama of Bunker Hill, saying, "There you shall see the whole business, the burning of Charleston and all, with your own eyes, and hear the cannon and musketry with your own ears" (VI: 184). The next morning the excited children give Grandfather "a full account of the diorama of Bunker Hill" (VI: 185), and he moves on to other stories.

The device of presenting history through a staged exhibition is amplified, modified, and made more dramatic in "Main Street" (1849). Here Hawthorne presents a showman-historian who has created a pictorial exhibition that features a shifting panorama, puppet figures, and various wheels and springs—in short, a diorama. Hawthorne rolls out the history of Salem from its settlement by stern Puritans to its contemporary citizens, joining the showman's descriptions and banter and the responses of a few members of the audience, including "an acidulous-looking gentleman in blue glasses" (XI: 52).[10] Through his dour criticism, we realize that the diorama is a cheaply built exhibit; yet it vividly presents Salem's story if viewers are willing to suspend their disbelief and give free rein to their imaginations. As the showman says to the acidulous gentleman who insists that his scenes are not realistic enough and that his puppets are "stiff in their pasteboard joints," "Human art has its limits, and we must now and then ask a little aid from the spectator's imagination" (XI: 52). The man in the blue glasses refuses that aid and demands his money back. But while that happens, the showman acknowledges the uneven quality of the painted scenes and cranky operation of his machines and still manages to give spectators with good imaginations a lively sense of Salem's past. In this tale, painted scenes and pasteboard puppets are virtually one with the plot.

An episode in "Ethan Brand," the Dutchman's magic lantern exhibit, offers a group of Berkshire spectators views of Europe and foreign battles. The Dutchman's lantern functions not only as a teaching device but also as an instrument through which innocent little Joe can more fully apprehend the horror of Ethan Brand's piercing glance into the heart of man. Further, the show box connects Ethan to the Faust legend (Stein 97-100).

The hurdy-gurdy that Clifford spots in the street before the old Pyncheon mansion offers more than the siren call of music, though Clifford cannot see all the details the narrator singles out, details that have a direct bearing on Hawthorne's plot. When the young Italian operator turned the crank of his hurdy-gurdy, "the cobbler wrought upon a shoe; the blacksmith hammered his iron; the soldier waved his glittering blade; the lady raised a tiny breeze with her fan; the jolly toper swigged lustily at his bottle; a scholar opened his book, with eager thirst for knowledge, and turned his head to-and-fro along the page; the milk-maid energetically drained her cow; and a miser counted gold into his strong box" (II: 163). Amidst all this activity, a "lover saluted his mistress on her lips!" (II:163). The scene at once reveals Clifford's awakening to life beyond the walls of the Pyncheon house and his overly refined aesthetic sense, which was jarred by the money-grabbing antics and gross physicality of the Italian boy's monkey. Clifford

> had taken a childish delight in the music, and smiled, too, at the figures which it set in motion. But, after looking awhile at the long-tailed imp, he was so shocked by its horrible ugliness, spiritual as well as physical, that he actually began to shed tears; a weakness which men of merely delicate endowments—and destitute of the fiercer, deeper, and more tragic power of laughter— can hardly avoid, when the worst and meanest aspect of life happens to be presented to them. (II: 164-65)

Interesting as they are in and of themselves and symbolically suggestive as they often proved to be, Hawthorne did not have to depend on
magic lanterns or hurdy-gurdies to help him develop plots. Traditional
art objects also served him well, the first of these a portrait by an
unnamed colonial painter in "The Prophetic Pictures" (1837). Doubling
traditional art objects in this tale, Hawthorne adds to his plot the
clandestine drawing of a sketch of the couple sitting for their portrait.
Hawthorne built his plot on Gilbert Stuart's anecdote (encountered in
Dunlap's history of American art) of a painter who foresaw and depicted
the eventual insanity of a sitter. In Hawthorne's adaptation, a European
practicing his art in colonial America senses the capacity for murder in
Walter Ludlow, whose fiancée, Elinor, has already glimpsed his
potential for evil. Despite Walter's belief that the painter can see the
inward man even as he copies the outward, and even though Elinor
realizes that the painter senses something dreadfully amiss in Walter's
character, the couple are married. Though she has seen a prophetic
sketch of her likely fate, Elinor believes love can conquer all. Hawthorne
develops this story not only for the plot but also for the opportunity to
examine the psyches of both the painter and the sitters. But he does
leave unexplained and unexplored "a certain fanciful person" who saw
the portrait and then did a sketch that also captured Walter's
murderousness (IX: 177). That an unskilled artist could read the deepest
meaning of the Ludlow portraits must enter into readers' conclusions
about Walter, Elinor, and the prophetic painter (Fay, "Light from Dark
Corners," 22-23).

Another painting, a miniature, advances the plot of "Sylph Etherege"
to its melancholy conclusion when Sylvia's suitor crushes beneath his
feet the miniature of her supposed bridegroom that he had commissioned for her. So attached to the image has she become, so much of her
consciousness does it manifest, that Edgar (alias Edward) might as well
have stomped Sylph, for she refuses to exchange her phantom love for
the iconoclastic Edgar when he tries to jolt her back into reality. As a
woman of feeling, she cannot stand the shock.

As a character type, Edward-Edgar deserves more attention, but in
relation to the plot of this often-ignored tale, we should note why he had
the miniature drawn and what he asked the artist to express: "I did but
look into this delicate creature's heart; and with the pure fantasies that I
found there, I made what seemed a man,—and the delusive shadow has
wiled her away to Shadowland, and vanished there." (XI: 118).
Romantic portraits beheld by dreamy girls may work mischief, but
Hawthorne insists that callousness, however well intentioned, is more
destructive.

But no mischief resides in the bosom of Alice Vane in "Edward

Randolph's Portrait'' (1838). Though the act of cleaning a dark, faded picture seems to have been borrowed from Sophia Peabody—hence a reference in the Hawthorne circle to this tale as Sophia's story (XV: 28)—the plot of this piece comes from those Gothic fictions where portraits speak, change facial expression, and move in and out of the frame, as in ''Dr. Heidegger's Experiment'' (Lundblad 86-87, 123). Here a restored painting of Edward Randolph, whose surrender of the original charter of Massachusetts made him the foe of all democratically minded New Englanders, serves as a warning to Francis Hutchinson, who thinks of yielding a fort to British control. The job of cleaning the portrait is undertaken by his niece, Alice Vane, democratic despite her residence in Italy, where she studied art. She finishes the job in a few hours, an impossible accomplishment if we insist on being acidulous readers in blue glasses. If the story is to work, we must suspend disbelief, as we must also do in *The House of the Seven Gables.*

In that romance, the portrait of Colonel Pyncheon is an element of the plot and setting, as is evident in a talk between Matthew Maule and Gervayse Pyncheon in the interpolated story of Alice Pyncheon:

> This picture, it must be understood, was supposed to be so intimately connected with the fate of the house, and so magically built into its walls, that, if once it should be removed, that very instance, the whole edifice would come thundering down, in a heap of dusty rain. All through the foregoing conversation . . . the portrait had been frowning, clenching its fist, and giving many such proofs of discomposure. . . . And finally, at Matthew Maule's audacious suggestion of a transfer of the seven-gabled structure, the portrait is averred to have lost all patience, and to have shown itself on the point of descending bodily from its frame. (II: 197-98)

Confronting words such as these, modern readers must remove their blue glasses and give unbridled rein to their imaginations, expecting Hawthorne to make telling use of the Pyncheon portrait. Sympathetic identifications with Hawthorne's imagination and sensitivity to his narrative practices pay off in chapter 18, the death scene of Judge Pyncheon where a half-dozen generations of Pyncheons seem to gather around their ancestor's portrait. Their gathering, which recalls the narrative scheme of ''Main Street,'' recounts events and acts that thwarted their aristocratic hopes since the building of the house and foretells what will happen after the death of the Pyncheon who shares his ancestor's dream. The parade of Pyncheons before the Pyncheon portrait condenses the family history and then points to the forthcoming union of a Pyncheon and a Maule.

In addition to dioramas and portraits, Hawthorne twice uses a statue, or what passes for one, as an element of the plot: once in "Drowne's Wooden Image" and again in "The Snow-Image." In the first, the traditional New England craft of carving a figurehead is executed by a historical woodcarver of considerable local fame—Shem Drowne, born in Kittery, Maine, in 1683, who died in Boston in 1774 after carving such famous pieces as the weather vane shaped like a grasshopper on Faneuil Hall (Davis, 127-36). Inspired by his love for his model, Drowne far exceeds anything he has heretofore achieved, winning praise from John Singleton Copley, who frequently visits Drowne's shop while the figurehead is being carved. "Drowne," says the famous painter, "if this work were in marble, it would make you famous at once; nay, I would almost affirm that it would make an era in the art. It is as ideal as an antique statue, and yet as real as any lovely woman whom one meets at a fireside or in the street" (X: 313). But this Bostonian Pygmalion seems capable of only one masterpiece, one fed by a "wellspring of inward widsom" flowing from his love of his subject (X: 313). Deprived of the source of inspiration, Drowne "was again the mechanical carver that he had been known to be all his lifetime" (X: 319). Hawthorne suggests that for "the Oaken Lady," Drowne's reach exceeded his usual grasp because "in every human spirit there is imagination, sensibility, creative power, genius, which, according to circumstances, may either be developed in this world, or shrouded in a mask of dulness until another state of being" (X: 319-20).

But those traits may be more alive in children than in adults who have been taught that the realities of life demand common sense rather than creativity, an issue addressed in both "The Artist of the Beautiful" (1844) and "The Snow-Image" (1850). Owen Warland's efforts to create a mechanical butterfly that will seem real evoke censure and doubt from the commonsensical Peter Hovenden, his daughter Alice, and her husband, Robert Danforth. Because his dedication to spiritualizing matter overbalances his dread of unsympathetic reception, Owen fashions two *objets d'art*, an emblematic ebony box, which survives to record his achievement, and a butterfly, which is crushed by the Danforth baby but attains a kind of immortality as the spiritual possession of the artist.

A spiritual possession of their creation is all that Violet and Peony Lindsey attain in "The Snow-Image" after their father sits their snow maiden before a blazing Heidenberg stove and the family maid, Dora, wipes up the remains with a towel. Violet and Peony created a playmate out of snow, a playmate their imaginative mother could accept as real, but commonsensical Mr. Lindsey lacks sympathetic imagination and believes only what his eyes tell him. In his eyes, his children have wrought no miracle. The narrator comments ironically on this not-too-distant cousin of the man in the blue glasses:

> But, after all, there is no teaching anything to wise men of good Mr. Lindsey's stamp. They know everything—Oh, to be sure!—everything that has been, and everything that is, and everything that, by any future possibility, can be. And, should some phenomenon of Nature or Providence transcend their system, they will not recognize it, even if it comes to pass under their very noses. (XI: 25)

In "The Snow-Image," as in other tales and in *The House of the Seven Gables*, Hawthorne thus makes an art object—albeit an unusual and fleeting one in this tale—central to the plot.

A recurrent use of art objects in Hawthorne's fiction was for foreshadowing, beginning with "The Prophetic Pictures" when the prophetic artist did a secret sketch that forewarned Elinor, and possibly Walter also, of the terrible deed that Walter would one day attempt. Foreshadowing is also a function of Hawthorne's elaborate description of the scenes carved on Pandora's box: among all the figures of "graceful men and women, and the prettiest children ever seen," and all the vines, trees, and flowers, Pandora "once or twice fancied that she saw a face not so lovely, or something or other that was disagreeable, and which stole the beauty out of all the rest" (VII: 69). Her attempts to confront that ugliness resist intense gazing and touching. She ends by rationalizing what she had seen: "Some face, that was really beautiful, had been made to look ugly by her catching a sideway glimpse at it" (VII: 69). Had she heeded the warning on the box, she would not have opened the box, but she proves herself a type of Grecian Eve by thinking independently. As Hawthorne's aesthetic child she seizes upon the deeper meaning of the carving by a "sideway glimpse."

Another of Hawthorne's Gothicized Grecian tales, "Circe's Palace," uses another art object, a marble fountain, to foreshadow later events. Ulysses's crew was warned that when it looked at the fountain and saw the water "constantly taking new shape, not very distinctly, but plainly enough for a nimble fancy to recognize what they were. Now it was the shape of a man in a long robe, the fleecy whiteness of which was made out of the fountain's spray; now it was a lion, or a tiger, or a wolf, or an ass, or, as often anything else, a hog, wallowing in the marble basin as if it were a sty" (VII: 276). Of course, the crew members will not pause to exercise their powers of fancy or heed the warning when their stomachs are growling from hunger. The men will become hogs.

By a kind of inverted use of an art object, one carved by nature herself—the Great Stone Face—Hawthorne foreshadows the development of man to his noblest heights in his tale of Ernest, the White Mountain boy who grows up to fulfill the legend about the coming of a man bearing "an exact resemblance to the Great Stone Face" (XI: 28). Hawthorne's description of the gigantic profile prepares the reader for Ernest's noble appearance as he grows into manhood. Such use of an *objet d'art*, albeit sculpted by nature, not only provides foreshadowing but gives an index to character as well.

Frequently, Hawthorne relates works of art to characters by referring to types of figures in paintings or statues, as when he associates Hester with the Madonna and Zenobia with Eve; by having portraits painted of fictional characters like Elinor and Walter Ludlow, whose inner lives are open to the painter who pierces beneath their prenuptial bliss; by offering clues to personalities through a particular piece of art, as with Gervayse Pyncheon's purchase of a Claude landscape; and, finally, by revealing character through the project of a real or would-be artist, as with Owen Warland, Shem Drowne, Wiggleworth, Hester, Pearl, the Lindsey children, and the main characters of *The Marble Faun*. Surprisingly, Peter Goldthwaite belongs on this list by virtue of his youthful attempts to decorate the walls of the family home with "charcoal sketches, chiefly of people's heads in profile. These being specimens of Peter's youthful genius, it went more to his heart to obliterate them, than if they had been pictures on a church wall by Michel Angelo" (IX: 396). But his now destructive urges, spurred by greed, overpowered his fondness for his early sketches. Among those drawings is yet another prophetic picture. Destroying it distressed Peter deeply, for in it he could see himself revealed both as a prophetic artist and as a victim. The sketch showed a thin, ragged man leaning on a spade and bending over a hole in the earth, one hand extended to grasp something that he had found. But close behind him was a fiendishly laughing figure with horns, a tufted tail, and cloven hooves.

> "Avaunt, Satan!" cried Peter. "The man shall have his gold."
> Uplifting his axe, he hit the horned gentleman such a blow on the head, as not only demolished him, but the treasure-seeker also, and caused the whole scene to vanish like magic. (IX: 396)

Peter is unusual because, except for Oberon in "The Devil in Manuscript," Hawthorne's artists rarely destroy what they create.

From the start of his career Hawthorne used works of art for characterization, though the description of his heroine in *Fanshawe* was at once tentative and apologetic:

> If pen could give an adequate idea of Ellen Langton's loveliness, it would achieve what pencil (the pencils at least of the

Colonial artists who attempted it) never could, for though the
dark eyes might be painted, the pure and pleasant thought that
peeped through them could only be seen and felt. But descriptions of beauty are never satisfactory. It must therefore be left to
the imagination of the reader to conceive of something not more
than mortal—nor, indeed, quite the perfection of mortality—but
charming men the more, because they felt, that, lovely as she
was, she was of like nature to themselves. (III: 340-41)

How much surer of himself and of his trust in his readers is the man
who wrote of Hester Prynne,

Had there been a Papist among the crowd of Puritans, he
might have seen in this beautiful woman, so picturesque in her
attire and mien, and with the infant at her bosom, an object to
remind him of the image of Divine Maternity, which so many
illustrious painters have vied with one another to represent,
something which should remind him, indeed, but only by
contrast, of that sacred image of sinless motherhood, whose
infant was to redeem the world. Here, there was the taint of
deepest sin in the most sacred quality of human life, working
such effect, that that world was only darker for this woman's
beauty, and the more lost for the infant that she had borne. (I: 56)

The allusion to the pictorial tradition of the Madonna and Child is
arresting, thought-provoking, functional. The reader must ponder the
implicit comparison and the explicit contrast, contemplating ideals of
womanhood and Hester's relation to them. This image of Hester as
Madonna informs her meeting with Chillingworth in the prison cell,
where he sees her as ''a statue of ignominy'' (I: 74). But the images of
Hester as Madonna and as ignominious wife are later displaced by
Hawthorne's negative construction of blighted passions:

There seemed to be no longer any thing in Hester's face for Love
to dwell upon; nothing in Hester's form, though majestic and
statue-like, that Passion would ever dream of clasping in its
embrace; nothing in Hester's bosom, to make it ever again the
pillow of Affection. (I: 163)

But Hawthorne demands even more attention to his clusters of iconic
images in the third scaffold scene when Hester again stands ''statue-
like'' (I: 244). This time she stands alone, Pearl ''playing at her own will
about the market-place'' (I: 244), a circumstance suggesting that Hester
has gained the strength to face life alone, even though just at the

moment she is eagerly anticipating a time when her bosom may serve again as a "pillow of Affection."

When in his second novel Hawthorne invited readers to think of Clifford Pyncheon as the subject of a miniature, one in "[Edward] Malone's most perfect style" (II: 31), and when he allowed Phoebe to see daguerreotypes of the Pyncheon portrait and of Judge Pyncheon, he was using a kindred strategy for making an art object a tool of characterization. His purpose here is not merely to invite contrasts and comparisons between a character and the art object but rather to enlist the art object in helping him to describe his characters, a practice begun years earlier in "Sylph Etherege" (1838) when a miniature presented Edgar Vaughan:

> The beauty of the pictured countenance was almost too perfect to represent a human creature, that had been born of a fallen and world-worn race. . . . It seemed too bright for a thing formed of dust. . . . There was that resemblance between her own face and the miniature, which is often said to exist between lovers whom Heaven has destined for each other. . . . Those heavenly eyes gazed for ever into her soul, which drank at them as at a fountain, and was disquieted if reality threw a momentary cloud between. (XI: 114-15)

Of course, Hawthorne's method is transparent: his real purpose in using the miniature is to characterize Sylph.

When aged Hepzibah removes a miniature from her escritoire, she gazes at an image far different from her own, "the likeness of a young man, in a silken dressing-gown of an old fashion, the soft richness of which is well adapted to the countenance of reverie, with its full, tender lips, and beautiful eyes, that seem to indicate not so much capacity of thought, as gentle and voluptuous emotion" (II: 31-32). This description prepares the reader for Clifford's appearance and provides insight into the characters of both Hepzibah and her brother as relics of a past age.

Moments after putting the miniature aside, Hepzibah steps into a low-studded room and contemplates the portrait of Old Colonel Pyncheon. She stares with a scowl at "the stern features of a Puritanic-looking personage, in a scull-cap, with a laced band and a grizzly beard; holding a Bible with one hand, and in the other uplifting an iron sword-hilt" (II: 33). This portrait both defines her heritage and suggests what Phoebe will detect in Judge Pyncheon when she studies Holgrave's daguerreotype.

Even when Hawthorne did not present an actual portrait to a fictional viewer, he could achieve the same effect by having his readers imagine one. That is the tactic Miles Coverdale used to describe Hollingsworth in the climactic moment when Zenobia is on trial for her life. To show

Hollingsworth's stern inflexibility, Coverdale says, "I saw in Hollingsworth all that an artist could desire for the grim portrait of a Puritan
magistrate, holding inquest of life and death in a case of witchcraft" (III:
214). That comparison sustains Hawthorne's image of Hollingsworth as
a man of iron will and grim determination, a man as bent on prison
reform as those first settlers were on building a city on the hill in the
New World. Coverdale, a bookish visitor to galleries, uses the same
potent device in describing Zenobia, who "should have made it a point
of duty . . . to sit endlessly to painters and sculptors" (III: 44). Before
reaching this conclusion, Coverdale had behaved verbally like some
sculptor imaging Eve before the Fall:

> Something in her manner . . . irresistibly brought up a picture
> of that fine, perfectly developed figure, in Eve's earliest gar-
> ment. I almost fancied myself actually beholding it. . . . One felt
> an influence breathing out of her, such as we might suppose to
> come from Eve, when she was just made, and her Creator
> brought her to Adam, saying—'Behold, here is a woman!' (III: 17)

Coverdale's heated imagination stirs the reader to conjure up an Eve as
naked as any rendered by an artist uninfluenced by Victorian prudery. It
is fitting that Coverdale, a sometime visitor to art galleries, should
associate his circle of friends with art objects or respond to "the
wonderful exhibition of the Veiled Lady" with his critical eye on the
composition achieved by Westervelt by "all the arts of mysterious
arrangement, of picturesque disposition, and artistically contrasted light
and shade" (III: 6). The Veiled Lady is a piece of staged supernaturalism, in a loose sense a *tableau vivant* meant to mystify the
onlookers, and her presentation in this manner anticipates a crucial
episode when Zenobia, after leading Blithedale residents to do *tableaux
vivants* based on "several splendid works of art—either arranged after
engravings from the Old Masters, or original illustrations of scenes in
history or romance" (III: 106)—tells her legend of a veiled lady and flings
a piece of gauze over Priscilla, thus transforming her into the same kind
of "wonderful exhibition" Westervelt had presented and would present
again.

Thus in *The Blithedale Romance* Hawthorne associated all of his major
characters except Coverdale with art objects: Hollingsworth with
portraits of the old Puritans, Moody with Dutch and Flemish renderings
of topers, Priscilla with nineteenth-century *tableaux vivants* used to
augment lectures of many kinds, and Zenobia with those old masters
who, as sculptors and painters, rendered woman in her quintessential
beauty and majesty. These associations were both a continuation of
earlier practices and a forecast of the more probing associations
Hawthorne would make in *The Marble Faun*. The increasing density of

such associations at once suggests how fruitful Hawthorne's acculturation in the visual arts had become and requires his readers to consider more and more carefully how his knowledge of artists and their works helped to shape his own creative efforts.

While art objects helped him open an intercourse with his readers, such artistic techniques as chiaroscuro (the treatment of light and shade in a drawing or painting) and the tableau (a striking picture or dramatic scene) were equally important. It is impossible to determine whether he was more indebted to such literary masters as Spenser, Shakespeare, Milton, Bunyan, or Scott or to the theorists of the visual arts in his handling of light and shade, though he probably took hints from writers and painters as well as aesthetic philosophers like Alison. That he did make distinguished use of these techniques has long been recognized.[11]

From his children's stories to his unfinished romances, Hawthorne manipulated light and shade with a master's touch, as when he presents Young Goodman Brown entering the forest outside Salem or describes Pearl, Hester, and Dimmesdale meeting in the forest near Boston. Here and elsewhere, Hawthorne worked as carefully as any master painter would have to establish atmosphere through the counteracting and complementary play of light and shade. This contrastive use of light and shade added potent evocative registers to his symbols, as in his move from the dark vigil around the limekiln to the glorious light of day when Ethan Brand dies. And in yet another way, characterization, his handling of light and shade served well, as in his presentation of Phoebe, associated with light, and Hepzibah, associated with darkness.

More important, chiaroscuro is crucial to Hawthorne's theory of the romance. To reach that neutral territory where the sunlight of realism could merge with the moonlight of fantasy, Hawthorne believed that the right mix of shade and light would enable him to write a romance acceptable to readers with growing appetites for realistic novels. His enunciation of this theory comes in "The Custom House" essay in *The Scarlet Letter*, but the practice had long preceded the theory, for Hawthorne well knew by 1850 that his imagination demanded an amount of light somewhere between the bold glare of the sun and the dim glow of the moon.[12]

Hawthorne's use of the tableau was recognized at least as early as 1902 when George Woodberry observed that Hawthorne told *The Scarlet Letter* "in that succession of high-wrought scenes, tableaux, in fact, which was his characteristic method of narrative, picturesque, pictorial, almost to be described as theatrical in spectacle" (191). That observation applies equally well to the other romances and to many of the tales, too, as in the window-framed portrait of Sylph Etherege: "The girl's slender and sylph-like figure, tinged with radiance from the sunset clouds, and overhung with the rich drapery of the silken curtains, and set within the deep frame of the window, was a perfect picture; or, rather, it was like the original loveliness in a painter's fancy, from which the most finished picture is but an imperfect copy" (XI: 111-12). Treated much the same way in his romances are Clifford as he stands looking into the Salem street and Zenobia as she appears before a window in Boston.

Tableaux vivants, which have almost a Spenserian richness in Hawthorne's fiction, function symbolically like the static ones. To catalogue his use of them would require listing almost his whole fictional canon. A few examples must suffice: Father Hooper preaching behind his veil, Tobias Pearson coming upon the gentle Quaker boy, Young Goodman Brown kissing Faith goodbye, Dimmesdale holding his midnight vigil, Coverdale encountering the Blithedale masqueraders, and Hilda seeing Miriam return the gaze of Donatello. The iconicity of these tableaux, and the hundreds of others crowding his fiction, adds emblematic richness while assuring verbal economy. In short, tableaux became essential to Hawthorne's mode of depicting the human condition in relation to the past, to the present, and to the eternal.

While Hawthorne used art objects and appropriated artistic techniques to help describe a setting or delineate a character, he also used artists as characters. Whether they were central or minor characters, Hawthorne examined their minds, hearts, talents, and temperaments. They might act as advisers to the sick or misguided, as fabricators of decorative, utilitarian, or artistic objects, as advocates for art, or as tormented protagonists whose talents were not fully understood or properly valued.

Hawthorne's artist-figures who advise sick or misguided people include George Herkimer, Alice Vane, Hester, and Holgrave. Herkimer, a sculptor in "Egotism; or the Bosom Serpent" (1843) who has lived and worked in Italy for several years, returns from Florence to help his cousin cure her husband, whose jealousy and envy have reduced him to near lunacy. Herkimer is a man of sympathy, insight, and faith who prays for heavenly wisdom "to discharge [his] errand aright!" (X: 268). Trained as he is to seek hints of character in facial expression or complexion, he quickly notes that Roderick's skin "had a greenish tinge over its sickly white, reminding him of a species of marble out of which he had once wrought a head of Envy, with her snaky locks" (X: 269). Through Herkimer's plan, Roderick hears the curative words of his wife, Rosina: "Forget yourself, my husband . . . forget yourself in the idea of another!" (X: 283). After the serpent leaves Roderick's bosom, Herkimer remains to pose a deep question: "Can a breast in which so much egotism in the form of jealousy was lodged be purified?" The answer comes from Rosina, "Oh, yes!" she says, "the serpent was but a dark fantasy, and what it typified was as shadowy as itself. The past, dismal as it seems, shall fling no gloom upon the future. To give it its due importance, we must think of it but as an anecdote in our Eternity!"

(X: 283). In bringing a separated couple together, Herkimer does much the same thing that Kenyon will later do in Perugia's marketplace, though more eloquently. Herkimer is little more than a tool of the plot and is given an even smaller role in "The Christmas Banquet" (1844), where he must simply listen as Roderick reads a story.

The purpose of Alice Vane, the heroine of "Edward Randolph's Portrait," is larger than restoring an egomaniac to the magnetic chain of humanity. Her youthful idealism and her belief in a democratic form of government put her in opposition to her misguided uncle, Lieutenant-Governor Hutchinson. When reasoned opinion and heartfelt words fail to persuade him to disobey an order to turn Castle William over to a British officer, Alice tries another tactic. The means Alice chooses to reach her uncle's mind and heart, since his ears are closed to her pleadings, is cleaning a portrait of Edward Randolph.

When Alice removes a veil that she has placed before the restored portrait, allowing her uncle and the Selectmen to see it, Hutchinson chides her: "Girl! . . . have you brought hither your painter's art—your Italian spirit of intrigue—your tricks of stage-effect—and think to influence the councils of rulers and the affairs of nations, by such shallow contrivances?" (IX: 268). Her strategy fails, and the patriotic Alice asks God to forgive her uncle. But Hawthorne has given her a unique place among his artists by allowing her to defend the cause of liberty. In choosing *Vane* as her surname, Hawthorne probably wanted his readers to think of Henry Vane the younger, once governor of Massachusetts and champion of parliamentary causes in England. Hawthorne believed Hutchinson's loyalty to the king made him hostile to republicanism, a point Hawthorne returned to in *Famous Old People:* "A devoted monarchist, Hutchinson would heave no sigh for the subversion of the original republican government, the purest that the world had seen, with which the colony began its existence" (VI: 138). Obviously, Alice had not forgotten these king-resisting men and thus showed her uncle that she kept the spirit of independence alive.

As one who lived among those grim and stern Puritans whom Hutchinson betrays in yielding to the demands of the British crown, Hester Prynne, an artist whose medium is embroidery, gained a respectable place not only by meeting the ceremonial and burial needs of Puritan Boston but also by performing charitable deeds for her fellow townsmen. While some iconoclastic Bostonians censured her artistically wrought "A," taking the symbol of shame on her bosom as yet another sign of her consort with evil, other citizens, in time, took it to stand for angel, a token appropriately signifying her selfless services to the community. Meanwhile, Hester scorned her Puritan neighbors' attempt to convert her and her letter into a symbol "at which the preacher and moralist might point, and in which they might vivify and embody their images of woman's frailty and sinful passion" (I: 79). Not to resist would mean "giving up her individuality" (I: 79). Hester affirmed through her art and good deeds that she intended to let no one break her link in the magnetic chain of humanity. Her conduct and struggle to keep the claims of heart and head balanced served as an antidote to the misguided dependence on the intellect that her Puritan neighbors adopted.

Although his artistic mode is much more mechanical than that of Hester, another artist whose "inward strength" Hawthorne celebrates is Holgrave, the warmhearted and flexible daguerreotypist:

> Altogether, in his culture and want of culture; in his crude, wild, and misty philosophy, and the practical experience that countered some of its tendencies; in his magnanimous zeal for man's welfare, and his recklessness of whatever the ages had established in man's behalf; in his faith, and in his infidelity; in what he had, and in what he lacked—the artist might fitly stand forth as the representative of many compeers in his native land. (II: 181)

Here then is an artist for a democratic people, an idealistic descendant of Alice Vane and an heir to Hester Prynne. Holgrave appears to be preparing himself to live agreeably and productively in a society where aristocracy must yield to Jacksonian notions, where the common man should have his due, as does Uncle Venner. Hawthorne will neither allow Holgrave to turn his intellectual powers inward and become isolated, a Digby or an Ethan Brand, nor violate the sanctity of another human heart by using his hypnotic powers. The dark side of Holgrave's nature responds to the sunshine of Phoebe's, making him realize that, as a daguerreotypist accustomed to catching the inmost secrets of his subjects through sunlight, he can best hold his place in the chain of humanity as an active participant in life. He cannot hide out in some obscure gable of the house if he wants to be whole. But we must conclude that Holgrave will in time become a Jeffersonian democrat, if not a Whig, because of his willingness to assume the role of a country gentleman. How much of a friend he will be to society at large remains a question. Once again Hawthorne was to use an artist-figure as an antidote to misguided social and political ambitions, this time the Pyncheons' aspirations to live like aristocrats. A man less friendly than Holgrave would have let these last relics of Salem aristocracy crumble to the ground.

A more limited act of friendship emerges in John Singleton Copley's support of Shem Drowne, the self-taught woodcarver from Maine whose figure heads and other woodcarvings had won fame. "These specimens of native sculpture had crossed the sea in all directions, and been not ignobly noticed among the crowded shipping of the Thames, and wherever else the hardy mariners of New England had pushed their adventures" (X: 308). Out of "the dearth of any professional sympathy" (X: 310), Copley came to Drowne's shop to meet him and to examine his work, most of it marked with cleverness, fancy, and skill, but lacking a "life-giving touch." Then Copley's eyes fall on the half-developed figure of a woman in the corner of Drowne's shop:

> "What is here? Who has done this?" he broke out, after contemplating it in speechless astonishment for an instant. "Here is the divine, the lifegiving touch! What inspired hand is beckoning this wood arise and live? Whose work is this?"
> "No man's work," replied Drowne. "The figure lies within that block of oak, and it is my business to find it."
> "Drowne," said the true artist, grasping the carver fervently by his hand, "you are a man of genius." (X: 311)

Copley divines the secret of Drowne's success, love for his subject: "Strange enough!" said the artist to himself. "Who would have looked for a modern Pygmalion in the person of a Yankee mechanic!" (X: 312). Returning almost daily to watch Drowne's progress, Copley thinks that if the statue was marble, Drowne could become famous. Because Copley wants him to treat the figurehead as if it were marble, he suggests the radical departure of leaving it unpainted. Drowne refuses, saying,

> "Mr. Copley," . . . "I know nothing of marble statuary, and nothing of a sculptor's rules of art. But of this wooden image— this work of my hands—this creature of my heart—" and here his voice faltered and choked, in a very singular manner—"of this—of her—I may say that I know something. A wellspring of inward wisdom gushed within me, as I wrought upon the oak with my whole strength, and soul, and faith! Let others do what they may with marble, and adopt what rules they choose. If I can produce my desired effect by painted wood, those rules are not for me, and I have a right to disregard them."
> "The very spirit of genius!" muttered Copley to himself. "How otherwise should this carver feel himself entitled to transcend all rules, and make me ashamed of quoting them." (X: 313)

Copley also advises Drowne to send the Oaken Lady to England, where she might bring him a thousand pounds.

> "I have not wrought it for money," said Drowne.
> "What sort of fellow is this!" thought Copley. "A Yankee, and throw away the chance of making his fortune! He has gone mad; and thence has come this gleam of genius." (X: 315)

When Copley later sees the young lady from Fayal and realizes exactly what released Drowne's genius, he says, "You have been a truly fortunate man. What painter or statuary ever had such a subject! No wonder that she inspired a genius into you, and first created the artist who afterwards created her image" (X: 318-19). This remark is over Drowne's head, since he does not fully sense the importance of a Galatea. "This image! Can it have been my work? Well—I have wrought it in a kind of dream" (X: 319).

Throughout this story, then, Copley is a man of good will, sensitivity, and insight. His praise of Drowne's work places a value on the woodcarver's achievement that elevates Drowne to a place among American artists and argues, implicitly at least, that America could produce notable art within native traditions (Davis, 127-31).

Drowne's one piece of inspired art, his one moment when the ideal passed from his soul and dreams through his hands into a fully realized expression of his genius, could be adequately judged only by Copley. In a time and place where art was valued for its utility more than for its expression of the beautiful and the ideal, a Copley was invaluable. But Drowne sinks back to his accustomed role after this one inspired piece.

Hawthorne created two other colonial artists in Boston who work to satisfy the demands of their Puritan customers. One of these, of course, is Hester, whose needle produces "manifold emblematic devices" (I: 82) as well as ruffs, gloves, and robes. The other is the unnamed painter of "The Prophetic Pictures" who limns faces and spends his time and oils depicting "a few ells of broadcloth and brocade" (IX: 171) for the richest and proudest of his sitters. The bride and groom who come to him thought it was most proper "to obtain their portraits, as the first of what, they doubtless hoped, would be a long series of family pictures" (IX: 169). In discussing their portraits with the painter, they reject a joint portrait representing them engaged in some appropriate action because so large a space of canvas would have been too large for their parlor (IX: 171-72). But in sitting for two separate half-length portraits that fit their decoration scheme, they got more than they bargained for, distressing insight into souls. Though he easily might have done so, Hawthorne here makes no issue of Elinor and Walter's philistinism. The satiric glance at their bourgeois tastes quickly gives way to his far deeper interest in the characters of the painter and his subjects.

That interest in artist-figures as upholders of aesthetic values differing from those of the customers they serve continues in Hawthorne's presentation of Owen Warland and Wigglesworth. Owen's customers expect him to do useful work, the kind that Peter Hovenden had done to satisfy his. Owen can be the artist of the beautiful only by extraordinary efforts. The useful will earn him praise and money. To strive for the beautiful is to lose money, evoke scorn, and risk lunacy. Unlike Owen, Wigglesworth is willing to give the customer what he wants and to keep his thoughts to himself. Like the Danforths and Hovendens of this world, Wigglesworth cannot accept the narrator's opinions about gravestones, opinions Owen might have voiced:

> "Every grave-stone that you ever made is the visible symbol of a mistaken system. Our thoughts should soar upward with the butterfly—not linger with the exuviae that confined him. In truth and reason, neither those whom we call the living, and still less the departed, have any thing to do with the grave."
>
> "I never heard any thing so heathenish!" said Mr. Wigglesworth, perplexed and displeased at sentiments which controverted all his notions and feelings, and implied the utter waste, and worse, of his whole life's labor,—"would you forget your dead friends, the moment they are under the sod!" (IX: 418)

But this outburst from a man carrying on one of Puritan New England's best-known uses of graven images, this defense from a man with the same surname as a memorable New England divine, captures the ambivalence of Puritans: even as they marched to the Celestial City they clung to the earth with the grip of a Mammon. Little wonder then that a latter-day Puritan, Peter Hovenden, could not understand what Owen wanted to express by creating a butterfly. Hawthorne expressed his own artistic frustration through these dramatized encounters between seekers of the ideal and the beautiful and customers who restrain the role of the artist. Owen emerges as a flawed artist though as a strong advocate of art, his advocacy all the stronger because Hawthorne evidently shared his passion for creating something beautiful and enduring, even if duration is ultimately, or especially, a "spiritual possession." Like Owen, Hawthorne believed that the imperfect, the incomplete, is more glorious than a finished work. What appears to be resignation and defeat is illusory. In conception lies triumph. To the commonsensical, such notions are absurd; to the artistic, they can be sparks to creativity.

But Hawthorne does not usually create artists to serve as doctrinaire champions of art or mere mouthpieces for himself. Typically, he is far more interested in probing their psyches than he is in forcing one of them to shoulder a placard. One of the most intriguing artist-figures is Aylmer, the young scientist of "The Birthmark" (1843). Aylmer may be considered an artist, though his means and methods may appear unusual, because he strives for aesthetic perfection, assuming the role of Pygmalion and plying his craft upon his wife to transform her into a perfect Galatea. Like Hawthorne's other artists, Aylmer is flawed himself and will never achieve the goal his idealistic eyes envision. Aylmer's flaw is hubris. His singlemindedness renders him heartless, and these are conditions that Hawthorne finds most destructive to the magnetic chain of humanity. Aylmer's enthusiasm for aesthetic improvement through the transforming powers of science links him with the unnamed colonial artist of "The Prophetic Pictures," whose encomium to art sprang from the same sort of belief that Aylmer placed in science.

> "Oh, glorious Art!" thus mused the enthusiastic painter, as he trod the street. "Thou art the image of the Creator's own. The innumerable forms, that wander in nothingness, start into being at thy beck. The dead live again. Thou recallest them to their old scenes, and givest their gray shadows the lustre of a better life, at once earthly and immortal. Thou snatchest back the fleeing moments of History. With thee, there is no Past; for, at thy touch, all that is great becomes forever present; and illustrious men live through long ages, in the visible performance of the very deeds, which made them what they are. Oh, potent Art! as thou bringest the faintly revealed Past to stand in that narrow strip of sunlight, which we call Now, canst thou summon the shrouded Future to meet her there? Have I not achieved it! Am I not thy Prophet?" (IX: 179)

But his dedication to art, despite the human concern that led him to warn Elinor of her impending fate and later to restrain Walter's hand, has made him less than a whole man: "He had no aim—no pleasure—no sympathies—but what were ultimately connected with his art. Though gentle in manner, and upright in intent and action, he did not possess kindly feelings; his heart was cold; no living creature could be brought near enough to keep him warm" (IX: 178).

Since coldhearted people in Hawthorne's fiction are often doomed to suffer (or inflict suffering), the unnamed artist seems to present the narrator of "The Prophetic Pictures" with a challenge because the artist's deeds from beginning to end belie the narrator's ascription of a cold heart. Words and deeds are at war, suggesting that Hawthorne was uncertain whether creative solitude and the insights it brought were worth the price of isolation.[13] The story should perhaps be marked as a failed piece of Gothicism in which a Byronic painter obtrudes into the lives of two psychological cripples and saves them from themselves. From its opening paragraphs, the story drops hint after hint that Walter glimpsed the truth about himself and his capacity for violence. Elinor's heart, the reader sees, counts for more than her ears and eyes. She does not achieve a counterpoise of head and heart. Thus it could be argued that a prophetic picture, a *tableau vivant*, existed before the painter agreed to do portraits of the couple:

"For Heaven's sake, dearest Elinor, do not let him paint the look which you now wear," said her lover, smiling, though rather perplexed. "There: it is passing away now, but when you spoke, you seemed frightened to death, and very sad besides. What were you thinking of?"

"Nothing; nothing," answered Elinor, hastily. "*You paint my face with your own fantasies.* [Italics added.] Well, come for me tomorrow and we will visit this wonderful artist." (IX: 167)

If we thus exonerate the artist from meddling, his advocacy of art loses the self-serving note of a Gothic wielder of power and becomes a paean that Drowne or Owen might have quoted approvingly, realizing as they did its exaggerated claims.[14] Yet any paean must perhaps be qualified by something bubbling up from Hawthorne's Puritan past, something he voiced while sitting for Thompson after the publication of *The Scarlet Letter.* "The pursuit [of portrait painting] has always interested my imagination more than any other; and I remember, before having my first portrait taken, there was a great bewitchery in the idea, as if it were a magic process" (VIII: 492-93). Perhaps Hawthorne retained some vestigial fear of graven images, some question about the right of the artist to play the role of creator, some confusion as to whether an artist might be no more creative than a Paul Pry, Mother Rigby, or Aylmer. Hawthorne's "great bewitchery" is indeed provocative.

While troubling questions arose as he depicted artist-figures, Hawthorne used them to his advantage to encourage readers to consider an artist's place in society, as in the roles Drowne and Owen play in their communities. By reaching far beyond his usual grasp just once, by finding a way to show "that in every human spirit there is imagination, sensibility, creative power, genius," Drowne stands by example and achievement as an advocate of art. No matter that he sinks back to the status of a mere mechanical carver, for just this once he has realized his potential, a height he achieved because a Galatea empowers and inspires him for a time. Drowne's achievement suggests that the quality of art in America will depend on the quality of its inspiration. Luckily, Drowne found his Galatea; Owen Warland looked in vain for one.

Annie Hovenden, the thimble-bearing daughter of the man of iron and fiancée of a blacksmith, cannot realize her highest potential and become Owen's inspiration. If Annie and other upholders of practicality rebuke the artist, he needs inward strength to carry on alone: "It is requisite for the ideal artist to possess a force of character that seems hardly compatible with its delicacy; he must keep his faith in himself, while the incredulous world assails him with its utter disbelief; he must stand up against mankind and be his own sole disciple, both as respects his genius, and the objects to which it is directed" (X: 454). These words

Melville would later mark as worthy of thought, as he did a later passage
in "The Artist of the Beautiful":

> Alas, that the artist, whether in poetry or whatever other
> material, may not content himself with the inward enjoyment of
> the Beautiful, but must chase the flitting mystery beyond the
> verge of his ethereal domain, and crush its frail being in seizing it
> with a material grasp! Owen Warland felt the impulse to give
> external reality to his ideas, as irresistibly as any of the poets or
> painters, who have arrayed the world in a dimmer and fainter
> beauty, imperfectly copied from the richness of their visions.
> (X: 458)

The pain of isolation, the frustration of failure, the sense of being held
captive by both time and money—all could be better endured if a
supportive, loving, sympathetic person stood by the artist. Without
that, the artist must content himself with the act of creating, with the joy
of shadowing forth at least part of his glimpse of the ideal, going beyond
dull realities to the realm of the imagination. Granted hope of that
accomplishment, regardless how fleeting, since the ideal as transmuted
into art form will not last eternally, an artist will make extraordinary
sacrifices, suffer great indignities, and perform demanding tasks to
share his talents. Before his work comes into being, and even after its
destruction, an artist has spiritual or imaginative possession of it. To
render this possession into marble or to express it by brush and paints is
but to give it material existence. That is why Owen remains so calm after
the Danforth baby crushes the butterfly. "He had caught a far other
butterfly than this. When the artist rose high enough to achieve the
Beautiful, the symbol by which he made it perceptible to mortal senses
became of little value in his eyes, while his spirit possessed itself in
enjoyment of the Reality" (X: 475). Typically, Hawthorne's artists
temper their advocacy of art and the artist's life, as Owen does here, by
admitting the price they must pay to pursue the ideal.

One step beyond artists serving as characters are those people in
Hawthorne's fiction whose lives—in some measure—imitate art.
Zenobia's use of "engravings from the Old Masters" as models for her
tableaux vivants is the simplest example. More complex is Pearl's
"inherited . . . gift for devising drapery and custom." When she
fashions an "A" from eelgrass in imitation of her mother's embroidered
scarlet letter, Pearl does not simply display a green "A" upon her
bosom; she "bent her chin upon her breast, and contemplated this
device with strange interest; even as if the one only thing for which she
had been sent into the world was to make out its hidden import" (I: 178).
When Pearl declares that the reason Hester wears the "A" is the same

reason that Dimmesdale holds his hand over his heart, Hester thinks her child might be nearing a "meeting-point of sympathy" (I: 179). Pearl has displayed signs of the true artist's disposition and ability. No longer would she be limited to mere surface meanings. Her act of imitation and her probing beneath surface meanings bring insight and promise maturity. She is becoming adept at reading emblems and begins to understand what they reveal about the human condition.

A far more adept reader—and manipulator—of symbols appears in *The Blithedale Romance*. Zenobia, as "womanliness incarnated," should have been willing to pose "endlessly" for sculptors and painters, thought Miles Coverdale, "because the cold decorum of the marble would consist with the utmost scantiness of drapery, so that the eye might chastely be gladdened with her material perfection, in its entireness" (III: 44). Her picturesque manner and dress indeed remind Coverdale of a statue or portrait. She was too much of an artist herself, however, to sit as a model. Agreeable though her staging of *tableaux vivants* was, Zenobia at last grew weary of putting them on, explaining, "Our own features, and our own figures and airs, show a little too intrusively through all the characters we assume. We have so much familiarity with one another's realities, that we cannot remove ourselves, at pleasure, into an imaginary sphere" (III: 107). At this moment, she turns from her roles as stage director and scenic designer to become another kind of artist, a storyteller. Her narrative art matches her theatrical skill; in fact, the two blend during her tale about Theodore and the Veiled Lady. Since this tale in some respects mirrors Priscilla's own role as a lyceum performer, art here imitates both life and another form of art (staged picturesque supernaturalism). Realizing how apt the parallel is, Priscilla nearly faints as the story comes to an end. When Zenobia next imitated art, the outcome was disastrous. Ironically, the occasion for Zenobia's enactment of a scene from art originates in Hollingsworth's choice of Priscilla over her. Zenobia's loss of Hollingsworth drives her to commit suicide. Not unexpectedly, Coverdale pointedly suggests that Zenobia found art an inspiration for her last desperate act: "She had seen pictures, I suppose, of drowned persons, in lithe and graceful attitudes. . . . [T]here was some tint of the Arcadian affectation that had been visible enough in all our lives, for a few months past" (III: 236-37).

Just what pictures this romantic and tragic heroine might have seen, Hawthorne does not say, though his invocation of Shakespearean drama suggests that he might have been thinking of Eugene Delacroix's illustration of Ophelia's death, which had been engraved in 1843. Delacroix's Ophelia seems less "lithe and graceful" than Sir John Everett Millais's Ophelia, but Millais's Ophelia was not available in lithograph until 1853, a few months after the publication of *The Blithedale Romance*. Delacroix depicts Ophelia as a statuesque figure with one exposed breast. She clutches posies in her right hand, which is pressed tightly against the right breast, and holds not very firmly onto a branch of a tree as she slides into the water. The stream, trees, and grass provide ample hints of Arcady. A scene so quiet and pretty diminishes the depravity and finality of her act. The fateful twist of the last act of staging is that Zenobia creates a haunting and horrible *tableau mort* for the dwellers at Blithedale.

THE LIFE AND WORK OF AN ARTIST: HAWTHORNE ON BENJAMIN WEST

Although they were at odds over many things, one dislike united Puritans and Quakers—their scorn of graven images. The story of how one Quaker boy overcame that obstacle and became the most celebrated painter of colonial America would be told by a descendant of a persecutor of Quakers when Hawthorne chose Benjamin West for one of the six *Biographical Stories for Children* (1842). Probably drawing upon John Galt's *The Life, Studies, and Works of Benjamin West* (1832) or an anonymous abridgment of Galt, Hawthorne focused his story on the familiar theme of transformation, claiming "There are fewer stranger transformations than that of a little Quaker boy" (VI: 228) who steadfastly developed his art and became an artist of the beautiful and true.

Hawthorne emphasized the strength and integrity of West's character as he recounted how the Pennsylvania boy met every challenge to his determination to become an artist, whether by cutting fur from the family cat for a homemade brush or by courageously opposing the prevailing standards of art in eighteenth-century London. Jacksonian democrat that he was, Hawthorne seemed pleased to report that West had kept his hat on when introduced to a European prince. His focus on West's integrity and refusal to bow to pressure, artistic or political, finds a parallel in Hawthorne's treatment of such artists as Owen Warland and Shem Drowne.

More interested in narrating dramatic or telling episodes in West's life than in describing or criticizing his paintings, Hawthorne mentioned only two, *The Death of Wolfe* and *Christ Healing the Sick*. Even then he did not deal with the paintings themselves but noted that the Quakers were disturbed by the war scene in the first and that fees for viewing *Christ Healing the Sick* had supported thirty patients in the hospital to which West had given it. Hawthorne's aim in this sketch, as in others in these biographies for children, was to inculcate good moral lessons, to hold up good examples. Of his six subjects—West, Sir Isaac Newton, Oliver Cromwell, Samuel Johnson, Benjamin Franklin, and Queen Christina— all but Christina (whose life exemplified the disastrous effects of a bad education) directly serve that purpose.

The fact that Hawthorne said virtually nothing about West's painting suggests distaste for rather than ignorance of West's work. He later pointed directly to a problem with his work when he saw a West altarpiece in Greenwich Chapel: "Over the altar . . . is a strangely confused picture by West, out of which I could not have made head or tail with the aid of a catalogue" (EN: 372. Quotations are taken from Hawthorne's *English Notebooks*). When he revised the notebook entry for an article in *The Atlantic Monthly*, he frankly explained his dislike of West and the painting:

> I never could look at [the altar piece] long enough to make out its design; for this artist (though it pains me to say it of so respectable a countryman) had a gift of frigidity, a knack for grinding ice into his paint, a power of stupefying the spectator's perceptions and quelling his sympathy, beyond any other limner that ever handled a brush. In spite of my many pangs of conscience, I seize this opportunity to wreak a life-long abhorrence upon the poor, blameless man, for the sake of that dreary picture of Lear, an explosion of frosty fury, that used to be a bugbear to me in the Athenaeum Exhibition. Would fire burn it, I wonder! (V: 230-31)

Whether or nor he saw West's *King Lear* when it was first exhibited in the Boston Athenaeum in 1829, he had fourteen other chances to encounter it before sailing for England (Perkins and Gavin 150). This vinegary outburst specifically explains why he wrote in his notebook, "I hate to think of" West's works (*EN:* 217). But Hawthorne's "pangs of conscience" remind us that he respected the man, admired his dedication to art, and considered him a worthy model for children. More important, it reveals that Hawthorne unsuccessfully struggled to appreciate West's work. The process of acculturation that he had embarked upon in America had given him some aesthetic convictions he would always retain, chiefly his belief that an artist's heart must enter into his creation if he is to evoke the viewer's sympathetic understanding.

Hawthorne's "pangs of conscience" seem to betray a concern that he had been less than honest with his young readers when he highlighted West's efforts to overcome obstacles. Writing dispassionately as a biographer, Hawthorne had ground some ice into his own paint and refused the role of critic.

THE AMERICAN PHASE: EAGERNESS WEDDED TO AMBIVALENCE

Through reading, through visits to galleries and exhibitions, through conversations with friends on the subject of art and artists, through

marriage to a practicing artist, and, more important, through his efforts
to understand artistic creativity by writing about it, Hawthorne climbed
his ladder of taste. He enjoyed hanging original works of art on his
walls, especially if they were by Sophia, and he enjoyed displaying
prints of a few celebrated masterpieces. To assist him in climbing the
ladder of taste, he turned to Winckelmann on classical art and to Ruskin
on modern artists. For the children he bought books containing
engravings of famous works. Sitting for a portrait by Cephas Giovanni
Thompson brought out old thoughts about the "bewitchery of art." He
shared Sophia's dream of seeing the art treasures of Italy. And he was
confident enough about his judgment to tell a publisher that William
Ellery Channing offered sound criticism in his book on art.

All this seems to suggest that he bounded up the ladder of taste
quickly and easily, but that was far from the case. No sooner had he
struggled up a rung or two than he worried about acquiring the glibness
of a dilettante. More than that, he felt uneasy about an artist's alleged
powers of penetrating to the human soul, about the artist's potential for
violating the sanctity of the human heart. He worried about his
relatively uninstructed visions and his receptivity. He wanted to criticize
American philistinism, but he also viewed the American distrust of art
as a safeguard against the corruption of Europe.

His climb up the ladder of taste had brought satisfying joys and
candidly admitted anxieties, but when he and his family sailed for
England on the *Niagara* in July 1853, he eagerly looked forward to a
deeper immersion in the arts.

NOTES

1. The staff at the Bowdoin Museum kindly compiled a list of the artworks in
the Bowdoin collection during Hawthorne's undergraduate years.

2. For a discussion of Hawthorne's use of Bell's theories on hands, see John
L. Idol, Jr., "A Show of Hands in 'The Artist of the Beautiful,'" *Studies in Short
Fiction* 22, no. 4 (Fall 1985): 455-60.

3. Hawthorne refused a project that Hammatt Billings suggested as a joint
venture. As he explained to Sophia, "I would rather write books of my own
imagining than be hired to develope the ideas of an engraver" (XV: 677). When
his imaginings led him to complete *A Wonder-Book for Girls and Boys*, he asked his
publisher, Fields, to engage Billings to illustrate it with "fanciful designs." He
assured Fields that his stories would "bear out the artist in any liberties he may
be inclined to take" (XVI: 437). He added, "Billings would do those things well
enough, though his characteristics are grace and delicacy rather than wildness of
fancy" (XVI: 437). Hawthorne's apparent ease with commonplaces of Victorian
criticism suggests considerable sophistication, though he might have been
passing along Sophia's judgment.

4. See Margaret Fuller Ossoli (Pt. II, 108-21); Oliver Wendell Holmes (358-81); Elizabeth Palmer Peabody (30-62).

5. At least one of Clarke's paintings of Kentucky is still in the Athenaeum. Clarke was one of Sophia's bridesmaids.

6. He did have a match holder decorated with drawings from John Flaxman, a gift from his sister Elizabeth.

7. Emerson gave Sophia prints of works by Raphael, Michelangelo, and Da Vinci, which were later displayed in revered places in various Hawthorne homes.

8. His remarks on *Venus de Medici* or Hiram Powers's *The Greek Slave* more truly represent Hawthorne on nudity than do the often quoted comments of Hilda and Miriam in *The Marble Faun*.

9. For a discussion of Hawthorne's use of the Claude landscape, see Fritz Gysin, "Paintings in the House of Fiction: The Example of Hawthorne," *Word & Image* 5, no. 2 (April-June 1989): 159-72.

10. For an informed treatment of Hawthorne's use of the diorama, see Jean Normand, *Nathaniel Hawthorne: An Approach to an Analysis of Artistic Creation*, translated by Derek Cox (Cleveland, Ohio: The Press of Case Western Reserve University, 1970): 308-33.

11. More recently, three unpublished dissertations have given more extensive attention to Hawthorne's manipulation of light and shade: William A. Cook, "Hawthorne's Artistic Theory and Practice," Lehigh University, 1971; Judith Kaufman Budz, "Nathaniel Hawthorne and the Visual Arts," Northwestern University, 1973; and Patricia Dunlavy Valenti, "Hawthorne's Use of Visual Elements," University of North Carolina, 1977. The studies of Benjamin Lease and J. Gill Holland on Hawthorne's knowledge of dioramas, daguerreotypes, and photography suggest that Hawthorne learned something about the artistic handling of light and shade from these contemporary visual devices.

12. For a succinct account of Hawthorne's theory of fiction, see Terence Martin, *Nathaniel Hawthorne* (38-48).

13. Gupta's (1972) position on the painter's role (65-80) is more convincing than Dichmann's (188-202).

14. Stephanie Fay, "Lights from Dark Corners: Works of Art in 'The Prophetic Pictures' and 'The Artist of the Beautiful,'" *Studies in American Fiction* 13, no. 1 (Spring 1985): 15-29 joins a long list of discussions of Hawthorne's use of the unnamed colonial artist and Owen Warland by Baym, Bell, Curran, Dichmann, Doubleday, Fairbanks, Fogle, Gupta, Liebman, and West.

The European Experience

ENGLAND

Hawthorne's experience of art in England was remarkable only in its sparseness at the beginning and its richness at the end of his four-year stay. From his first view of his consular office in August 1853, Hawthorne might have anticipated that Liverpool would not foster his education as a connoisseur of art: his room contained a "hideous colored lithograph of General Taylor, life-size, and one or two smaller engraved portraits; also three representations of American naval victories; a lithograph of the Tennessee State-house, and another of the Steamer Empire State" (*EN:* 3). Yet at the annual exhibitions of the Liverpool Academy, Hawthorne might have looked at recent works by William Holman Hunt, Edwin Landseer, John Millais, and dozens of other artists, including many that had been shown at the Royal Academy. Reviewing those exhibitions, the London *Art-Journal* reported that the quality was high and hundreds of paintings were sold every year; but if Hawthorne saw any of them, he did not say so. Nor did he say anything about the paintings he undoubtedly saw whenever he dined with the local gentry. But at the beginning of his second year as consul, he noted that the mayor held a soiree at the town hall, "adorned for the occasion with a large collection of pictures, belonging to Mr. Naylor," the works of "modern artists, comprising some of Turner, Wilkie, Landseer, and others of the best English painters."[1] If Hawthorne's aesthetic education was not making rapid advances in Liverpool, it was hardly at a standstill.

The easy reference to "the best English painters" indicates he felt sure about which were the best, however he acquired that certainty. Further, his following comment that Turner's work "seemed too airy to have been done by mortal hands" suggests an initial appreciation of the controversial painter whose "airiness" later gave him problems (*EN:* 88). An even more interesting indication of early familiarity with English painting is a spare notation for 3 April 1854. Following the description of a regiment marching to embark for war, he wrote, "March to Finchley," casually invoking a Hogarth painting he would enthusiastically praise three years later in Manchester for its truth "to English life and character" (*EN:* 59, 549, 556-57). Whether the soldiers Hawthorne saw in 1854 reminded him of Hogarth's painting or an engraving of it, Hogarth's robust images had already made an indelible impression.

Like most of his contemporaries, he assumed the existence of a hierarchy in art, parallel to a hierarchy in literature. Imitations of ordinary life were at the bottom; sacred and heroic subjects were at the top. Mimetic exactitude was crucial at the bottom; but even at the top, nobility and beauty had to comport with truth to human experience. Thus Hogarth deserved his popularity, but (as Hawthorne later said of Wilkie) his achievement was limited and "low," readily accessible to the most limited taste. Hawthorne's highest praise was reserved for a work of art—whether a painting or a novel—that convincingly, skillfully, and beautifully embodied a noble conception of reality, interpreted with enough intelligence and passion to enlist the perceiver's (or reader's) imagination.

Meanwhile, he had been training his eyes to appreciate "English life and character" in other ways. He had come to England with a predisposition to view things pictorially; and (possibly with the aid of Hogarth) he could regard even the dark, dirty, and crowded slums of Liverpool as "very picturesque in their way" (*EN:* 13). He could more readily enjoy the picturesque countryside, particularly the ivy-covered ruins he would fondly remember in Italy. But whether in the city or the country, on a casual ramble or a concerted sightseeing trip, he would dutifully record "characteristics" and "remarkables" in his notebook, though complaining even in his first year abroad of a limited attention span and a weariness of "antiquities."

Yet he did not visit a major repository of art until September 1855, when the family spent a month in London before Sophia sailed for Portugal. During their visits to the standard tourist attractions few works of art arrested Hawthorne's attention, though he did say that in the chapel at Greenwich he saw "a large picture of [Benjamin] West— whose works I hate to think of," and he merely noted that one of the paintings of naval battles in the great hall was by Turner (*EN:* 217). A few weeks later when he and Sophia wandered into a gallery of modern painting along Oxford Street and looked at several works by Benjamin Haydon, all but a sketch of Wordsworth seemed "exceedingly disagreeable." But his contempt for the gallery's other artists suggests more familiarity with contemporary English painting than the notebooks otherwise indicate: he concluded that the gallery was primarily "a receptacle for pictures by artists who can obtain places nowhere else." He then reached a surprisingly pessimistic generalization that he would hold onto even in Italy: "There is very little talent in this world, and what there is, it seems to me, is pretty well known and acknowledged. We don't often stumble upon geniuses in obscure corners" (EN: 241).

Then the very next day he was even more distressed by his encounter with "well known and acknowledged" works, not stumbled upon in an obscure corner but seen by design in the British Museum. What happened would occur repeatedly in art collections in England and on the Continent: he felt overwhelmed by the extent of the exhibits and their unfamiliarity, and he was disheartened by the depredations of time. Sweepingly dismissing almost everything as "rubbish," he said the beauty of the shattered Elgin marbles must be "guessed at, and seen by faith," and he suspected that most of those "who seem to be enraptured by these fragments, do not really care about them; neither do I. And if I were actually moved, I should doubt whether it were by the statues, or by my own fancy" (EN: 242).

On his second extended visit to London the following spring, he made a more concerted effort to appreciate the art treasures of England, taking an excursion to Hampton Court and visiting the National Gallery as well as the British Museum. Characteristically, as with the Elgin marbles, he approached each of the famous art objects dutifully but without any anticipation of pleasure. Repeatedly, he deprecated his own ability to respond adequately, and he was quick to complain if the work was in poor condition or poorly displayed. At best, he offered only sparse praise, aware of prevailing critical opinion but refusing to be bound by it.

Thus he did "not pretend to admire, nor to understand" the celebrated Raphael cartoons in Hampton Court:

> I can conceive, indeed, that there is a great deal of expression in them, and very probably they may, in every respect, deserve all their fame; but on this point I can give no testimony. To my perception, they were a series of very much faded pictures, dimly seen (for this part of the palace was now in shadow) and representing figures neither graceful nor beautiful, nor, as far as I could discern, particularly grand. But I came to them with a wearied mind and eye; and also I had a previous distaste to them through the medium of engravings. (EN: 286)

Like most of his contemporaries, Hawthorne placed works of beauty and grandeur at the top of an established aesthetic hierarchy; but he could not see beauty or grandeur in the cartoons. Such scrupulous phrases as "to my perception" and "as far as I could discern" qualify his comment, and he readily granted that his weariness, the pictures' faded color, the palace's dim light, and his "previous distaste" might account for his response. But he did not join the almost universal chorus of praise for Raphael, and he would not do so steadily even after encountering his major paintings in Italy.

The same mixture of self-trust and self-mistrust that Raphael provoked is evident in his more fully developed account of visiting the National Gallery of Art two days later. Again he felt dismayed by the apparent limits of his receptivity; but he did not despair. "It is of no use for me to criticise pictures, or to try to describe them," he said, "but I have an idea that I might get up a taste, with some little attention to the subject; for I find I already begin to prefer some pictures to others. This is encouraging." Yet, characteristically, he immediately undercut even this cautious optimism: he would not remain in London long enough to "get up a taste." Even when recording his artistic preferences, he cautiously qualified his response: he did not say "Murillo's are the best" or "I like some by Murillo best," but "I think I liked some by Murillo best." Nevertheless he tried to sort out his preferences: "some of Claude's" seemed more beautiful than two Turners he looked at, but a Canaletto seemed "wonderful—absolutely perfect—a better reality" (EN: 292-93). He would later formulate his aesthetic criteria more explicitly but without essential change: the perfect work of art told truths about this world but suggested a better one.

Finally, however, people interested him more than art. Even when his taste was most highly developed, he preferred works of art that enlarged his understanding of human predicaments and possibilities; but even "low" behavior engaged him. Thus, on his first visit to the National Gallery, he relished the sight of three spectators grinning at a "lascivious" Venus observed by a satyr even more than he enjoyed the painting itself (EN: 293).

His visit to the British Museum the following day was far less satisfying. The "dead weight" of the past that had burdened him on his first visit had not lifted. "It quite crushes a person to see so much at once," he said, and wished "(Heaven forgive me!) that the Elgin marbles and the frieze of the Parthenon were all burnt into lime" (EN: 294). The very fact that Hawthorne visited the museum a second time demands attention: as events in Manchester and in Italy would further prove, he was never stymied by frustration. Even though his subsequent third visit to the British Museum was again "wearisome and depressing," he could then grant that some of the old sculptures were "doubtless grand and beautiful in their day." Nevertheless, he added a characteristically negative qualification: "It is by no means plain to me that their merit has not been vastly overestimated" (EN: 591). His patience was better rewarded the following month when at last he felt "on more familiar terms" with the collections and not "weighed down by the multitude of things to be seen." Shifting to the metaphor of eating (one he would use repeatedly in Italy), he said he could never "devour and digest the whole enormous collection," but (varying the metaphor slightly) he was pleased to extract "a little honey" from individual objects.[2] Familiarity enabled him to discern "grace and nobility" even in the "battered and shattered" remains of Greek sculpture, and he could then move beyond aesthetics to praise its "potency to educate and refine the minds of those who look at it, even so carelessly and casually as I do" (EN: 609).

But depressed though he was by those maimed and corroded Greek marbles, and revolted though he was by the "human shapes and beast-heads" and other "monstrosities" in the British Museum's Egyptian galleries, he was remarkably receptive to the portrait statues in Westminster Abbey—not that he responded uncritically. Even on his first visit, he was connoisseur enough to say that most of the statues were mediocre and some "little less than ridiculous." Further, the "preponderance of nobodies" surmounted by "great piles of sculpture" made him question the wisdom of "bestowing the age-long duration of marble upon small, characteristic individualities." But he was not impeded by critics' praise; the statues were in relatively good condition and well displayed, and he had time to view them at leisure. He particularly enjoyed recognizing "the mould and fashion of English features through the marble and was inclined to believe that many of the statues and busts preserved "faithful likenesses." Consequently he thought a statue could bring its subject "nearer to the mind" of the viewer, enabling him to "see the man at but one remove, as if you caught his image in a looking-glass." The process of appropriating such objectified individuality would always tantalize Hawthorne whenever he examined portraits, whatever their medium, as when a year later he felt "startled at recognizing myself so apart from myself" in a group portrait taken by England's foremost photographer, Philip Henry Delamotte (EN: 422; Gollin, Portraits, 43-46). But in September 1855 he could declare confidently, albeit with careful qualification, "The bust of Gay seemed to me very good; a thoughtful and humorous sweetness in the face" (EN: 236). If he had not yet seen the world's most celebrated statues, Hawthorne's main criteria for judging them were already in place, though he would refine and expand them in Italy as he dealt with such issues as aesthetic rules, inspiration, nudity, and the appropriateness of color and costume.

Although he was not quite as careless or casual about sculpture as he suggested, paintings were initially more familiar and more immediately accessible to his imagination. "I remember fancying in myself an

increasing taste for pictures," he said after his second visit to the
National Gallery (*EN:* 294). The word "fancying" suggests skepticism,
but evidently his responsiveness pleased him.

A visit to the Vernon Gallery of English painting at Marlborough
House a few months later was even more enjoyable. With his usual
qualification, he said, "I think nothing pleased me more than a picture
by Sir David Wilkie—the Parish Beadle," but he thought he enjoyed
such paintings more than the Old Masters in the National Gallery only
because "my comprehension has not yet reached their height" (*EN:*
389). The word "yet" is crucial, a clear signal that Hawthorne expected
his "comprehension" to improve.

Hawthorne monitored his responses to works of art in the same
thoughtfully cautious way that he monitored his responses to any other
visual experience. Even his earliest notebooks are filled with patient
observations of particular localities and of himself as observer. If he felt
relaxed in surroundings that combined familiarity with some element of
novelty, he could perceive intently, without feeling surfeited or overwhelmed; and if he assimilated the perceptions completely, they became
accessible to his imagination. Like most contemporary travel writers, he
would first describe a scene in his notebooks and then record the
thoughts and emotions it inspired. But his strategy of observation and
meditation was unusually deliberate. He attempted patient surrender to a
scene as he attempted self-surrender before a work of art, singling out
"characteristic" and "remarkable" elements. Sometimes he attained a
profound feeling of intimacy that he expressed as incorporation: he
would "swallow" and "digest" what he observed. But his limited ability
to take in new experiences kept him from being a perfect tourist or a
perfect gallery goer: he needed time and space to process his perceptions.

In these terms, he explained why he enjoyed his second view of
Rydal-water more than the first: "I find that it is impossible to know
accurately how any prospect or other thing looks, until after at least a
second view, which always essentially corrects the first. This, I think, is
especially true in regard to objects which we have heard much about,
and exercised our imagination upon; the first view being a vain attempt
to reconcile our idea with the reality, and in the second we begin to
accept the thing for what it really is" (*EN:* 171). Years before at Niagara
Falls he had a similar experience—not until a second visit could he
separate his own impressions from those of travel writers. His initial
rejection of the Raphael cartoons was partly the result of a comparable
problem: he had "a previous distaste to them through the medium of
the engraving." Always Hawthorne insisted on the importance of
seeing what is "really" there. Perception might be impeded by precon-
ception, overwhelming novelty, or boring familiarity.

At the same time, Hawthorne realized that he required a measure of
mystification at the height of aesthetic pleasure. He enjoyed feeling that

a scene or object eluded his complete comprehension. Thus he was delighted by Gothic cathedrals. He could enjoy their intricate complexity as well as their majestic unity, certain that increased attentiveness would result in increased appreciation. Whether looking at a cathedral, a mountain scene, a painting, or a sketch, he valued "suggestiveness," which would activate and enlarge the observer's imagination. The suggestiveness of a Gothic cathedral was a direct consequence of its conjoining the majestic and the minute; thus St. Michael's in Coventry was "so huge, so rich, with such intricate minuteness in its finish, that, look as long as you will at it, you can always discover something new directly before your eyes. I admire this in Gothic architecture—that you cannot master it all at once—that it is not a naked outline, but as deep and rich as human nature itself" (*EN:* 137). Implicit in this statement is a criterion of aesthetic value he would later apply to paintings and statues: the best seemed to have a "deep and rich" life of their own. In responding to the aesthetic challenge of Gothic cathedrals, Hawthorne was expressing and expanding a taste that would have repelled his New England forbears.

Yet he recognized that aesthetic grandeur and complexity could daunt a spectator who felt unequal to his/her experience. This explains his ambivalence about the Lichfield Cathedral. "I hated to leave gazing at it, because I felt that I did not a hundredth part take it in and comprehend it," Hawthorne said, "and yet I wanted to leave off, because I knew I never should adequately comprehend its beauty and grandeur" (*EN:* 149). This admixture of humility and frustration would recur in Italy whenever he tried to "comprehend" what mystified him, such as the painting of Beatrice Cenci or the statue of Venus de Medici. He felt at once elated and frustrated by any confrontation that eluded his complete "mastery."

In these terms it is easy to understand why Hawthorne enjoyed looking at sketches more than at finished paintings: they expanded his imagination without perplexing it. Thus the drawings by Raphael and Michelangelo that he saw in Oxford were "far better, for my purpose, than their finished pictures; that is to say, they bring me much closer to the hands that drew them, and the minds that imagined them. It is like looking into their brains, and seeing the first conception, before it took shape outwardly" (*EN:* 414). As in "The Artist of the Beautiful," Hawthorne placed an artist's conception above his finished work, and what best served his "purpose" of self-development was entry into a great artist's mind.

His experience at the Manchester Exhibition of Art in the summer of 1857, near the end of his four years as consul in Liverpool, was the culmination of all his previous ventures into connoisseurship and a preparation for his immersion in art in Italy. Diffident though he remained about his taste throughout his weeks in Manchester, he sensed improvement in it, and (both as a cause and a consequence) he increasingly enjoyed his role as a spectator. Meanwhile, whatever ambivalence he expressed, he judged works of art by the same standards that he applied to literature: he looked for truthful images of this world and intimations about the next.

He went to Manchester almost as if enrolling in an academic course—"our principal object being to spend a few weeks in the proximity of the Arts Exhibition." His first visit to the National Gallery a year earlier had made him think "it is no use for me to criticise pictures or even to describe them," but he was now determined to "educate himself" to do both. He had long believed it "the best definition of happiness to live throughout the whole range of his faculties and sensibilities" (I: 40), and the Manchester Exhibition of Art Treasures of the United Kingdom—celebrated as "the largest and most valuable collection of works of art, Ancient and Modern, ever collected"—provided an unprecedented way to develop his aesthetic faculty.[3] He would thus "get some real use and improvement out of what I see" (*EN:* 549). As John Steegman notes in *Victorian Taste*, there was a growing emphasis on individual taste at mid-century, and the Manchester Exhibition was part of a concerted effort to raise the taste of the general populace. Like Prince Albert and the organizers of the exhibition, Hawthorne considered it an educational opportunity. Perhaps he thought he might come closer to Sophia's level of knowledge and so share more fully in her aesthetic pleasures when they reached the Continent. Hawthorne's journal entries from 22 July to 6 September attest that he embarked on his self-appointed but typically Victorian chore with patience and humility, carefully monitoring his responses to art. And while "gradually getting a taste for pictures," he was also laying bases for far-reaching transformations in his attitudes toward art, artists, and spectators.

However, during his first visit to the exhibition (as during his first visit to the British Museum), he felt overwhelmed. "Nothing is more depressing than the sight of a great many pictures together," he declared. Entering the gallery of British painters, he found himself confronting "hundreds of pictures; any one of which would have interested me by itself; but I could not fix my mind on one more than another; so I left my wife there, and wandered away by myself, to get a general idea of the exhibition." Like the efficient tourist who takes a city bus tour before launching out alone, Hawthorne wanted to get a sense of the whole before choosing what he would return to and "digest." He felt numbed by the onslaught of new impressions, "and it was dreary to think of not fully enjoying this collection, the very flower of Time, which never bloomed before, and never by any possibility can bloom again." Although he undercut this tribute by remarking that "every great show is a kind of humbug," his chief reservations were about his "capacity to take in even the whole of this" (*EN:* 547-48).

He tried to take in the whole by dividing it into parts, persistently, deliberately, even stubbornly. On his second visit he concentrated on British painters, conscientiously formulating a "general idea" that he had been gestating for years. The artists succeeded to the extent that they captured ordinary "English life and character," he said, and Hogarth and a few others managed to interpret it; but he concluded that none of them could "paint anything high, heroic, and ideal. . . . They are strong in homeliness and ugliness; weak in their efforts at the beautiful." Reflecting on the group as a whole led him to a puzzling but unavoidable conclusion: the achievements of English painters were "much inferior to those of the English poets, who have really elevated the human mind" (EN: 549-50).

In these terms Hawthorne tried to define his dissatisfaction with the controversial "modern" paintings by Turner and the Pre-Raphaelites; and his comments clarify his literary goals as well as his aesthetic standards. It is difficult to explain his rejection of most of the Pre-Raphaelites' canvases, since they were undeniably accurate in detail, and William Holman Hunt and several others could "really take hold of the mind." He "could have looked all day" at Holman Hunt's realistic yet heavily moralized Strayed Sheep. Yet Hawthorne found most of the Pre-Raphaelites' paintings devoid of beauty and even "disagreeable," as acerb as unripe fruit. "Every single thing represented seems to be taken out of life and reality, and, as it were, pasted down upon the canvas," he said. "They almost paint even separate hairs." Contemptuously appraising one of the exhibition's most discussed paintings, John Millais's Autumn Leaves, he said each leaf seemed "stiffened with gum and varnish, and then put carefully down into the stiffly disordered heap." Such unselective meticulousness pained him: it was as if each separate object pressed "baldly and harshly upon the spectator's eyeballs."[4] Here Hawthorne was not echoing Samuel Johnson's injunction to avoid numbering the streaks when delineating an ideal tulip, but was expressing his awareness that the eye perceives reality selectively. His judgment that the Pre-Raphaelites' "life-like reproductions" were "stiff and unnatural" is wholly consistent with his theory of romance. He required in art and literature what he called "a proper light and shadow" to highlight important details and obscure others, thus suggesting and inviting interpretation. A veil of "semi-obscurity" might bring their canvases "nearer to nature," and perhaps the artists might "hereafter combine their truth of detail with a broader and higher truth" (EN: 550). This remark could have been lifted straight from the pages of Alison's Essays on Taste, which Hawthorne had read three decades earlier.

Turner's paintings presented Hawthorne with an opposite aesthetic problem, one he frequently confronted as a writer. If the Pre-Raphaelites seemed bogged down in detail, Turner seemed to dissipate in mist. "As for Turner, I care no more for his light-colored pictures than for so much lacquered ware, or painted gingerbread,'' Hawthorne wrote, using curiously deflating analogues. Yet, perhaps recalling Ruskin's high praise of Turner, which he had encountered nine years earlier in *Modern Painters,* he humbly declared, ''Doubtless, this is my fault—my own deficiency—but I cannot help it; not, at least, without sophisticating myself by the effort'' (*EN:* 550).[5] He dutifully tried to sophisticate himself by repeated visits until eventually he could see ''something wonderful even in Turner's lights, and mists, and yeasty waves,'' but he still felt ''I should like him still better if his pictures looked in the least like what they typify'' (*EN:* 556).

He would venture a more complex version of this same balanced judgment in London a few months later. Some of Turner's landscapes now seemed ''full of imaginative beauty, and of the better truth etherealized out of the prosaic truth of Nature,'' but he complained that it was ''impossible actually to see it. There was a mist over it; or it was like a tract of beautiful dream-land, seem dimly through sleep, and glimmering out of sight if looked upon with wide-open eyes.'' This heavily qualified praise recalls Hawthorne's ambivalent comments about his own fictional ''dream-land.'' Like many of his early tales, Turner's landscapes seemed woefully insubstantial. But what remains most engaging about Hawthorne's response to Turner is his patient open-mindedness. After doing his best to appreciate Turner's paintings at Marlborough House, he said, ''I mean to buy Ruskin's pamphlet at my next visit, and look at them through his eyes'' (*EN:* 614).[6] Whether or not Ruskin was responsible, he later reported, ''I begin to appreciate Turner's pictures rather better than at first'' (*EN:* 617).

The British historical portraits that Hawthorne examined ''pretty faithfully'' on his third visit to the Manchester Exhibition presented different problems. Again applying the broad standard of realism, he said most of the older portraits seemed ''cold and stiff,'' yet trustworthy, while the graceful portraits by Vandyke ''do not look like Englishmen.'' Expressing the same doubt he had voiced while sitting for his own portrait years before, he declared, ''I have a haunting doubt of the value of portrait-painting, that is to say, whether it gives you a genuine idea of the person purporting to be represented.'' He thought most painters distorted the truth, whether by flattering their sitters or following ephemeral standards of taste, and ''considering how much of his own conceit the artist puts into a portrait, how much affectation the sitter puts on, and then again that no face is the same to any two spectators; also, that these portraits are darkened and faded with age, and can seldom be more than half seen, being hung too high, or somehow or other inconvenient—on the whole, I question whether there is much use in looking at them'' (*EN:* 551-52). Typically, Hawthorne found more ''use'' in looking at real people: he paid far more attention to the "picturesque" Tennyson than to any portrait. "Gazing at him with all my eyes, I liked him well, and rejoiced more in him than in all the wonders of the Exhibition," Hawthorne said, the words "all my eyes" and "rejoiced" conveying an intensity of pleasure that at this point art could not bring (*EN:* 553).[7]

Nonetheless, the next day he returned to the exhibition, this time concentrating on the Old Masters and finding to his surprise that he was now "able to appreciate" portraits by Murillo, Velázquez, and Titian. This new responsiveness made him modify his earlier contemptuous judgment: "I see reason for allowing (contrary to my opinion expressed a few pages back) that a portrait may preserve some valuable characteristics of the person represented" (*EN:* 555). Even that concession must have been gratifying for a man who had put portraits to fictional use and repeatedly sat for his own portrait.

Of all the paintings he saw at the exhibition, only one group provided immediate and unmitigated pleasure—the Dutch Masters. "Even the photograph cannot equal their miracles," he marveled. "The closer you look, the more minutely true the picture is found to be." He rejoiced to think that "these painters accomplish all they aim at—a praise, methinks, which can be given to no other men." Unlike the Pre-Raphaelites, they pleased his eye while engaging his imagination. The Pre-Raphaelites' insistent detail seemed artificial, but the Dutch drew from life and invited viewers into that life. "And it is strange how spiritual, and suggestive the commonest household article—an earthen pitcher, for example—becomes when represented with entire accuracy. These Dutchmen get at the soul of common things, and so make them types and interpreters of the spiritual world" (*EN:* 556). Years before, he had praised Thoreau's writing in almost identical terms, for being "so true, minute, and literal in observation, yet giving the spirit as well as letter of what he sees (VIII: 355). In such sketches as "Foot-prints on the Sea-shore," he had tried to do the same, and he had deliberately tried to give *The House of the Seven Gables* the finish of a Dutch painting.

Thus Manchester reinforced an early predilection that he never outgrew, though after learning to value the art of Renaissance Italy he would come to regard it as a sign of low taste and regret that Dutch painters expended "pains on such undignified subjects" (Julian Hawthorne, *Hawthorne and His Wife*, II: 142). He would then wish what he knew was impossible—that Dutch minuteness might be combined with the grandeur of a painting like Raphael's *Transfiguration*. The connection with his goals as a writer is obvious. Throughout most of his career he, like the Dutch, tried to "get at the soul of common things, and to make them types and interpreters of the spiritual world," though in *The Marble Faun* he would also try to incorporate the grandeur of the *Transfiguration*.

He valued the Dutch as a group, but only one painter at the exhibition seemed "noble" enough to win Hawthorne's rhapsodic praise. "Murillo seems to me about the noblest and purest painter that ever lived, and his 'Good Shepherd' the loveliest picture I ever saw," he asserted with none of his usual uncertainty, and he insisted after his next visit that "there can be no mistake about Murillo;—not that I am worthy to admire him yet" (*EN*: 558-59). Such praise was consonant with the sentimental taste of the period, but perhaps it was also a consequence of familiarity. Hawthorne had enjoyed encountering Murillo years before at the Boston Athenaeum, and he was now taking pleasure in an artist his receptive faculty had already assimilated. This fond respect would continue in Italy, even after his taste had developed to the point that he knew Raphael was greater, because Murillo accomplished what Hawthorne aspired to in fiction—producing noble and beautiful images of reality infused with "natural passion" and high spiritual truth.

Given his criteria, it is easy to understand why Hawthorne (like most Victorians) had a special problem with paintings of nudes. Although he protested that he did "not mind nudity, in a modest and natural way," he thought immodest self-display was unnatural. He suspected that most painters of nudes were prurient, and he scorned their sensual indulgences. Predictably, he condemned the full-bodied nudes of William Etty. In this regard, the only surprise is Hawthorne's robust good humor. "The most disagreeable of English painters is Etty, who had a diseased appetite for woman's flesh, and spent his whole life, apparently, in painting them with enormously developed bosoms and buttocks," he declared. "Etty's women really thrust their nakedness upon you so with malice aforethought, and especially so enhance their posteriors, that one feels inclined to kick them." But he returned to aesthetic grounds for his final complaint: "The worst of it is, they are not beautiful" (*EN*: 556).[8] The beautiful brazen nudes he would see in Italy would present more complicated aesthetic problems.

On August 9, over two weeks after his first visit to the exhibition—the same day that Hawthorne commented on Etty and the Dutch Masters and the same day that he reported he could see "something wonderful even in Turner's lights, and mists, and yeasty waves"—Hawthorne made his first extended evaluation of his growing attainment as a "man of taste":

> I looked at many of the pictures of the Old Masters, and found myself gradually getting a taste for pictures; at least, they give me more and more pleasure, the oftener I come to see them. Doubtless, I shall be able to pass for a man of taste, by the time I return to America. It is an acquired taste, like that for wines; and I question whether a man is really any truer, wiser, or better for possessing it. (*EN*: 556)

Hawthorne's changing tone in this passage reflects a fundamental irresolution that he never overcame. At first gratified that his taste was improving, he more modestly shifts the ground to a simple report of pleasure. Next he gently mocks himself for expecting he could "pass for a man of taste" in America, as if his accomplishment was somehow bogus. And finally he belittles taste itself, as merely a matter of sensual discrimination that has nothing to do with morality or intelligence.

The same contradictory attitudes emerge more forcibly from two successive journal entries, dated August 16 and 20. The first reports his ongoing attainments as a man of taste:

> I am making some progress as a con[n]oisseur, and have got so far as to be able to distinguish the broader differences of style; as for example, between Rubens and Rembrandt. . . . I do begin to have a liking for good things, and to be sure that they are good. . . . I see more merit in the crowd of painters than I was at first competent to acknowledge. I could see some of their defects from the first; but that is the earliest stage of con[n]oisseurship, after a primal and ignorant admiration. Mounting a few steps higher, one sees beauties. But how much study, how many opportunities, are requisite, to form and cultivate a taste! (*EN:* 558)

Aside from his naive pleasure in distinguishing a Rubens from a Rembrandt, what emerges most clearly is Hawthorne's assumption that there are absolute aesthetic standards and that study enables the spectator to mount the ladder of taste.

But his next journal entry expresses profound doubts about the importance of making that effort. The connoisseur, he says, "is not usually, I think, a man of deep poetic feeling, and does not deal with the picture through his heart, nor set it in a poem, nor comprehend it morally. If it be a landscape, he is not entitled to judge of it by his intimacy with Nature; if a picture of human action, he has no experience or sympathy of life's deeper passages" (*EN:* 559). He even wonders briefly if connoisseurs might have laid down "wrong principles" for determining merit. Unlike Ruskin, who believed sympathy and morality are integral to taste, Hawthorne deprecated taste as merely a limited and artificial attainment, a position he would carry to its logical conclusion in Florence.

Yet he never stopped working at the attainment. "I have been two or three times to the Exhibition, since my last date," he wrote on August 30, "and enjoy it more as I become more familiar with it" (*EN:* 560). Such familiarity had its limits, however. Although he felt "a picture cannot be fully enjoyed except by long and intimate acquaintance with it" (*EN:* 559), by his fifth week in Manchester, the exhibition "was fast becoming a bore; for you must really love a picture, in order to tolerate the sight of it many times" (*EN*: 565). After his last visit to the exhibition, he lamented that he had "got but a small part of the profit it might have afforded me." Yet this self-deprecation did not overshadow his awareness of his newly refined aesthetic sensibility. "Pictures are certainly quite other things to me, now, from what they were at my first visit," he said. "It seems even as if there were a sort of illumination within them that makes me see them more distinctly" (*EN*: 562). He was still a naive viewer, but he had acquired a measure of taste and the confidence to apply it, moving from concern with self-improvement to consciousness of aesthetic pleasure. Even though his self-deprecation would continue, he was ready for the art treasures of Italy.

FRANCE AND ITALY

Consular duties finally behind him, Hawthorne traveled with his family for an extended stay in Italy, expecting to improve his taste and develop his mind, heart, and spirit by contemplating the Western world's most celebrated works of art. He was out to see the best, not only because that was what cultured travelers did, but because he thought it would be good for him. He would share the fulfillment of Sophia's lifelong dream, and he thought Italy would also be good for her health and important for the children's education.

Nevertheless, during his year and a half on the Continent, Hawthorne continued to represent himself as a dutiful but reluctant tourist, often with the same self-mockery apparent in his statement that he was glad to have seen the Pope "because now he may be crossed out of my list of sights to be seen" (XIV: 150). He was so easily surfeited by sightseeing that when he said it was Sophia's "enterprise, much more than mine, that impels us to see new things" (XIV: 32), he was understating the case. Despite her delicate health, Sophia would remain in churches or galleries marveling at paintings and statues long after her exhausted husband had left to refresh himself by wandering through the streets.

Paris and the "Moral Charm" of the Gothic

Hawthorne's week in Paris added little to his aesthetic education. Although he visited the Louvre twice, he confessed that "the vast and beautiful edifice struck me far more than the pictures, sculpture, and curiosities which it contains; the shell more than the meat inside" (XIV: 15). Even on his second visit he admired the magnificent exhibition rooms more than the works they contained, and paid more attention to the people in the museum—the visitors, guards, and copyists—than to the rooms or the artworks. Part of the problem was that he did not have enough time to formulate an adequate "general idea" of the Louvre's collections, a prerequisite for enjoying any particular works. Walking through the sculpture halls that opened interminably before him, he saw "only two or three things which I thought very beautiful," and he did not even identify them, though he was connoisseur enough to recognize that the well-displayed collection "shamed the sculpture gallery of the British Museum out of sight" and even guessed (mistakenly, he would discover) that the "world has nothing better, unless it be a world-renowned statue or two in Italy." His main object that day was to see the Louvre's collection of pencil drawings by great artists, done when they "had the glory of their pristine idea directly before their mind's eye." He thought that the artists enjoyed producing their "off-hand" sketches more than the finished paintings, and he was sure other artists would find the entire collection "intensely interesting," but to him at that moment it was "merely curious" and even "wearisome." But he blamed himself for being overcome by a "dreary and desperate feeling" which came upon him "when the sights last[ed] longer than [his] capacity for receiving them" (XIV: 23-25).

By contrast, he felt exalted by Notre Dame Cathedral. Six months before, after a final visit to York Cathedral, Hawthorne said he and Sophia had "seen [so] much splendid architecture" that their eyes had become "educated" and they had "grown in some degree fitted to enjoy it." The cathedral perfectly conjoined majesty with sweetness and beauty, he declared. It was "the most wonderful work that ever came from the hands of man." With an unusual burst of devoutness, he thanked "God that I saw this Cathedral again, and thank Him that he inspired the builder to make it, and that mankind has so long enjoyed it" (*EN*: 544-45). But Notre Dame impressed him even more. Though its interior was under repair, he and Sophia agreed as they walked around the choir "that it was the most magnificent Gothic edifice . . . [they] had ever seen." Despite the workmen's scaffolds, "it gave to my actual sight what I have often tried to imagine in my visits to the English Cathedrals; the pristine glory of those edifices when they stood glowing with gold and picture, fresh from the architect's and adorner's hands." His response went beyond aesthetics to reverence for structures that "receive our pettiness into their own immensity" (XIV: 30-31). Like Ruskin, Hawthorne rejoiced in the grandeur and brilliant organicism of Gothic architecture, unconcerned about Catholicism.

His enjoyment of Notre Dame expanded a taste already established and confirmed in England, unusual only because Hawthorne never wavered about it. The Gothic cathedral always provided a gratifying analogue for the human condition. Spatial metaphors were always congenial to his imagination, from the earliest notebook images of the heart as a cavern to the towers and underground chambers of *The Marble Faun* and the last romances. The sense of being at once diminished and exalted in such enclosures invited speculation about the self in the universe, and the Gothic cathedral was a particularly congenial model because its vast loftiness stretched the viewer's comprehension and intimated spiritual liberation. Further, in its fluorescence, its transcendence of individuality, its emergence over a period of time, and its susceptibility to the ravages of time, it seemed "natural." Standing in a Gothic cathedral, aware of himself as an observer yet absorbed, uplifted, and challenged by its immensity, Hawthorne attained the state he hoped to induce in the minds of his readers.

His appreciation of the Gothic as a natural mode (consistent with Ruskin but not dependent on him) would expand even further in Italy, where classical architecture and sculpture seemed coldly intellectual and oversimplified. It was easy to explain his pleasure in such exuberant statuary as the monument to Pope Benedict XI in Perugia: "I like this overflow and gratuity of device, with which Gothic sculpture works out its designs, after seeing so much of the simplicity of classic art in marble" (XIV: 259). Even on his first view of "the thousand forms of Gothic fancy" adorning the cathedral in Siena, he praised their "majesty and a minuteness: neither interfering with the other; each assisting with the other; this is what I love in Gothic architecture" (XIV: 445). The word "assisting" recalls his conception of the Gothic as a living entity, thus necessarily an entity he could only partly understand. But this limitation was never troublesome. Admiring the Campanile in Florence, he felt the "moral charm in this faithful minuteness of Gothic architecture," even though it "perhaps may never be studied out by a single spectator. It is the very process of Nature, and, no doubt, produces an effect that we know not of" (XIV: 404-5). No sense of personal inadequacy impeded his appreciation of the Gothic, even when he was most weary and travel jaded. Thus on his way back to England, his first glimpse of the Cathedral of Lyons made him feel its grandeur was "unspeakably more impressive than all the ruins of Rome." Characteristically, he moved to a moral ground to explain his response, though this time a more private ground than usual: "It did me good to enjoy the awfulness and sanctity of Gothic architecture again, after so long shivering in classic porticos" (XIV: 549-50). Gothic architecture always vitalized and uplifted his imagination; classic architecture cooled it.

There is another way of understanding Hawthorne's deep response to the conjunction of majesty and minuteness in the Gothic. What most fully engaged his imagination was the joining of opposite conditions or capacities. Thus his ideal of a neutral territory of romance where actual and imaginary could meet "and each imbue itself with the nature of the other"; his regret that Aylmer in "The Birth-mark" was unable to "look beyond the shadowy scope of Time, and . . . find the perfect Future in the present"; his praise of human tenderness in a painting of a Madonna and Child, and spirituality in a Dutch master's pan or pitcher; his fascination with the turbulence and calm of the *Laocoön*; and his focus in *The Marble Faun* on the mysteries of guilt and innocence. Any conjunction of opposites provoked his imagination to consider both the separate extremes and their implosive conjunctions or syntheses. Analogously, his notebooks and his fiction often proceed from minute particulars to generalizations charged with wonder, consonant with his praise of Gothic cathedrals: "They receive our pettiness into their own immensity."

What Hawthorne admired in the Gothic implicitly explains most of his other aesthetic preferences. For example, he disliked the Baroque because, unlike the Gothic, its "overflow and gratuity" did not exist within a large controlling design. More important, he preferred English to classical ruins because the marble in Italy not only keeps its color but "remains hard and sharp, and does not become again a part of Nature, as stone walls do in England"; thus the ruins of a Roman temple seemed "beyond time, and without the kind of impressiveness that arises from suggestions of decay and the Past."

More than a taste for the picturesque is at stake in the statement. A partisan of this solid earth, Hawthorne accepted and even welcomed evidence of the cyclical processes of growth and decay. Repeatedly on his walks through Rome, he complained that "Nature does not take a Roman ruin to her heart as she does the old feudal castles and abbeys of England, covering them up with ivy," so that the beauty of a classical "ruin is the remnant of what was beautiful originally, whereas an English ruin is more beautiful, often, in its decay than ever it was in its primal strength" (XIV: 58, 107)—a judgment he would repeat in *The Marble Faun*. The conjunction of decay with ongoing life confirmed Hawthorne's belief in a providential universe. By the same logic, his distaste for shattered statues and battered, faded paintings was more than a matter of aesthetics: not only was it difficult to concentrate on vestiges of beauty or to imagine a ruined work's original splendor, but there was no compensatory form of renewal in its decay. Thus the disgust that Hawthorne felt while looking at the nearly obliterated fresco was proleptic of what he felt during his last years when he speculated that life might end with the grave.

The same sensibility that enabled him to find reassuring challenges to his imagination in Notre Dame led him to locate and admire the picturesque, which he encountered more frequently in Italy than ever before. While this interest in pictorial complexity was wholly consonant with period taste, his comments also reflect the way his imagination processed new experiences. As a dutiful and articulate traveler trying to sharpen his powers of perception and retain what he saw, he recorded precise descriptions of scenes Claude Lorrain or Thomas Cole might have painted: spacious sunlit landscapes filled with steeply rising mountains and precipitous gorges, ruined towers, whirling rivers, and views of distant valleys dotted with vineyards and villages. Isolating the details that made one village, one building, or one individual more picturesque than another, he created word pictures drenched in visual detail though surprisingly drained of moral content. Thus a particularly shabby group of villagers had "little picturesqueness of costume or figure"; and later he neutrally described the neglected houses beneath the Uffizi, with nets hanging from their windows, as "picturesquely various in height, from two or three stories to seven; picturesque in hue, likewise, pea-green, yellow, white, and of aged discoloration, but all with green blinds; picturesque, also in the courts and galleries that look upon the river, and in the wide arches that open beneath" (XIV: 410). In such passages he did not move to moral commentary but concentrated on amassing the plethora of unfamiliar raw material while it was still fresh. Yet at some level Hawthorne must have been aware of a moral problem in enjoying any sight of shabbiness and neglect, whether in a Liverpool slum or along the Arno River. He would further explore the moral underside of the picturesque in *The Marble Faun*. Observing "wretched cottages" that were "picturesquely time-stained," for example, the narrator suggests "that a people are waning to decay and ruin, the moment that their life becomes fascinating either in the poet's imagination or the painter's eye" (IV: 296). Usually, however, both in Hawthorne's journals and his fiction, the picturesque (like the Gothic) gives evidence of the plenitude and complexity of this world that augurs well for the next; and both Kenyon and the narrator repeatedly offer such evidence in *The Marble Faun*.

The Receptive Faculty: "Surprised into Admiration"

Soon after arriving in Rome, Hawthorne saturated himself in art as never before by visiting museums, churches, and palaces, calling on artists in their studios, and simply wandering through the streets. Most important to his development as a man of taste, of course, were his confrontations with masterworks of art. After immersing himself in art at the Manchester Exhibition, he had been glad to learn that there were "better things still to be seen" in Italy, and he was now out to see them. Often with his wife, and sometimes his children, Hawthorne began systematic visits to major repositories of art. In recording his experiences, he proceeded as he had in London, Manchester, and Paris, giving an overview of a building and then its display rooms before venturing comments on a particular collection, finally focusing attention on particular artworks. The luxury of extended residence in Italy meant he never felt compelled to pay more than a short visit to any gallery; thus he could familiarize himself gradually with a work of art, hoping to apprehend its vital center.

Like his countrymen who came to Italy in increasing numbers at mid-century, Hawthorne brought high expectations of particular works of art, which were often fulfilled but sometimes thwarted. Sometimes he attributed his disappointment to the work and sometimes to personal limitations. Whenever he looked at a work of art, he was also looking at himself; and as in England he was skeptical and wavering in judging both his own taste and the importance of developing it. In Italy, however, not only were the swings greater, but Hawthorne pondered the psychology of aesthetic perception more deeply and more concertedly than ever before. As Nathalia Wright observes, while receptive capacity in this activity was limited" (*Tennessee Studies in Literature*, 143), though Wright does not explore his understanding of that capacity.

After his first visit to the Manchester Exhibition, Hawthorne had complained that he lacked the capacity to take it all in but concluded that "something (according to the measure of my poor capacity) will really be taken into my mind" (*EN: 549*). After reaching Italy, he formulated a more complex notion of his limited capacity. Trained by the Scottish school of philosophy to assume that the mind operates through separate faculties, he now postulated the existence of a "receptive faculty," which was essentially mechanistic and passive, and with curious spatial, generic, and temporal limits. Commenting about his first Italian sightseeing venture in Genoa, he praised the Balbi Palace as "the stateliest and most magnificent residence that I had ever seen," but he complained of his limits as tourist and connoisseur: "I soon grew so weary of admirable things that I could neither enjoy nor understand them. My receptive faculty is very limited; and when the utmost of its small capacity is full, I become perfectly miserable, and the more so, the better worth seeing are the things I am forced to reject." He expressed his misery by expanding on the familiar metaphorical comparison of art to food: "I do not know a greater misery; to see sights after such repletion is, to the mind, what it would be to the body to have dainties forced down the throat long after the appetite was satiated" (XIV: 49). Such complaints recurred throughout his stay in Italy, though sometimes with surprising good humor. He departed from a Perugian chapel that Sophia was still enjoying because he had seen as many pictures as he could digest; he thanked heaven that there were only two picture galleries in one Roman museum and only four in another;

and he said Sophia was as delighted to see the early Italian paintings of the Franciscan convent in Assisi as he was "delighted, not to have seen it" (XIV: 257, 253).

Not only did Hawthorne assume that his receptive faculty had a limited tolerance on any particular day: he also thought he had a limited receptivity for any particular kind of aesthetic experience. After only a month in Rome, he concluded that he had "long ago exhausted all my capacity of admiration for splendid interiors of churches"—no doubt a dismaying thought, given the many such famous interiors he had yet to enter (XIV: 95). Often he stressed his feeling of inadequacy by measuring his own limited receptivity against Sophia's, which seemed limitless and fresh. He even formulated a curious quantitative notion. He speculated that once he reached his limit of receptivity for a particular kind of aesthetic experience, the stamp of each such successive impression would obliterate an earlier one.

He evidently thought his receptivity had an active component, which was itself limited. The ability to attend sympathetically to a work of art was like a limited sum on deposit in a savings bank of the soul, to be expended only with great care. Thus, even while acknowledging that adequate response to an excellent work of art required sympathetic self-surrender, he often held back from such surrender because he was reluctant to give some of his "soul" to individual paintings, especially those he was viewing for the first time. He was depressed by the very idea of going from one picture to the next and leaving some of his "vital sympathy" behind at each one (XIV: 115).

But if receptivity was in part a matter of capacity, it was also in part a matter of mood. On some days he could not make any adequate response to art. Trying to understand why he did not enjoy the celebrated paintings of the Borghese gallery, he speculated, "I think I was not in a frame for admiration, to-day, nor could achieve that free and generous surrender of myself which . . . is essential to the proper estimate of anything excellent" (XIV: 110-11).

Sometimes his condition was worse than simple unimpressibility: it was more like a disease. He sometimes sensed a "peculiar lassitude and despondency" coming upon him, as he viewed works of art. When this occurred one day in the sculpture galleries of the Villa Ludovisi, he simply "sat down wearily upon a chair, and left [his] wife to see and admire, to her heart's content" (XIV: 147). He treated such weariness as a kind of physical ailment that might come without warning, and might even be catching. Thus when Julian felt "utter distaste" on his first visit to the Uffizi, Hawthorne in turn felt afflicted by the same "weary lack of appreciation that used to chill [him] through and through, in . . . earlier visits to picture-galleries; the same doubt, moreover, whether we do not bamboozle ourselves in the greater part of the admiration which we learn to bestow" (XIV: 350). In such a state even the *Venus de Milo* or a

Raphael canvas could make no claims on his receptive faculty; and he sadly reported that when he could "perceive them only by the grosser sense, missing their ethereal spirit, there is nothing so heavily burthensome as masterpieces of painting and sculpture" (XIV: 429-30).

But if he had bad days when no work of art found him "impressible," or when he wondered "whether the pictorial art be not a humbug," he had good days when he felt that "the pictorial art is capable of something more like magic—more wonderful and inscrutable in its methods—than poetry" (XIV: 306). He therefore proposed a kind of double-entry aesthetic ledger: we should give a work of art credit for what "it makes us feel in our best moments," but never judge it in "the coldness and insensibility of our less genial moods" (XIV: 308-9). This caution underlay all his reports and assessments of his own responsiveness. In his "best moments," he was never a puritanic iconoclast, a Victorian prude, or an obtuse Babbitt. And his sense of well-being in Florence made him feel "that a process is going on—and has been, ever since I came to Italy—that puts me in a state to see pictures with less toil, and more pleasure, and makes me more fastidious, yet more sensible of beauty where I saw none before" (XIV: 317).

On the most memorable occasions, he was at once "sensible of beauty" and of the "ethereal spirit" within a work of art. Such epiphanic moments were not, however, generated only by the visual arts. He wrote of St. Peter's Cathedral:

> At times, a single, casual, momentary glimpse of its magnificence gleams upon my soul, as it were, when I happen to glance at arch opening beyond arch, and I am surprised into admiration when I think least of it. I have experienced that a landscape, and the sky, unfold their deepest beauty in a similar way, not when they are gazed at of set purpose, but when the spectator looks suddenly through a peep-hole among a crowd of other thoughts. (XIV: 91)

In certain privileged moments, paintings and statues similarly revealed themselves.

But his recognition of the fortuitous suddenness of such experiences must have presented paradoxes to Hawthorne the gallery goer. Looking too closely at a work of art might prevent him from sensing its inner beauty; yet he had learned long before that he could not adequately respond to any images, whether in a landscape or a work of art, until they were in some measure familiar. Thus he developed a policy of patient attentiveness in the galleries of Rome and Florence, repeatedly submitting himself to a painting or statue and observing it closely. Then at some marvelous but unexpected moment, it might suddenly open up before him so that a casual glance would penetrate to its deepest meaning. He would then be "surprised into admiration."

Hawthorne regarded such a work as a living entity. Just as he felt it a rare privilege to penetrate the inner depths of another human being, convinced that only loving respect warranted such penetration, so he felt that only patient and loving attentiveness to a work of art entitled the viewer to genuine admiration, to the rare felicity of perceiving its essential beauty. Although he believed that the grandest art was ordinarily beyond human appreciation, for single fortuitous moments even such grandeur might become wholly evident.

Delighted by the illusion of life, he felt as gratified by a realistic statue as the most naive viewer. He admired Michelangelo's *Lorenzo de Medici*, for example, because "after looking at it a little while, the spectator ceases to think of it as a marble statue; it comes to life"; and the Perugian statue of *Pope Julius III* "seems to have life and observation in him, and impresses the spectator as if he might rise up from his chair, should any public exigency demand it" (XIV: 327, 260). But the receptive faculty had to cooperate fully before a marble deity seemed fully alive. Thus on one visit to the Vatican's sculpture gallery, the *Apollo Belvedere* suddenly seemed "ethereal and godlike; only for a flitting moment, however, and as if he had alighted from heaven, or shone suddenly out of sunlight, and then had withdrawn himself again" (XIV: 125). After a later visit he complained that the Vatican's "statues kept, for the most part, a veil around them, which they sometimes withdrew, and let their beauty glow upon my sight—only a glimpse, or two or three glimpses, or a little space of enjoyment; and then I see nothing but a discolored marble image again"; yet he then reported succinctly but with evident delight, "The Minerva Medica revealed herself to-day" (XIV: 165-66). This led him to wonder whether other viewers "invariably find their way to the inner soul of a work of art," but he doubted it. All too aware that his aesthetic capacity was limited, he did not consider himself below average.

It was far easier for Hawthorne to respond to the illusion of life in paintings than in statues, particularly paintings of the human figure. Partly it was a matter of lifelike coloration and partly a matter of familiarity. Cephas Thompson's *Georgian Slave*, for example, immediately seemed "warm and rich . . . and with an expression of higher life and feeling within" (XIV: 128). But the reward of close attention was rarely immediate. If he looked too intently at Guido's *Hope*, for example, its charm vanished. Conversely, he might be looking intently at one painting when he suddenly "caught" the charm of another; thus in the Uffizi he sometimes "caught the divine pensiveness of a Madonna's face, or the glory and majesty of the babe Jesus in her lap, with his Father shining through him." His language conjoins religious with aesthetic gratification: "This is a sort of revelation, whenever it comes" (XIV: 318).

Hawthorne's most concerted efforts to understand the involuntary operation of such a revealing glimpse appear in his speculations about the painting of Beatrice Cenci, a painting that entered deeply into his conception of *The Marble Faun:* "Its peculiar expression eludes a straightforward glance, and can only be caught by side glimpses, or when the eye falls upon it casually, as it were, and without seeking to discover anything; as if the picture had a life and consciousness of its own, and were resolved not to betray its secret of grief or guilt" (XIV: 520). Hawthorne's concentration on Beatrice's "peculiar expression" is consistent with his usual attentiveness to facial expression in paintings, itself an index of his belief that good art is imbued with life. In this he was a man of his age. Ruskin, for example, also interpreted facial expressions as indices of moral character, and most Victorian critics expatiated on their emotional reactions to facial expressions. Every travel book on Rome had something to say about Beatrice's sorrowful countenance. But Hawthorne concentrated on the unfathomable mysteries her expression could only suggest, while examining his own need to be taken by surprise.

More than the receptive faculty was at stake in such a response: Hawthorne recognized that even transitory or partial penetration into the mystery of an artwork depended on assent to its apprehended meaning. Thus the landscapes of George Loring Brown were immediately accessible as "beautiful and true" because Hawthorne saw in them intimations of an even more beautiful afterlife. Conversely, he felt disappointed by any image that violated his own deepest convictions. Thus, although he considered Raphael's *Transfiguration* a marvelous painting, he criticized the face of Jesus as too human: divinity did not beam forth. While granting that Michelangelo's *Last Judgment* was "a great picture," he was repelled by its image of God as inexorable judge. But he could more enthusiastically praise a lesser painting, Guido's *St. Michael Overcoming Lucifer*—and Miriam's and Hilda's responses to the painting are integral to *The Marble Faun*—because its central statement was so morally congenial: "the immortal youth and loveliness of virtue, and its irresistible might against evil" (XIV: 100). Hawthorne could call even a mosaic copy of the painting "one of the most beautiful things in the world" because it confirmed one of his most deeply held beliefs—that this world is a place of love and beauty despite human grief and guilt, and that eternity is under the dominion of a just and benign god.

His understanding of the moral suggestiveness of great art in part derived from his training in Scottish Common Sense School philosophy, which explained that we value most those works of art that we associate with enjoyable experiences or ennobling ideas. Thus, Hawthorne understood, we may enjoy looking at a beautiful painting of a ruined castle beside a turbulent river on a sunlit mountain because it reminds us of similar paintings and similar scenes, but also because it arouses gratifying emotions and provokes speculation about the beauties and limits of this world as contrasted with the perfection of eternity. Yet Hawthorne never wholly accepted the associationalists' contention that the meaning of a work of art and its value lie within the perceiver's mind. He was both too much of a relativist and too much of an absolutist— too skeptical about his own aesthetic responses to trust them completely, though at the same time (as we will see) a firm believer in unchanging laws of beauty intelligible to any individual of cultivated taste. To the extent that he agreed with the Scots, however, he also agreed with Ruskin—that the greatest art is that which excites in the spectator's mind the greatest number of the greatest ideas. Further, his concern about the moral suggestiveness of art was a consequence of his habit of symbolic thought. Here he was on the same ground as Emerson and Thoreau, Carlyle and Wordsworth, and other distinguished contemporaries who valued the imagination as a power that could apprehend the beautiful surfaces of this world yet penetrate beyond space and time to apprehend eternal truths.

His receptivity to the *Laocoön* is typical of Hawthorne's response to any work of art he came to admire. On his first visit to the statue, he just looked at it briefly; but on his second visit, he moved beyond visual experience to assimilate the experience imaginatively, locating its essential if paradoxical nature. He then felt the *Laocoön* "very powerfully, though very quietly; an immortal agony, with a strange calmness diffused through it, so that it resembles the vast rage of the sea, calm on account of its immensity, or the tumult of Niagara, which does not seem to be tumult because it keeps pouring on, forever and ever" (XIV: 125). On his next visit, his imagination moved beyond these associations with powerful and complex natural phenomena to recognize the statue as a type of our mortal predicament, "of human beings struggling with an inextricable trouble, and entangled in a complication which they can never free themselves from by their own efforts, and out of which Heaven will not help them." This generalization in turn made him conclude that the sculptor must have had "a most powerful mind, and one capable of reducing a complex idea to a unity" (XIV: 138). His final comment on the statue was evoked by a supposedly fine copy in the Uffizi: the copy lacked the "mighty and terrible repose" of the original, he said, "a repose growing out of the infinitude of trouble" (XIV: 296). The final judgment, a fusion of the earlier ones, so exactly fit Hawthorne's approach to the human predicament that it transcended merely aesthetic description. Later, in *The Marble Faun*, he would attribute this response to Kenyon, saying that the sculptor's mood of despondency after Hilda's disappearance made him unusually responsive to the *Laocoön*'s "immortal agony . . . as a type of the long, fierce struggle of Man, involved in the knotted entanglements of Errour and Evil"; its hard-won repose made it seem "the one triumph of Sculpture" (IV: 391). Kenyon's mood is not projected onto the sculpture but allows him to see it more clearly, though at the same time it precludes a valid response to any other work of art.

Hawthorne's awareness that a spectator can see only what he is prepared to see worried him frequently as he walked through the galleries of Italy. Even when he felt most gratified and stimulated by the work of art, his skeptical principle intruded. He insisted that the viewer is never sure how much of what he sees is his own creation. Although his friend William Ware claimed to see "prophetic depth of feeling" in a Michelangelo Madonna, Hawthorne suspected that "it was one of the many instances in which the spectator sees more than the painter ever dreamed of" (XIV: 350). Repeatedly he worried that we may be mistaken in thinking a particular work is a masterpiece.

Even if it is indeed a masterpiece, he further asserted, we may never fully understand it. Looking at the *Three Fates*, for example, a painting then attributed to Michelangelo, he was reminded that over the centuries, various viewers had interpreted the painting in various ways; and he thought that the artist might have intended a meaning different from all of them. Indeed, he may not have wholly understood his own creation. Hawthorne's tolerance for mystery nevertheless enabled him to conclude that if the public feels a certain picture is great, it must be so, "a great symbol, proceeding out of a great mind"; but he acknowledged that its meaning might remain forever indeterminate, as with the *Three Fates:* "If it means one thing, it seems to mean a thousand, and often opposite things" (XIV: 335).[9]

Among the Artists

Trying to come to terms with a work of art during his years in England, Hawthorne usually concentrated on the work itself and his own response, but in Italy he became increasingly interested in an artist's responsibility for his creative achievement. Although Sophia's copying and sketching had, of course, been an intimate part of the life she shared with her husband, before coming to Rome Hawthorne had few opportunities to exchange ideas about art with professional artists and few occasions to inspect their recent works and works in progress. With few critics to aid or impede him, Hawthorne faced the challenge of assessing the capacities and achievements of his contemporaries.[10]

On February 12, three weeks after reaching Rome, the Hawthornes inaugurated a long series of social calls on American artists by visiting the Boston-born sculptor William Wetmore Story and then Cephas

Thompson, who had painted Hawthorne's portrait in Boston eight years earlier. A few days later, he began sitting for his marble bust portrait in the studio of Louisa Lander, like himself a native of Salem. Thus from the first, his encounters with artists were far more intimate than those of ordinary American tourists who included a few studios on their itineraries after ascertaining the artists' addresses and specialties from published brochures. Although Hawthorne never fully participated in the expatriate artists' social life—refusing, for example, Emelyn Story's invitation to a fancy ball—he encountered painters and sculptors at the dinners and evening parties he did attend, and he formed friendships with several of them. Louisa Lander accompanied the Hawthornes on many of their early sightseeing tours; Paul Akers took them to visit painters' studios; and, in Florence, Hawthorne pursued a relationship with Hiram Powers that included both of their families. As he observed and even shared the lives of artists, Hawthorne measured his own sensibility and aesthetic beliefs against theirs, and he later incorporated his experiences and conclusions into his fiction.

When Hawthorne entered an artist's studio—usually as a friend or at least a social acquaintance—he was alert to his surroundings and eager for new discoveries. In his notebook accounts of these visits, he described artists at work and tried to fix his initial impressions of their talent and achievements, usually by describing several of their works and then pondering whatever aesthetic issues they provoked. Thus after visiting Story's studio for the first time, he described the sculptor gravely modeling his statue of *Cleopatra*. He had chosen "a grand subject, and he appears to be conceiving it with depth and power, and working it out with adequate skill," attempting more in his art than sculptors who produced "beautiful nudities" baptized with classical names. Although Hawthorne thought several of Story's finished statues were both beautiful and noble, the word "adequate" suggests reservations about his talent; yet the offhand remark about "beautiful nudities" conveys contemptuous disapproval of the commonplace neoclassical works of most of the other expatriate sculptors. What Hawthorne found most disconcerting in Story's studio was the unexpected sight of a stone cutter translating one of the sculptor's plaster casts into marble. "It is not quite pleasant to think that the sculptor does not really do the whole labor on his statues, but that they are all but finished to his hand by merely mechanical people," he said (XIV: 73-74)—a thought that might have well recurred when he received Lander's disappointing portrait bust a few months later. But at this point, a sculptor's studio was so novel to him that it provoked far-ranging ideas about the relation of an artist's conceptions to his skill and emotional power, about nudity in modern sculpture, and about the relation of a sculptor's initial stages of creation to his finished work—issues that would become central to *The Marble Faun*, where the *Cleopatra* herself would reappear.[11]

A month later, Hawthorne visited the studio of Thomas Crawford, who had died six months before, and sweepingly dismissed the statues of that celebrated artist as merely competent contrivances. They seemed without "force of thought or depth of feeling," a case of reputation far exceeding merit, Hawthorne declared, differing from prevailing opinion.[12] As in Story's studio, he brooded about the sculptor's dependence on stone cutters to translate his model from plaster to model, which seemed analagous to the mystical change from flesh to spirit (XIV: 129-30). Both in his journal and in his last completed novel, he would pursue the analogy further as he tried to come to terms with this apparent disjunction between the creator and the creation.

Statues in other sculptors' studios led him to ponder more precise issues, including the matter of nudity. The tinted statues of the patriarchal Englishman, John Gibson, were a special case. Hawthorne found "something fascinating and delectable in the warm, yet delicate tint of the beautiful nude Venus," although he seemed to stutter while performing a rhetorical about-face, not "at all certain that I should not, in the end, like the snowy whiteness better for the whole statue. Indeed, I am almost sure I should; for this lascivious warmth of hue quite demoralizes the chastity of the marble, and makes one feel ashamed to look at the naked limbs in the company of women" (XIV: 157). Later Powers would argue that white marble was a spiritual substance that "gave chaste permission to those nudities which would otherwise be licentious," and on the whole—recalling his response to Gibson's *Venus*—Hawthorne would agree. He found Gibson's color unsettling; it was not lifelike, yet it made an unwonted appeal to the senses. He resented the sense of shame its impropriety provoked, a reaction he would restate in *The Marble Faun*.

He later came to a more sweeping conclusion, however. In a world that contained the wonderful *Venus de Medici*, not even the best of the modern "beautiful nudities" (including Hiram Powers's *Greek Slave*) were needed and their proliferation in enduring marble seemed absurd. Granting that Edward Bartholmew's *Eve* was "pretty in some points," Hawthorne complained that it lacked the energetic conception of Story's clothed *Cleopatra*, and its "awful volume of thighs and calves" made him declare, "I do not altogether see the necessity of ever sculpturing another nakedness" (an idea he would later give Miriam). Then, dropping the tentativeness of the word "altogether," he firmly concluded, "Man is no longer a naked animal; his clothes are as natural to him as his skin, and sculptors have no more right to undress him than to flay him" (XIV: 177). His conviction that modern statues should be clothed was more a matter of decorum than squeamishness, an issue he discussed more fully with Anna Jameson and Hiram Powers—often wittily, as when he looked at Powers's clothed statue of Washington and imagined the alternative: "Did anybody ever see Washington naked! It is inconceivable. He had no nakedness, but, I imagine, was born with his clothes on and his hair powdered" (XIV: 281). Nudity was appropriate for the Golden Age but not for modern times.

What Hawthorne most looked for and most enjoyed in a sculptor's studio is evident in his account of visiting Harriet Hosmer to see her nearly completed model of Zenobia. First he described the lofty room and then the jaunty woman, but he concentrated on her "noble and remarkable" statue of the tranquil captive queen, "as yet unfinished in the clay." He speculated about the sculptor's skill in suggesting motion and rendering drapery, and he pondered the queen's inner state as if she were alive. Wondering "whether there is some magic in the present imperfect finish of the statue, or in the material of clay, as being a better medium of expression than even marble," he declared that he had "seldom or never been more impressed by a piece of modern sculpture" (XIV: 509). He was as challenged and delighted by the unexpected accomplishment of the "brisk little woman" as by the imperfectly finished work itself; and the independent life and enterprising career of Harriet Hosmer, as well as Louisa Lander and other young American women working as artists in Rome, led to his conception of Hilda and Miriam as artists (though, to be sure, he conceived them as painters rather than sculptors).

In the more familiar world of painters' studios, Hawthorne also pondered issues of the artist's conceptions, emotions, and skill, though without worrying whether any subjects or treatments might be particularly appropriate to the nineteenth century. His terms of praise for Thompson are those he had formulated while judging paintings in England: one of St. Peter, for example, was beautiful and "deeply and spiritually conceived," and he concluded that there was no painter as "earnest, faithful, and religious in his worship of art." He felt no shame in confessing that he enjoyed Thompson's paintings more than works by Old Masters. But here Hawthorne made an important distinction: it was not that Thompson was a better painter but rather that there was "something in the productions of the day that takes the fancy more than the works of any past age" (XIV: 128).

He made a similar claim for the landscapes of George Loring Brown, which seemed beautiful, true, and even magical, more pleasing than Claude's, "and the fact serves to strengthen me in the belief that the most delicate, if not the highest charm of a picture is evanescent," particularly because pigment deteriorates (XIV: 176). After visiting the studios of the American landscapist Hamilton Wilde and the Swiss Rudolph Muller, Hawthorne generalized his praise of modern artists who patiently and lovingly reproduce the beauties of nature. Without downplaying the achievements of Claude, Poussin, or Salvator Rosa, he said, "the glory of a picture fades like that of a flower" (XIV: 188-89).

Hawthorne's praise of the moderns is remarkably homogeneous, suggesting that in Rome he encountered no painters who perturbed him like the Pre-Raphaelites, puzzled him like Turner, or disgusted him like Etty. Perhaps his friends guided him only to painters they assumed he would find congenial. Many of the paintings he saw in Roman studios delighted him, however disconcerting it was to view them in the artists' presence, though none ensnared his imagination as did Story's *Cleopatra*, Hosmer's *Zenobia*, or the portrait of Beatrice Cenci.

Although Hawthorne tried to be fair, even to artists whose works gave him little pleasure (such as those of the sculptor Joseph Mozier), his journal comments about the group as a whole are surprisingly censorious. For example, after a large dinner party, he declared that all the sculptors and painters except Gibson and Thompson seemed devoid of taste and refinement, leading him to suspect that they had nothing more than mechanical skill. But he quickly proposed the alternative possibility that artists could "only express themselves in their own art" and resolved to "know them better through their work." He pondered a different kind of problem after spending a casual evening with a few painters: the artists—who created a comfortable society for themselves in Rome—were "not gracious critics of one another." This time, however, the explanation had nothing to do with the artists' capacities: because their public was "more limited than that of the literary men, . . . they have the better excuse for these petty jealousies" (XIV: 220). In each case we recognize the familiar patterns of Hawthorne's thought. From immediate impressions of individual artists, he moved to generalizations about the group, then ventured broader hypotheses.

Not only did he try to understand their problems but he became so concerned about the career difficulties of the artists he knew best that he made direct (if unsuccessful) efforts to help them. He asked his friend Ticknor to arrange publicity and commissions for Louisa Lander when she planned her visit to America (before the scandal that made him join the artists' colony in snubbing her); he praised Story to both Ticknor and Fields, hoping to generate broader public acclaim for his statues; he told Ticknor that Cephas Thompson needed such acclaim to help him "flower"; and, most specifically, he praised Hiram Powers to his old friend Pierce, urging him to arrange payment of government funds already appropriated for the sculptor's work.[13]

But his most enduring advocacy of the expatriate artists was in his last completed novel. In his introduction to *The Marble Faun*, he served as a publicist, naming particular artists and their works, gracefully explaining his fictional appropriation of statues by Akers and Story, and saying he had also considered using others by Rogers and Hosmer.[14] Then in his fifteenth chapter, "An Aesthetic Company," he repeated both the general criticisms of painters and sculptors entered into his journal and his specific praise of those he admired, concluding that on the whole the artists constituted a pleasanter group than the average because even the pettiest was ennobled by pursuit of the beautiful. He amplified that conclusion through his Man of Marble, his ideal copyist, and his temperamental painter, who emerged from the studios of Rome as surely as from their metaphorical equivalent, the alembic of the writer's imagination.

Critics, Rules, Taste, and the "Sturdy Goth"

The main arenas where Hawthorne worked to develop his taste were not artists' studios but Italy's world famous galleries of paintings and statuary. Like most cultured tourists, he entered them with a Murray's guidebook and familiarity with books by other travelers, ranging from Byron's *Childe Harold* and Madame de Staël's *Corinne* to Anna Jameson's books on Christian art and his friend George Hillard's *Six Months in Italy* (1853).[15]

Hundreds of travel books about Italy were issued by American publishing houses shortly before the Civil War, typically (like Hillard's) written to record a brilliant "episode" that had engendered "beautiful and enduring memories." But their chief purpose was to refresh the memories of previous travelers and help others prepare for the "land of promise." While *Six Months in Italy* was probably the best seller, the well-established genre included dozens of popular books by other well-respected Americans, whose titles suggest their slightly different emphases. Harriet Beecher Stowe's *Sunny Memories of Foreign Lands* (1854), James Jackson Jarves's *Italian Sights and Papal Principles* (1856), and Charles Eliot Norton's *Notes of Travel and Study in Italy* (1860) were all advertised by Ticknor and Fields along with *The Marble Faun* and Hillard's *Six Months in Italy* as "The Best Guides to Italy." Sophia Hawthorne's *Notes in England and Italy* (1869) was a belated entry into the same field.

Hawthorne's Italian notebooks were primarily a storehouse of rich material, not a book shaped for publication, though many of his experiences, assumptions, and attitudes coincide with those of the published travel writers. They were all dazzled by their first confrontations with Italy's celebrated works of art; they assumed (as Hillard put it) that "the legitimate function [of art is] to make us better men"; and all condemned works of art that "degrade and sensualize the mind," particularly the nudes of painters and sculptors who seemed to light their "torch at the fires of sense" (119-21). Thus they welcomed the intellectual challenge of such complex works as Raphael's Vatican frescoes, marveled at the suggestiveness of such art, reported on their own emotional responses as evidence of visual and moral sensibility, and reserved their highest praise for works that seemed modes of divine revelation. But always they "read" works of art, evaluating them in terms of the ideas they seemed to embody. Although most of the travel writers reported occasional boredom and fatigue and expressed doubts about their taste, these did not prevent them from venturing confident judgments about the merits of particular artists and particular artworks.

Like most of his countrymen, Hawthorne was at once reverent, sentimental, and skeptical about the visual arts, though he was never quite as philistine or provincial as some critics claim. Because he had trained his eye to respond to the particularities of individual works, he alertly reported whatever surprised him—whether the difference between one day's response and another's, the difference between his reaction and someone else's, or specific differences between two works by the same artist. Even more interesting than his specific aesthetic judgments are his reports of his mind's reflections, refractions, and grapplings for certainty. For all his similarities to other writers who preceded him in the field—Stowe, for example, was as disappointed in the Louvre as Hawthorne, and struggled to validate her taste—Hawthorne's accounts are much more richly speculative as he tried to understand why one work of art vitalized his imagination while another left it inert.

Hawthorne used travel books as guides and sounding boards, concentrating on the major sights and art objects recommended by Murray, "that necessary nuisance," particularly those also singled out by other writers such as Hillard or Byron. He compared his responses with theirs, and his treatment of such informants and advocates was always judiciously self-monitoring: Bernini's statue of Apollo and Daphne, for example, was "not so good as Hillard's description of it made me expect" (XIV: 175). While a modern reader can easily recognize that such cautious judgments conform as closely to period taste as his more sweeping enthusiasms or antipathies, Hawthorne formed them independently and reported them honestly even when they ran counter to the experts or counter to his own expectations; and he was prepared to change them only on the evidence of immediate experience.

Although Hawthorne became increasingly confident about his opinions throughout his stay in Italy, he complained to the very end that his taste remained unformed and imperfect. In fact, such complaints are not essentially different from those he made in London before beginning his role as a connoisseur. On his first visit to the Pitti Palace he thought that in a year he might develop "some little knowledge of pictures," but (although he was glad to find he could appreciate one painting more than another) he felt "I still know nothing" (XIV: 306-7). What seems particularly poignant is that despite his persistent efforts to develop his taste, he so frequently denigrated the attainment as merely a matter of intellect, separated from the heart and the spirit. Thus he complained that the Italian masters address "a formed intellectual taste" and that "there is something forced, if not feigned, in our tastes for pictures of the old Italian schools" (XIV: 112, 115). Later, when Hiram Powers declared that taste "was something very different and quite apart from the moral sense, and that it was often, perhaps generally, possessed by unprincipled men of ability and cultivation," Hawthorne agreed: "I have had this perception myself; a genuine love of painting and sculpture, and perhaps of music, seems often to have distinguished men capable of every social crime, and to have formed a hard and fine enamel over their characters. Perhaps it is because such tastes are artificial, the product of cultivation, and, when highly developed, imply a great remove from natural simplicity" (XIV: 321). Nevertheless, Hawthorne kept trying to work up his taste, monitoring his emotions as well as his intellectual responses while confronting works of art. Perhaps his conviction that his taste remained imperfect was at some level gratifying, proof that he remained a man of principle whose "natural simplicty" could not be enameled.

The reverse side of his self-criticism was self-congratulation. As an innocent abroad who deplored slick sophistication, he preserved a more valuable "natural sympathy." Repeatedly when he represented himself as an innocent with unrefined tastes, he comically exaggerated his limitations. Thus he reported that Anna Jameson correctly assumed he knew nothing at all about art: "The only mystery is, how she came to be so well aware of my ignorance on artistical points" (XIV: 207). But if her taste was better than his, that did not mean it was excellent. Hawthorne's relativism as well as his characteristic mix of diffidence and confidence is evident in his statement that despite Jameson's vast store of knowledge about art, her common sense, and her "elevated views," he doubted "whether she has quite the finest and highest perceptions in the world" (XIV: 208).[16]

That same careful relativism underlies his conviction that while his own taste was relatively unrefined, most Americans were even less sophisticated. Thinking about such federally commissioned statues as Greenough's *George Washington,* he concluded, "There is something false and affected in our highest taste for art," and he supposed that only Americans "seek to decorate public institutions, not by the highest taste among them, but by the average, at best" (XIV: 432). Even at the far swing of his pendulum of self-trust, he felt sure that his own taste was well above the American average.

He assumed that there are certain universal aesthetic rules and that he was capable of absorbing them, and one day after enjoying two or three "wonderful" statues at the Vatican, he said, "I am partly sensible that some unwritten rules of taste are making their way into my mind; that all this Greek beauty has done something towards refining me," even though he still remained "a very sturdy Goth" (XIV: 165-66). Most of his judgments distinguish understanding from emotion, as when after confronting a colossal head of Juno that was reputedly the greatest treasure of the Villa Ludovisi, he declared, "I did not myself feel it to be so, nor, indeed, received any strong impression of its excellence" (XIV: 147). Many analyses of his own responses to celebrated works are both more explicit and more grudging, as when he said he was "willing to accept" the merit of Leonardo's *Vanity and Modesty*, "although one of the faces has an affected smile"; but sometimes he merely distinguished general opinion from his own, saying for example that he preferred the "least celebrated" of the two Guido Madonnas (XIV: 124).

Ultimately, rules and established reputation were far less important to him than the overall effect of an artwork. In his discussions with Hiram Powers, he felt free to challenge the earnest, honest Yankee who argued as a practitioner and whose opinions often differed from those of connoisseurs. Sometimes Hawthorne presented opinions he had arrived at in discussions with others. Thus because he agreed with Anna Jameson that buttons and breeches "degrade the marble," though without relinquishing his belief that contemporary statues should be clothed, he objected both to Powers's predilection for nudity and to the fussily detailed clothing of his statue of George Washington. On the other hand, he praised Powers's statue of Daniel Webster though it was finished "to a seam and a stitch," since "this true artist has succeeded in showing him through the broadcloth" (XIV: 209, 433).

Because effectiveness was always Hawthorne's final concern, however, he was not persuaded by Powers's disparagement of Michelangelo's *Lorenzo de Medici*: "He allowed that its effect was very grand and mysterious; but added that it owed this to a trick—the effect being produced by the prearrangement of the hood, as he called it, or helmet, which throws the upper part of the face into shadow." Instead of denouncing such a "trick," Hawthorne admired it for enlisting the spectator's imagination and contributing to "the whole effect of this mighty statue" (XIV: 336). While taking Powers's professional judgments into consideration, Hawthorne relied on his own responses.

Yet Powers did make Hawthorne aware of sculptors' options while elucidating his own criteria for success, and in one notable instance he did alter Hawthorne's judgment of a celebrated statue. The *Venus de Medici* had given Hawthorne such immediate delight on his first visit to the Uffizi that he wrote, "Contemplation of the statue will refine and elevate my taste" (XIV: 308). But after Powers argued that the statue's eyes were like buttonholes and the ears were too low, he went back for another look. Although he could now perceive what Powers considered defects, particularly the "unnatural" eyes, he nonetheless asserted,

"Whatever rules may be transgressed, it is a noble and beautiful face; more so, perhaps, than if all rules had been obeyed" (XIV: 316). Yet Powers had refined his perception and undermined his enthusiasm. Never again was he as rhapsodically enthusiastic about the beauty or intelligence of the *Venus de Medici* as when he first saw her; and when he saw the newly unearthed Venus on the Roman Campagna, he declared it was far better than that other Venus with the "buttonhole eyes."

Though he was willing to entertain other people's opinions and was sometimes persuaded by them, and though his views were largely those of the standard authorities, he accepted none without challenge, not even those of his beloved Sophia. Not surprisingly, many of the judgments and even the metaphors in his *French and Italian Notebooks* and her *Notes in England and Italy* are virtually identical, indices of shared beliefs and closely shared experiences. Both praised the brilliant sunshine of Guido's *Aurora* and felt profoundly moved by his *Archangel Michael*; both considered Perugino a superb painter and Sodoma's *Christ Bound* a noble achievement; both thought Raphael the most consummate painter and criticized the English Pre-Raphaelites for "painting every hair on the skin"; and both preferred the delicate womanliness of the *Venus de Medici* to the "earthly" *Fornarina*. They were not always in agreement, however. Sophia was at once more rigid about morality and more flexible about mimetic conventions. Although both of them disapproved of eroticism, condemning the coarse sensuality of Titian's *Magdalen,* and thus (implicitly) of its painter, Sophia simply detested the picture and thought it was shameful that Titian "knew a person and contemplated her so minutely" and painted her so well (392), while Hawthorne could appreciate its pictorial values. But if Sophia read into paintings more singlemindedly than her husband, she could more readily accept unfamiliar styles and conventions. Thus the Hawthornes' judgments of the early Italian masters diverged. Sophia was enraptured by the devotional art of Giotto and Fra Angelico, but, although Hawthorne could see her point, he was put off by the painters' archaisms.

As his responses to Powers's criticisms of the *Venus de Medici* indicate, Hawthorne remained open-minded and responsive to his own developing taste. He had serious reservations about Raphael's celebrated cartoons at Hampton Court, and near the beginning of his stay in Italy he considered Francia more "devout" than Raphael. But gradually, as "some unwritten rules of taste" made their way into his mind, he found "Raphael grows upon me; several other painters—Guido, for instance— are fading out of my mind" (XIV: 315). Eventually, even when confronting faded frescoes and even in an unreceptive mood, he could accept the contemporary consensus that Raphael was a consummate artist, and he agreed with the majority in considering the *Madonna della*

Seggiola "the most beautiful picture in the world" (XIV: 305). Yet, not even Raphael got blanket approval. Hawthorne criticized the two-part composition of the *Transfiguration* (as in fact most contemporary critics did), but he took pains to discriminate exactly what he admired in its conception and execution before concluding as Hillard and Murray did that it was on the whole a splendid creation. He would give Kenyon his own perception that a spectator's mood can transfigure even the *Transfiguration*, though he also would have Miriam criticize Kenyon's relativism, just as Hawthorne himself came to recognize that the "life and expression" of Raphael's masterpiece eluded a copyist's skill and transcended subjectivity.

Some of his initial aesthetic responses, however, remained essentially unchanged even when his connoisseurship had advanced beyond them. In England he had unstintingly praised the Dutch Masters, and in Italy he felt a sense of relief when encountering any Dutch paintings. Yet he said, "It is the sign, I presume, of a taste still very defective, that I take singular pleasure in the elaborate imitations of Van Mieris, Gerard Dou, and other old Dutch wizards who painted such brass-pots that you can see your face in them." He did not desire or expect this aspect of his "defective" taste to change, though he wished for what he knew to be an impossibility—that "Raphael had painted the *Transfiguration* in this style, at the same time preserving his breadth and grandeur of design." He desired that synthesis without in the least expecting it, but he felt impelled to praise "the vast scope of this wonderful art, when we think of two excellences so far apart as that of this last painter and Raphael." The balance of the passage, however, makes it clear which "excellence" he preferred: Hawthorne focuses on the "petty miracles" of Dutch tulips and birds' nests, which can take "hold of us in our most matter of fact moods; whereas, the merits of the grander style of art may be beyond our ordinary appreciation, and leave us in doubt (nine times out of ten that we look at them) whether we have not befooled ourselves with a false admiration." Continuing to generalize his own responses through the plural pronoun, he condoned his delight in the Dutch as an acceptable consequence of limited taste: "Until we learn to appreciate the cherubs and angels that Raphael scatters through the blessed air, in a picture of the Nativity, it is not amiss to look at a Dutch fly settling on a peach, or a humble-bee burying himself in a flower" (XIV: 317-18). If Hawthorne felt he rarely reached the heights of appreciation Raphael requires, he could meanwhile (like George Eliot) take pleasure in the homely details of the Dutch. There he was on safe ground. Even if he did not feel spiritually uplifted by a Dutch fly or humble-bee, he had no worries about whether his admiration was justified; with the Dutch he would never befool himself.

As he walked through the chronologically arranged galleries of the

Uffizi and the magnificent collections of the Pitti Palace and the Academy of Fine Arts, becoming increasingly confident as a connoisseur, Hawthorne formulated broad generalizations about historical developments as well as achievements of particular schools and particular artists. He had acquired far more knowledge about art history and artists' techniques than during his weeks in Manchester, though he continued to demand credible representations of the world we inhabit as well as suggestions of deeper and higher truths.

Thus he explained his dislike of such early Italian painters as Giotto and Cimabue, devout and skillful though they were: except in faces and figures, they did not aim at "a lifelike illusion. . . . The trees are no more like real trees than the feather of a pen; and there is no perspective, the figures of the picture being shadowed forth on a surface of burnished gold." Although he could imagine the original brilliance of their paintings and even feel their present power, that gave him little pleasure. He thought he might come to like Fra Angelico if he "thought it worth while," but then he rather arrogantly suggested, "It is enough to have an outside perception of his kind and degree of merit, and so to let him pass into the garret of oblivion, where many things as good, or better, are piled away, that our own age may not stumble over them" (XIV: 323-24). For Hawthorne the first painter of "genuine merit" was Perugino, and eventually he placed Raphael even higher, gradually gaining enough confidence to evaluate individual canvases. But he sweepingly concluded that most artists who followed Raphael displayed an increased technical ability that usually coincided with a decrease in devoutness, a judgment that would enter into *The Marble Faun*.

He made equally broad generalizations about the developments of sculpture. The ideal statues of the antique world he declared superior to those of modern times, many of which he dismissed as petty and absurd. Yet he thought Christian sculptors were more "earnest" and "sympathetic" than their predecessors, and therefore capable of such "marvels" as Michelangelo's *Lorenzo*. Further, though he agreed with Anna Jameson that most of the American expatriates were without "high aims," he admired the lofty conceptions of Story's *Cleopatra* and Hosmer's *Zenobia*, and he granted that many of the sculptors he encountered were fine technicians. He made the same points through the statues of *The Marble Faun*, which range across all periods from the Greek *Faun* to the Roman *Marcus Aurelius*, to Christian *Pope Julius*, and the contemporary *Cleopatra*. But in each what Hawthorne chiefly valued was essentially the same—a conception worthy of the endurance of marble. Therefore he came to misprize the representation of transience in marble. Though he had at first admired the *Dying Gladiator* "exceedingly," he later came to believe that such "flitting moments" were inappropriate for "the eternal repose of marble" (XIV: 511), a view he would ascribe to Kenyon.

Underlying such statements is Hawthorne's belief that a statue is potentially a higher form of art than a painting, at least to the extent that the sculptor aims at ideality and the painter at reality. Unaware of the Greek and Roman practice of painting statues, he assumed that whiteness was integral to the sculptors' pursuit of the ideal, and his uneasiness about Gibson's painted statues is at one level a consequence of his belief that color belonged to the province of painting. As he saw it, color in a statue distracted both the sculptor and the spectator from the pursuit of ideality.

Intermingled with such judgments, which he assumed conformed to universal rules of taste, Hawthorne expressed his private taste, though in each case he conformed to period taste more often than he thought. Like most Victorians, he was self-conscious in the presence of nudity in statues and paintings, although he was seriously disturbed only if they seemed ungainly or erotic. Thus he was enchanted by the "chaste and naked grace" of the *Venus de Medici* but merely glanced at Titian's "naked and lustful" *Venus* in the same room of the Uffizi (XIV: 298-99). He had more trouble with Titian's "coarse and sensual" *Magdalen*, whose "golden hair clustering around her naked body" permitted her "voluptuous breasts" to be seen. From a connoisseur's perspective the picture was splendid, but Hawthorne nevertheless erupted in moral judgment against the painter: "Titian must have been a very good-for-nothing old man" (XIV: 333-34).

Yet doubtless he was right in believing himself not unusually squeamish. After noting that some of the Titians and Veroneses at the Fine Arts Academy had once been concealed from the public eye, he said, "I did not think them noticeably indecorous, as compared with a hundred other pictures that are shown and looked at without scruple;—Calypso and her nymphs, a knot of naked women by Titian, is perhaps as objectionable as any" (XIV: 170). The "perhaps" suggests he had no great emotional investment in the issue. As for the "faded nudities" in Michelangelo's *Last Judgment*, "if they were ever more nude than now, I should suppose, in their fresh glow, they might well have startled a not very squeamish eye," presumably such as his own; but he was neither startled nor offended by their present "sprawl of nakedness" (XIV: 215-16).

Hawthorne's aversion to coarse or startling nudes is one aspect of his lively interest in works of art representing the human form. While he could readily appreciate landscapes and still lifes, his imagination was far more engaged by fictive, sacred, or historically based portraits. Whether they were painted or sculpted, presented singly or in groups (as in the *Transfiguration* or the *Laocoön*), Hawthorne pushed beyond their surfaces to search out moral identity. As he had delineated the character of Hester Prynne by describing her face, he "read" the character of Beatrice Cenci in her visage. Both processes conjoin in *The*

Marble Faun, as we will show, when the characters of Hilda and Miriam are revealed through their resemblances to the portrait of Beatrice. Aesthetic issues had virtually no role in such conceptual speculations about character, whether actual or invented. Thus looking at Roman portrait busts, Hawthorne wondered why Caracalla was so willing to have his ugliness preserved, and he wished someone had tried to fix Nero's character in marble. Details of physiognomy and facial expression served as clues to the mysteries of spirit and intelligence that could never be wholly understood. Thus it is easy to appreciate his excitement at seeing a well-modeled head placed on the body of a recently excavated statue of Venus: "It seemed immediately to light up and vivify the entire figure" (XIV: 517), a reaction he would incorporate into his novel.

In a sense, he was witnessing the completion of a work of art, but exciting though that was, he found intimations of character and inner experience most immediately accessible through unfinished works. Admirable though technical finish was, it offered no clues to human behavior, while sketches and clay models offered Hawthorne clues about the artist's subjects, the artist, and, ultimately, himself. In such works, clear detail merged with challenging mystery, as in successfully completed paintings, statues, or even Gothic cathedrals, though in a simpler and more suggestively concentrated form that directly invited the viewer's imagination to imitate that of the artist.

Thus sketches by famous artists in one of Cephas Thompson's portfolios impressed Hawthorne by their "fire and spirit." He said it gave him "a higher idea of the imaginative scope and toil of artists than I generally get from their finished pictures" (XIV: 221). Later in the Uffizi even the roughest and hastiest sketch interested him because "it seems as if the artist had bestirred himself to catch the first glimpse of an image that did but reveal itself, and vanish." That charm could not survive in the finished work. In its "forecasting thought, skill, and prophetic design," the sketch at once captured the artist's "celestial germ" and stimulated the perceiver's imagination (XIV: 402). Similarly, the clay models he saw in sculptors' studios gave evidence of the artist's seminal imagination (though not as in sketches the original inspiration), making Hawthorne wonder if there might be "some magic" in imperfect finish "or in the material of clay, as being a better medium of expression than even marble" (XIV: 509). His imagination was as stirred by evidence of process in unfinished works of art as in unfinished human lives.

Conversely, he was disheartened by faded or time-darkened paintings, or by shattered, headless statues. Sketches and clay models stimulated the imagination; ruined art works turned it off. Thus Michelangelo's faded frescoes in the Sistine Chapel were "forlorn and depressing," and the sight of Orcagna's *Last Judgment* in the Strozzi Chapel made Hawthorne feel "it was purgatory to look at this poor, faded rubbish'' (XIV: 214, 359). When vitality departed—whether from a work of art or a human life—only material "rubbish" remained. By contrast, he accepted the plaster cast of a clay model as a different and happier form of death. Unlike the dead remains of once-living works of art, the cast (as the dictum attributed to Thorvaldsen affirmed) was simply a stage preceding a marble "resurrection" (XIV: 133). A plaster copy was a different matter entirely; (and with the single exception of Hilda's in *The Marble Faun*) he relegated copies of paintings to an even lower order of existence. Copies and engravings of famous paintings and plaster casts of famous statues, like those that had depressed him at the Boston Athenaeum, were only minimally alive: they lacked the nobility and beauty of the originals.

In conformity with his idealistic conception of the visual arts, Hawthorne looked for beauty in surfaces and for thought in underlying designs. Thus he could detect the "skeleton of thought" in the Raphael rooms at the Vatican even though the beauty that "clothed" it had vanished (XIV: 164). Yet even while regarding beauty as tributary to thought, he felt refreshed by beauty and depressed by ugliness. As Sophia Hawthorne commented in her edition of the *French and Italian Notebooks*, ''Mr. Hawthorne's inexorable demand for perfection in all things leads him to complain of grimy pictures and tarnished frames and faded frescos'' (203). Not that he was an Aylmer: he had no illusions about achieving perfection, but the evidence of mortal decay saddened him.

The beauty in a painting's colors or design could give Hawthorne immediate pleasure as could the precise rendition of painted or sculpted detail, but he reserved his highest praise for works of art whose color, design, and detail were tributary to some statement about life's broadest and highest truths, some suggestion of the primacy of spirit. Because he had learned to separate judgments of beauty from a final judgment of a painting's value, he could call a Dolci painting "a miracle of pictorial art" but also "a master-piece of absurdity" (XIV: 371-72).

However, when beautifully executed surfaces coexisted with noble conceptions, Hawthorne was enthralled, reiterating the words *magic, mystery,* and *miracle* in his attempts to come to terms with an artist's achievement. Even the best copy of the *Madonna della Seggiola* could not capture "that mysterious something that renders the picture a miracle," he said (XIV: 306), and he used the word *miracle* in the same way for the *Venus de Medici* and Michelangelo's *Lorenzo*. He assumed that their creators must have "wrought religiously" to achieve such results, without themselves completely understanding what they did. Calling a work "miraculous" was his highest tribute, though he occasionally acknowledged that one person's—or one age's—miracle might not be another's: a Cimabue Virgin "deemed a miracle in its day" was devoid of charm for Hawthorne, and he could only wish it "reverently burnt"

(XIV: 359-60). Yet he was probably too aesthetically shortsighted to realize that later ages might feel the same about what he "deemed a miracle," such as Sodoma's *Christ* and the *Beatrice Cenci*. He said of the Sodoma, "by nothing less than a miracle, the great painter has not suffered the Son of God to be merely an object of pity. . . . He is redeemed by a divine majesty and beauty, I know not how" (XIV: 452). Hawthorne's uncertainty about the artist's creative methods, the "I know not how," both fascinated and dismayed him; and he had the same response to the pitiful figure of Beatrice Cenci. "I think no other such magical effect can ever have been wrought by pencil," he said (XIV: 520), and perplexity about that effect (as about the teasingly marvelous suggestiveness of Kenyon's *Cleopatra* and his bust of Donatello) became integral to *The Marble Faun*.

In Hawthorne's notebooks, an artist's or a spectator's inability to understand the "mysterious something" that makes a work of art is frequently linked to Hawthorne's problem of describing the effect. Paradoxically, he felt most inadequate and frustrated in the presence of works whose greatness was beyond doubt. In England he had attributed his relative inarticulateness to ignorance about art; later in Italy he speculated that one art was simply not translatable into another. "Cold criticism" could never convey the vitality of a work of art, he declared, while struggling to find adequate language for his own feelings. His efforts at description were "idle" and "futile," he said, mocking himself for throwing "heaps of words" at works of art he admired. Later still, he had another problem: he felt too experienced and too jaded to write adequately about what he saw. In Avignon, he complained that even the "newest things, now-a-days, have a sort of familiarity in my eyes; whereas, in that lost sense of novelty lies the charm and power of description" (XIV: 531). As he approached the end of his European travels, no aesthetic experience seemed wonderfully novel. All seemed familiar in his eyes, at once a relative and an ultimate problem for a perceiver determined to see with his eyes alone, deferring to no traveler or art critic.

In all his commentaries on art, Hawthorne focused on his own experiences as a perceiver, carefully qualifying his judgments. He left the bulk of his impressions of art in his notebooks, although (of course) he drew on them heavily for *The Marble Faun* and *Our Old Home*. Unlike writers of travel books like Jameson and Hillard, who provided full descriptions and background information to guide other travelers, Hawthorne subordinated such information to his personal response. But there was never any doubt about what he expected of the artist or about the standards he applied to the work of art itself.

First came the question of an artist's motives. He thought an artist should first conceive and then capture and communicate noble truths about earthly existence, subordinating personality to reverence and love. For such an artist he reserved the words *sincere, earnest,* and *devout.* But he was aware that an individual was easily deflected from such self-surrender by a desire for fame or fortune (which might lead to idiosyncrasy or mere modishness) or by his own lower nature.

Finally, Hawthorne demanded of the artist what he demanded of himself as a writer—the combined effort of imagination, heart, mind, and spirit, working to assimilate the data supplied by clear-eyed perception to create something new. He also realized that an artist's observations and insights could be communicated only by the exercise of patience and skill. The artist was a seer whose humble submissiveness to the phenomenal universe sometimes resulted in "miraculous" vision. Even when skeptical of his own responses to high art, he contended that an artist's inspired vision of the immense "mystery which envelopes our little life" (IV: 26-27) might last only for a moment; but in capturing such a moment, the artist virtually repeated the original process of creation.

While not even the most devoted Hawthorne scholar would consider him a sophisticated critic, his aesthetic criteria (though essentially conventional) are sound, clear, and flexible. He most valued a noble subject, a grand conception, truthful representation (including appropriate facial expression), skillful handling of color and design, and "suggestiveness." He did not require precise adherence to formal rules, but an organically unified work with a single central effect. Thus he never deviated from the position that he had formulated at Manchester, one wholly applicable to his own fiction: a work of art must be true to nature but subsume mimetic exactitude to broader and higher truths.

The reader who comes to *The Marble Faun* from the notebooks must recognize how thoroughly Hawthorne's encounters with the visual arts are assimilated in that novel. He draws freely on his comments about individual receptivity, about the lives and accomplishments of contemporary painters and sculptors, and about taste, historical change, and the legacies of particular painters and sculptors and particular works, concentrating on those crucial to his development of theme and character, such as the Praxiteles *Faun* and the *Beatrice Cenci.* Of course, works of art do not function in the novel exactly as in the notebooks: Guercino's *Petronilla,* for example, has no place in the journals; and Hawthorne invented the busts of Donatello. But in the notebooks as in the novel, except in isolated doleful passages, Hawthorne celebrates paintings and statues as modes of knowledge and loci of moral value.

Art and Character in *The Marble Faun*

When in *The Marble Faun* Hawthorne took occasion to praise an American painter living in Rome for "landscapes that seem the reality of a better earth, and yet are but the truth of the very scenes around us, observed by the painter's insight and interpreted by his skill" (IV: 133), he was articulating his long-held belief that the best artists combine "truth of detail with a broader and higher truth."[17] Years earlier he had similar praise for the poet in "The Great Stone Face": "Creation was not finished till the poet came to interpret, and so complete it" (XI: 43). Hawthorne never abandoned his belief that the ideal artist, whatever his medium, perceives concrete reality with such sympathy, intelligence, and insight that he could see and express ideal truths.

In *The Marble Faun*, however, most of Hawthorne's comments on painters and spectators reflect his carefully qualified opinion that this ideal was rarely attained. In establishing and developing his characters, particularly his two heroines, Hawthorne drew on ideas about painting that he had been developing for the past two years, ideas about the painter's sincerity and the spectator's subjective response. A painter might be earnest and even inspired, but he might merely be a skilled and venal technician; and no spectator can see what his own mood, taste, and experience have not prepared him to see. In his last finished novel, Hawthorne repeatedly made paintings the middle term in a complex interchange between the creator and perceiver, one that defines them both.

Both heroines of *The Marble Faun* are painters, though of opposite kinds. Miriam projects her own warmth and passion into images of human sorrows and joys; Hilda is a self-abnegating artist who subordinates her own "feeling and fancy" to recapture the ethereal visions of the great masters. Further, Hawthorne defines all four of his protagonists through their responses to paintings: prior experience and present consciousness determine what they see. At the same time, paintings articulate the novel's central thematic conflict of innocence and guilt.

In a series of three chapters, Hawthorne defines Miriam and Hilda in terms of where they paint, what they paint, and how they respond to paintings. The fifth chapter, "Miriam's Studio," establishes her in the dark room that "had the customary aspect of a painter's studio," all its windows curtained but one that admits only "partial light which, with its strongly marked contrast of shadow, is the first requisite towards seeing objects pictorially." It seems a place of magic, as Cephas Thompson's Boston studio had seemed to Hawthorne when he was having his portrait painted, "the outward type of a poet's haunted imagination, where there are glimpses, sketches, and half-developed hints of beings and objects, grander and more beautiful than we can anywhere find in reality" (IV: 41). Miriam is a typical artist, her imagination filled with ideal visions, but she is also haunted by shadowy fantasies of her fears and desires.

Hawthorne had already established that despite Miriam's limited "technical merit," she produced paintings so passionate and colorful that they "met with good acceptance among the patrons of modern art" (IV: 20). Now, through the innocent Donatello's response to her art, we learn more about both the artist and her spectator. Her passionate sketches of Jael and Sisera, Judith and Holofernes, and Salome and John the Baptist all show "woman, acting the part of a revengeful mischief toward man," and Donatello shudders in fear and disgust as he looks at them. Miriam had not intended him to see those impassioned drawings. "Ugly phantoms that stole out of my mind," she calls them, "not things that I created, but things that haunt me" (IV: 44-45). We have already been told that her sketches and paintings frequently include the "features, or some shadow or reminiscence" of her persecutor, the Model who "haunted her footsteps" in Rome, the man whose guilt somehow tainted her (IV: 32). Like the writers in such early sketches as "The Devil in Manuscript," Miriam is haunted; her art embodies the "things that haunt" her, and in turn her art haunts the viewer.

She shows Donatello a portfolio of sketches of "common life, and the affections that spiritualize it," hoping they will please him. Donatello, however, is not certain how to respond to these "productions of a beautiful imagination" rendered with "deep and true" sympathy because in the background of each sketch, Miriam portrays herself as a sad onlooker (IV: 45-46). But he is enraptured by the one painting Miriam shows him, the portrait of a woman "so beautiful, that she seemed to get into your consciousness and memory, and could never afterwards be shut out, but haunted your dreams." This work of apparent "witchcraft" is Miriam's self-portrait, the only one in Hawthorne's fiction. It immediately conveys "intimate results of her heart-knowledge" to Donatello, who soon comes to see its sadness (IV: 47-49). Miriam's art reveals her sorrow, and by perceiving it, he now begins to share it.

Miriam's art results from a passionate awareness of life's joys and sorrows, but Hilda's art gives proof of her detachment, as suggested by the title of the novel's sixth chapter, set where she lives and works—"The Virgin's Shrine." Men of taste in America had collected her sketches, "lacking, perhaps, the reality which comes only from a close acquaintance with life, but so softly touched with feeling and fancy, that you seemed to be looking at humanity with angel's eyes." But once in Italy, she relinquished her role as an original artist to devote her talents to the great masters. "She saw—no, not saw, but felt—through and through a picture; she bestowed upon it all the warmth and richness of a woman's sympathy." She became a copyist. In this role, she is at once a spectator and an artist, a "handmaid of Raphael," but not merely an imitator. Selecting "some high, noble, and delicate portion" of a great painting, she renders it "with her whole soul"; and sometimes, through her sympathy and skill, "the spirit of some great departed Painter now first achieved his ideal." Hawthorne praises the nobility of her complete self-surrender and her willingness to forego personal reputation: "Since the beauty and glory of a great picture are confined within itself, she won out that glory by patient faith and self-devotion, and multiplied it for mankind" (IV: 55-61). Hilda is at this stage his ideal spectator; no personal distraction keeps her from seeing into a painting. She is so spiritually pure, however, that she can see only what is pure and ideal in paintings. She is oblivious to what she cannot understand—anything low, ignoble, or indelicate.

In the next chapter, called "Beatrice," Hilda's copy of the inscrutable portrait gives proof of her great patience and skill. It is "Guido's very Beatrice," Miriam says. But more important, Miriam is defined by her response to the portrait. She is moved to such "painful sympathy" by Beatrice Cenci's "unfathomable depth of sorrow," as Guido had painted and Hilda copied it, that her "expression had become almost exactly that of the portrait." Miriam as spectator empathizes completely with Beatrice's guilt-stained innocence; Hilda is the startled witness of her reaction. Miriam asks Hilda to cover the "magical picture" (as disturbing portraits are curtained in "Edward Randolph's Portrait" and "The Prophetic Pictures"), so that she can stop pondering its mystery, particularly the question that applies most directly to her own anguish—whether Beatrice herself thought she was innocent or guilty (IV: 64-67). Later, after Hilda has become indirectly stained by witnessing the Model's murder, she sees her own face and the painting reflected in a mirror and fancies in horror "that Beatrice's expression . . . had been depicted in her own face" (IV: 205). The artist had sympathetically portrayed Beatrice's grief or guilt, and her own expression of grief or guilt leads to this shock of identification. For both young women, the *Beatrice* becomes a moral mirror, posing an enigma they cannot resolve.

A brief episode involving a fictitious Italian painter offers a paradigm of the sympathy that should obtain between painter, subject, and spectator. The expression of sorrow on Hilda's face after the Model's death "deeply interested" the painter. Observing her one day as she looked at Leonardo's *Joanna of Aragon* "but evidently without seeing it, (for though it had attracted her eyes, a fancied resemblance to Miriam had immediately drawn away her thoughts) this artist drew a hasty sketch, which he afterwards elaborated into a finished portrait," depicting the girl staring in horror "at a blood-spot which seemed just then to have been discovered on her white robe."[18] The intuitive artist entitles the portrait *Innocence, dying of a Blood-stain!* But the greedy and literal-minded art dealer who buys it calls it instead *The Signorina's Vengeance*, since "a more intelligible title" can command a higher price. The painting won fame, although the "coarse world" could not understand its moral profundity. Some "connoisseurs" saw a resemblance to

Guido's *Beatrice*, but Hawthorne suggests that such sympathetic spectators as Hilda, Miriam, or the Italian painter are rare (IV: 330-31).

But even as spectators, Hilda and Miriam have their limits. They differ significantly in their responses to a sketch of the *Archangel Michael Subduing the Demon*, an unsigned sketch that Hilda is certain was made by Guido himself. The sketch poses a riddle about the survival of evil, since its centuries-old image of the Demon bears as uncanny resemblance to Miriam's Model. Perhaps Guido imagined the face as the epitome of evil, or perhaps the evil Model has existed for centuries. Of more immediate importance, however, are the girls' reactions to Michael's averted eyes. Hilda approves of his turning "away his eyes in painful disgust," but Miriam scorns such "daintiness." This exactly anticipates their responses to the Model's murder. Hilda turns away "in painful disgust," but Miriam confronts her guilt; she looks "the Demon in the face," as neither Michael nor Hilda can do. Although this is only a sketch, Hawthorne says that in sketches "if anywhere, you find the pure light of inspiration"; the very incompleteness "is suggestive, and sets the imagination at work" (IV: 138-40).

When Miriam later sees Guido's finished painting in the Church of the Capuchins where the dead Model now lies, she more forcefully develops her objections to Michael's "daintiness," saying she does not admire the painting's "moral and intellectual aspect" as Hilda does. Her experience of evil had led her to discern what she considers to be defects in it. After battling evil, Michael should be stained and wounded, she says; the Demon is a powerful antagonist. Kenyon, who admires the angel's "expression of heavenly severity" as Hilda does, nevertheless suggests that Miriam should "paint the picture of man's struggle against sin, according to your own idea! I think it will be a master-piece." But Miriam responds, "I am sadly afraid the victory would fall on the wrong side." She speaks as one who had done "battle with Michael's enemy" (IV: 183-85). By contrast, when Hilda is later comforted by a mosaic copy of this painting, she is not conscious of embattled bodies, but only of the representation of virtue triumphant. Their different inner states impel Miriam and Hilda to respond in opposite ways to essentially the same work of art: Miriam is ineluctably aware of her unresolved emotional turmoil, while Hilda yearns for spiritual comfort.

Kenyon's discussion of Fra Angelico with Donatello more discursively develops the way predisposition affects vision. Kenyon praises the "religious sincerity" of Fra Angelico's paintings, saying, "When one studies them faithfully, it is like holding a conversation about heavenly things with a tender and devout-minded man." The guilt-wracked Donatello, however, asserts that only the innocent can delight in images of such pure saints and angels—"they are not for me." Kenyon praises the "moral depth" of Donatello's criticism; it helps him understand Hilda's delight in Fra Angelico. The exchange establishes Kenyon as a conscientious spectator and reaffirms Hilda's essential innocence, but its chief importance is to show that Donatello is no longer the innocent young man who had reacted so sensitively to Miriam's sorrow-laden art. Now his mind is filled with guilt and he sees only through its filter (IV: 310).[19]

The viewer can see only what she or he is prepared to see. Thus Hawthorne explains that the faithful Catholic can see beauty in "ugly little prints," such as those Donatello hangs in his tower bedroom, "representing the sufferings of the Saviour and the martyrdoms of Saints," appropriate to his anguish yet his hope of redemption. The deeply penitent Donatello would not perceive his copy of Titian's *Magdalen*, "clad only in the flow of her golden ringlets," as Hawthorne and later Hilda would, as an unlikely candidate for heaven depicted by a sensual old man (IV: 255; XIV: 334). The pictures Donatello contemplates express and extend his penitence; thus he refuses to look at "some admirable frescoes by Perugino" because old frescoes give him "pain, yet not enough of a pain to answer as a penance" (IV: 309-10).

Chapter 37, "The Emptiness of Picture-Galleries," is Hawthorne's fullest examination of how perception changes with changed emotions and beliefs. After Hilda has witnessed murder, she can no longer respond sympathetically to paintings she had previously considered beautiful. She can no longer help a painter with her own "resources of sensibility and imagination." In her depression, she "doubted whether the pictorial art be not altogether a delusion." In part this is because beauty is comprised of formal order and harmony, and her mind is disordered and inharmonious. But, more important, her indirect participation in guilt has made her aware of the dark complexities of human behavior, and now "her perceptive faculty penetrated the canvas like a steel probe," detecting emotional and spiritual shallowness in many renowned paintings. Now not even consummate skill can obscure a "deficiency of earnestness and absolute truth" (IV: 335-41). Hilda sees as Hawthorne did that the Italian masters often substitute "intellectual perception" for "sympathy and sentiment" or "put genius and imagination in the place of spiritual insight" (IV: 375). She comes to the sad conclusion that most paintings of the Virgin are merely flattered portraits of earthly beauties without intimations of divinity: many painters "deified their light and wandering affections, . . .offering the features of some venal beauty to be enshrined in the holiest places" (IV: 338). No longer is Hilda the innocent occupant of the Virgin's shrine.

She has not rejected all the old masters, however, nor has her new dark knowledge dispelled her faith in the ideal of her moral fastidiousness. She still reveres the paintings of Fra Angelico and Perugino, and she can emphatically share the agony Sodoma felt while painting his *Christ Bound*, but she hopes that art can give her specific moral consolation.[20] Art "cannot comfort the heart in affliction," Hawthorne says (IV: 340), but emotional turmoil makes Hilda put aside her role as self-effacing spectator to seek assurance that her sorrow can be overcome. Loss of innocence has not made her lose hope that virtue ultimately triumphs; and she finally encounters two works of art that seem to sustain that hope. Coming upon Guido's *Archangel Michael* in St. Peter's Cathedral, a mosaic copy of the painting whose moral "defects" Miriam had so passionately criticized, Hilda feels overwhelmed by its representation of "the immortal youth and loveliness of Virtue, and its irresistible might against ugly Evil." She kneels and sobs a prayer. At this moment, she sees the "Truth" she wants to see (IV: 352).

She is relieved, if only briefly. Then, as she looks into the next shrine, she see Guercino's picture of Saint Petronilla lowered into her tomb "while her beatified spirit looks down," and with this image as her analogue, she hopes it might be possible "to rise above her present despondency that she might look down upon what she was, just as Petronilla in the picture looked down at her own corpse" (IV: 352-53). Her hope for such self-transcendence leads her to the confessional booth in the following chapter. There she seeks fuller emotional relief than she can find in Guido or Guercino.

Hilda leaves the picture galleries during her time of sorrow, but she later returns with "fresh love . . . , and yet with a deeper look into the heart of things; such as those necessarily acquire, who have passed from picture-galleries into dungeon-gloom, and thence come back to the picture-gallery again" (IV: 375). In Hawthorne's last passage about painting in the novel, he fancifully speculates about where Hilda was during her absence from her friends. Displaying his own knowledge as a man of taste while paying tribute to Hilda's love of the ideal, he suggests that perhaps

> she had been snatched away to a Land of Picture; that she had been straying with Claude in the golden light which he used to shed over his landscapes. . . . We will imagine that, for the sake of the true simplicity with which she loved them, Hilda had been permitted, for a season, to converse with the great, departed Masters of the pencil, and behold the diviner works which they have painted in heavenly colours. Guido had shown her another portrait of Beatrice Cenci, done from the celestial life, in which that forlorn mystery of the earthly countenance was exchanged for a radiant joy. Perugino had allowed her a glimpse at his easel. . . . Raphael has taken Hilda by the hand [and shown] her his latest master-piece. (IV: 452-53)

But Hawthorne's fantasy ignores the fact that Hilda no longer has "true simplicity." She can never be as successful a copyist as before, since she can never again wholly surrender to a painting: "She had known such a reality, that it taught her to distinguish inevitably the large portion that is unreal, in every work of art" (IV: 375). What happened to Hilda is what finally happened to Hawthorne: "she saw beauty less vividly, but felt truth, or the lack of it, more profoundly" (IV: 338). Her changing role as a spectator measures and deepens her response to life; she moves from worship to critical assessment.

Hawthorne asserts through Hilda that for the spectator as well as the painter, art can lead to self-awareness and moral growth and that a sketch or a copy can involve the imagination more than a technically perfect work. Perhaps this explains why Hawthorne doggedly continued until death on his unfinished romances, pondering questions of guilt and mortality. As a writer, he was engaged in the earnest search for the truth that he valued in painters, and from his readers he hoped for that complex range of response that he and Hilda finally made to art. With awareness of his changing role as a spectator of art, however, he became increasingly diffident about his reader's responses. His preface indicates and his postscript acknowledges that in writing his last novel, Hawthorne felt he addressed an unknown and unpredictable audience. As no painter could be sure of his viewer's understanding or sympathy, so he felt he could not count on the understanding or sympathy of a "Gentle Reader."

Only if a painter was sincere, perceptive, and skillful could he express his insights about human experience or eternal truth, but only to the extent that a spectator yielded to the painting (as a reader to a work of fiction) could he share the vision or move beyond it. This Hawthorne said in his journals and developed in his last finished romance. The "inspired" painting of Beatrice Cenci is ultimately inscrutable, but Miriam and Hilda sympathetically enter into it and so learn more about themselves; Hilda praises the *Archangel Michael* and Miriam criticizes it, but both attentively examine the painting before reacting to its moral statement. Especially through these two young women and these two paintings, Hawthorne says that the serious artist and spectator should regard a work of art as a moral statement. Hawthorne's artist is not, as Nina Baym suggests, one who "draws upon the erotic, creative forces" of life ("Hawthorne's Elegy for Art," 361), but rather one who subordinates sensuality to spiritual vision, sympathetically rendering truths about this world, yet suggesting higher truths.

That Hawthorne became increasingly tentative about assigning precise value and even precise meaning to great paintings during his stay in Italy does not mean that he denigrated art. Both in his journals and in *The Marble Faun*, he concluded that a painter can set forth a riddle that he is unable to solve, and that each viewer may interpret "the hieroglyphic in his own way;" yet he continued to value the painting as the middle term in the complex transaction between creator and viewer. A painting that poses moral problems moves both painter and spectator to test old insights and move toward new ones.[21]

The role of sculpture in *The Marble Faun* is at once simpler and more pervasive, consistent with Hawthorne's conviction that sculpture is "substantial fact" while painting is illusory. The novel opens in a gallery of the Capitol that contains many famous statues, including a copy of the *Faun* of Praxiteles; and Kenyon, Hilda, and Miriam immediately recognize the *Faun* as "an amiable and sensual creature," simpleminded and morally undeveloped—the very type of young Donatello (IV: 5-9). Thus from the start, sculpture is integral to the novel's theme and character development.

In his introduction to the novel, Hawthorne tries to account for what has troubled many of his critics, the heavy weight of the "Italian objects, antique, pictorial, and statuesque." They had filled his mind in Italy; in the course of writing his novel in northern England, they flowed out with such vitality that he "could not find in [his] heart to cancel them" (IV: 3). Further, once he had conceived Kenyon as a sculptor, he had to provide him with appropriate creations, and to that end he appropriated Story's *Cleopatra*. But these explanations are only partial. The germ of the novel was Hawthorne's confrontation with the *Faun* of Praxiteles and his attempt to understand how in its composition "characteristics of brute creation meet and combine with those of humanity" (IV: 9). His pursuit of the theme of the fortunate fall then led him to invent two portrait busts—Kenyon's studies of Donatello's face after the murder. The narrator suggests that Donatello's initial resemblance to the ancient faun made Hilda, Miriam, and Kenyon wonder while looking at other statues, "Why should not each statue grow warm with life!" (IV: 17). From one point of view *The Marble Faun* is about works of art (analogously including Hawthorne's novel) with such vitality that they can "come to life" and help spectators understand human existence; but it is also about the complexities of our inner lives that resist the fixity of marble. In writing his novel, Hawthorne drew on everything he had seen and thought about in the expatriate sculptors' studios, on his conversations with the artists, on his own concerted efforts in the galleries of Italy to understand statues as embodied ideas, and on his own response to the unearthed *Venus of the Campagna*. But whether describing particular statues or pondering such technical matters as the relation of the clay model to the finished marble, he was developing central thematic issues: an individual's capacity for inner change, an artist's role in understanding and expressing moral and emotional identity, and a spectator's capacity to understand a work of art.

Even statues that elicit only a few lines of description and interpretation develop Hawthorne's theme, as does the one strategically

introduced at the end of the novel's first paragraph. The child with a
dove clasped at her bosom and a snake ready to strike her heel—at once
a timeless image and a statement of moral change—symbolically
announces and encapsulates the novel's central theme of endangered
and even doomed innocence; and it is also the first of many direct links
of a piece of statuary to a particular character—in this case, Hilda.
Through this statue, Hawthorne prepares the reader to read each work
of art in his novel—and the novel itself—symbolically. At two points,
one before the Model's murder and one after, bronze statues in public
places function as minor characters in the moral drama, implicitly
offering messages of hope to the troubled protagonists. Both the
equestrian *Marcus Aurelius* in Rome and the seated *Pope Julius III* in
Perugia appear as beneficent paternal figures, one secular and one
religious, whose commands are benedictions. These statues sustain a
belief in—or at least a hope for—the existence of a benign order in the
universe. Paradoxically, flawed sculptures also offer an implicitly
hopeful message, that the great heart of nature can redeem even man's
most foolish constructs. The Fountain of Trevi, where Donatello sees the
Model address Miriam, is a magnificently elaborate construction in poor
taste, but it is redeemed by cascades of water and appears beautiful by
moonlight; and the moss-covered ruins in the Borghese Gardens are
modified and improved by the ongoing life of nature.

But most of the complex uses of statues in the novel center on Kenyon,
particularly on a few of his creations. When Hawthorne describes the
sculptor's studio, he concentrates on evidence of different stages of a
work's progress—the block of marble, the hasty sketch, the rough
model, the "exquisite" model "more interesting than even the final
marble, as being the intimate production of the sculptor himself,
moulded throughout with his loving hands, and nearest to his imagination and heart," the plaster cast where "the beauty of the statue
strangely disappears," and finally the shining marble (IV: 114-15).
Kenyon discourses on such issues as the appropriate clothing for a
modern statue, the propriety of nudity, the effect of coloring, and the
merit of modern statues in general. But these are subordinate to the
relation between a sculptor's knowledge of his subject and his artistic
achievement. Kenyon's *Cleopatra* and his busts of Donatello define
complex individuals, one "ideal" and one actual, and also the artist's
limited yet profoundly sympathetic understanding of them. In discussing and describing these works, Hawthorne expresses his own beliefs
about the demands of the sculptor's medium and his parameters of
success.

Among the sources for the character of Miriam is Story's statue of
Cleopatra, "stolen" and given to Kenyon. Kenyon unveils for Miriam his
clay model of the beautiful queen, whose repose is the "repose of

despair." She has "latent energy and fierceness" within her, and her face betokens her complex mind and resolute spirit. Miriam marvels at Kenyon's ability to capture that passionate woman in a "lump of wet clay"; but while accepting her praise and acknowledging "it is the concretion of a good deal of thought, emotion, and toil of brain and hand," Kenyon admits, "I know not how it came about, at last." Despite his low emotional temperature, somehow in the process of creation he had captured the soul of the vengeful queen. For a moment, Miriam thinks Kenyon's statue means that he can be entrusted with her own terrible secret; but sensing his reserve, she disdainfully asserts that he is as cold and pitiless as marble itself (IV: 126-29). Both of them recognize that the statue is more than the product of its creator. It embodies a complex idea about earthbound womanhood as far beyond Kenyon's conscious understanding as is Miriam herself.

When Kenyon shows his statue to Hilda after it has almost wholly emerged from the block of marble, Hawthorne offers another set of comments about the artist and the spectator. In adapting Aristotelian theory, Hawthorne enlarges on his notebook statement that forms emerge from the sculptor's stone as if independent of the artist's vision; the sculptor who supervises the workmen's translation of his clay model into marble is a kind of deity, ordering life to emerge from inert matter. When Hilda first looks at *Cleopatra,* Hawthorne curiously attributes life to the created figure herself: she "had now struggled almost out of the imprisoning stone." Then he switches the image to credit the artisans with discovery: "the workmen had found her within the mass of marble" (IV: 377). Neither of these fanciful notions attributes any creativity to the sculptor. He is neither liberator nor discoverer. But Kenyon's disjunction from the passionate Cleopatra is congruent with his increased emotional distance from the trouble-laden Miriam.

Hilda's reactions to the statue reveal even more about her developing character than Miriam's comments did. "I am ashamed to tell you how much I admire the statue," she says. Whether her shame is caused by her intense awareness of Cleopatra's fiery nature or of Kenyon's skill, it suggests that the virginal copyist is almost ready to grow into her own womanhood. A different kind of maturity emerges when she comforts Kenyon after he complains that the *Cleopatra* no longer seems lifelike to him. Her consolation is at once Hawthornean, Melvillean, and Platonic: "Those who try to grapple with a great or beautiful idea" must inevitably fall short of their goals, since they have imagined "things too high for mortal faculties to execute." She then expresses Hawthorne's conception of the ideal "class of spectators" (like his ideal class of readers) "whose sympathy will help them to see the Perfect, through a mist of imperfection"; and she concludes with one of Hawthorne's firmest beliefs about any work of art: "Their highest merit is suggestiveness'' (IV: 378-79). Even the most successful work of art can only approximate an artist's vision, though it may convey to the sensitive viewer even more than the artist consciously intended. The work of art, like a living creature, has its own separate existence, its ultimate effects exceeding the artist's control. But as Hawthorne suggested through the *Cleopatra*, a powerfully conceived and well-executed work of art can expand the minds and imaginations of both the creator and the spectator. Even as the *Cleopatra* served to mark the gulf between Kenyon and Miriam, it anticipates the compassionate union of Hilda and Kenyon.

Kenyon's clay model of Donatello is more integral to the narrative, but it also implicitly asserts Kenyon's limited understanding—specifically, his inability to comprehend Donatello's changing moral character. While visiting Monte Beni, Kenyon asks permission to model the face of his guilt-stricken friend, which no longer resembles that of the marble faun. Donatello does not want "to be looked at steadfastly" but agrees to be "taken" when the sculptor promises to try to "catch the likeness and expression by side-glimpses, which . . . always bring home richer results" (IV: 228). Kenyon is perplexed by the discrepancy he senses between Donatello's genial features and his inner anguish; thus he cannot make the clay "the index of the mind within" (IV: 270). The problem is twofold: Kenyon is a man of limited acuity, and Donatello's character is developing so rapidly that it eludes the fixity of art. A statue requires a subject in repose, Hawthorne believed, but at this point Donatello is intellectually and emotionally agitated.

Intuitively recognizing his problem, Kenyon tries modeling with passionate recklessness, and when at one point he unintentionally shapes "a distorted and violent look," the remorseful Donatello urges him to fix that expression as an eternal reminder of his crime (IV: 272). Kenyon refuses. Without knowing that Donatello's face wore that distorted look at the moment of murder, he is certain that it is an ephemeral and uncharacteristic expression. He deliberately expunges it, arguing that Donatello should similarly eliminate the memory of evil.

Hawthorne concludes the passage on an even more comforting note. Without the notice of either Donatello or Kenyon, the sculptor's "last accidental touches" give the bust a "higher and sweeter expression than it had hitherto worn," proleptic of the next stage of Donatello's moral development (IV: 273). Hawthorne implicitly asserts that there is an inexplicable kind of magic in works of art that somehow capture truths not available to the consciousness of either the artist or his subject. Yet he is denying the artist the dignity of consciously achieved purpose. If the sculptor begat the marble Cleopatra by fiat, impulse and chance governed his reshaping of Donatello's clay features. Perhaps Hawthorne was moving toward the despair about his own creative enterprise that would prevent him from completing any subsequent romance. His sculptor is the efficient cause of the clay model and the final cause of the marble Cleopatra, but accident modifies one and "mechanics" shape the other. Hawthorne suggests that some inexplicable ultimate cause was also at work. Nevertheless, the sculptor conceived both projects, and Hawthorne's basic conception of his agency is positive. Without the seminal idea, there would be no artistic achievement at all.

Hawthorne presents other searching speculations about an artist's gropings toward knowledge and artistic achievement in the scene where Hilda and Kenyon examine his marble portrait bust of Donatello—not copied from a clay model or hacked by artisans from a plaster cast, but shaped from knowledge and memory by the artist's hands. The bust is still partly encrusted in the marble block and the features are not sharply defined, yet Kenyon has captured a recognizable expression, more characteristic of Donatello than either the face of the Praxiteles *Faun* or his own earlier clay portrait. At this point the narrator reminds the reader of "Thorwaldsen's threefold analogy;—the Clay-model, the Life; the Plaister-cast, the Death; and the sculptured Marble, the Resurrection," which seems validated by the spirituality of Donatello's emerging expression (IV: 380). Hawthorne had drawn on the same conception when first describing Kenyon's studio, speaking of the clay forms shaped by the sculptor's "loving hands," the plaster cast devoid of beauty, and the pure radiance of the completed marble. This more explicit authorial aside focuses on the emergence of the innate ideal, though the process is incomplete.

At this point Hilda's perceptive speculations help Kenyon come to terms with his accomplishment. She sees the bust as an image of the growth of the soul. When Kenyon says in surprise that he might have had such an idea in mind, Hilda apologetically suggests that the credit may not be his. She will not grant that the bust is wholly the product of his skill or intention, though in her characteristically Hawthornean way, she does not deny that possibility: she tentatively questions whether the statue's effect is "perhaps, the chance-result of the bust not being just so far shaped out, in the marble, as the process of moral growth had advanced, in the original?" At this point Kenyon does not say "you are right" but rather (with typically Hawthornean qualification), "I believe you are right" (VI: 380-81), and he agrees to leave the bust unfinished as a riddling representation not only of Donatello's transformation but of the growth of the human soul (IV: 379-80). It does not represent a "flitting moment," which Hawthorne considered improper for marble, but a stage of moral development. Hilda has served as the ideal spectator, helping the artist with her imagination, clarifying ideas he did not consciously apprehend. His bust is like one of the Old Masters' sketches Hawthorne admired, hastily limning a "celestial germ." Kenyon is as much a spectator of the marble form as Hilda is. He is a mystified man of faith, as was Hawthorne himself when dealing with the riddles of the spirit and the imagination.

The final and most richly suggestive statue in the novel is the long-buried and shattered *Venus* that Miriam and Donatello had encountered on the Campagna and then reburied for Kenyon to rediscover. The season is spring, and Hawthorne draws on seasonal myths of burial and resurrection that amplify Thorvaldsen's analogy. In no way is Kenyon the creator of this statue except as a creative perceiver. He puts together what has been broken apart as though solving a puzzle, finding proper places for missing pieces; and the reassembled statue (like the marble bust of Donatello) intimates the possibility of personal fulfillment. First he uncovers the earth-stained body, then finds the head and puts it in place, reminiscent of Donatello's growth from animality. "The effect was magical. It immediately lighted up and vivified the whole figure" (IV: 423), now apprehended as an ideal form of womanhood. Though temporarily lost to mankind (as Persephone-Hilda is at the moment), the risen goddess is proof and promise of the survival of love and beauty in this world. The magical moment of Kenyon's insight soon passes but like Miriam and Donatello before him, he has glimpsed its innate and immortal idea. Newly softened by adversity, he is capable of tenderness for both a marble and a fleshly Venus.[22]

Throughout *The Marble Faun*, Hawthorne ascribes an independent existence to art, separating it from human agency—possibly a reflection of his hopes about the survival of his fiction and doubts about his own creative role. Thus he presents the *Cleopatra* apparently struggling out of the marble, the developing soul in the marble bust of Donatello, the vital womanhood of the rediscovered *Venus*, and the self-protective *Beatrice Cenci*, concealing her dreadful secret from casual viewers and determined copyists alike. Hawthorne's view of a work of art as a vital entity with urgent messages for mankind is evident from his recurring journal entries about light emanating from inside a painting or statue, about glimpses of the spirit in a work of art, and about his delight when a work deigned to reveal itself. That conception is central to such stories as "The Artist of the Beautiful," "Edward Randolph's Portrait," and "The Prophetic Pictures," as well as *The House of the Seven Gables*. But in Hawthorne's last completed novel, the idea is amplified.

Even while complaining that the beauty of an artwork may fade or be wholly obliterated, he asserts that its essential meaning remains constant. The individual's ability to understand it, however, is affected by experience and mood. Thus Hawthorne used responses to paintings and statues as measures of a protagonist's character and emotions. Further, responses to works of art may serve as catalysts to awareness.

In this sense, works of art "come to life." If art cannot in itself comfort an afflicted heart, simple artworks can provide simple gratifications, while more complex works can expand the consciousness of artist and spectator alike. Viewing such works, individuals may formulate ideas that had not reached consciousness (as when Kenyon and Hilda contemplate the bust of Donatello), or move to more sympathetic awareness of what they already knew (as when Donatello admires Miriam's self-portrait or Miriam admires the clay *Cleopatra*). But Hawthorne insists that viewers can see only and understand what they are in some measure prepared to see. Thus during Kenyon's despair about Hilda's disappearance, he cannot see the radiant beauty of the *Apollo Belvedere*, but he thoroughly comprehends the *Laocoön*'s fierce struggle with error and evil. The changes are in the viewers, not in the paintings or statues.

Throughout his years abroad, Hawthorne worried about his receptivity to art and the refinement of his taste, worried that a work of art might seem alive one day and dead the next, and worried about the possibility of affixing meaning or value to any work that different spectators interpreted in different ways. More fundamentally, he worried that the universe might itself be meaningless: just as the beauty of a painted canvas might be simply a crust, so there might be nothing but an abyss beneath the crust of the earth. He tried to cope with these worries in *The Marble Faun* in several ways, usually by assigning his anxieties to protagonists or expanding them into authorial generalizations about the human situation. He had not at first appreciated Raphael; therefore the narrator explains that only a well-developed taste can appreciate him, implicitly asserting that Hawthorne had reached that stage. From the alembic of his concern about different spectators' reaching different interpretations of the same work of art, he drew Hilda's and Miriam's divergent responses to Guido's *Archangel Michael;* but he also showed that both were aware of the painting's polarity. And although a sorrowing Kenyon cannot appreciate the Apollo's beauty, that does not mean that the beauty has vanished: when his mood passes, presumably his appreciation will return. Proper understanding of an artwork requires a generous self-surrender as rare as a work of artistic excellence. The broken but reassembled statue of Venus serves as an index of Hilda's emotional condition: she has been shattered, but love can make her whole. If Hawthorne's art analogies are followed closely, Hilda does not emerge as a "monster of goodness" as some critics contend. She is a repressed young woman who must be vivified by the agency of love. Through his protagonists, Hawthorne dramatized tentativeness and relativity in aesthetic response, grateful for his moments of delight in the beauty of a Raphael Madonna or the benignity of a sculptured Pope, which seemed to presage ultimate resolutions of human sorrow.

What Hawthorne says about the ideal spectator applies directly to the ideal reader: he must sympathetically submit to the imaginative perusal of fictions, venturing to pursue their suggestiveness. Adequate response is in part an act of faith. The anxieties of Kenyon as an artist clarify those of Hawthorne as a novelist. Kenyon worried about finding the proper form for his conceptions, worried that he did not wholly comprehend or control his work, and feared that the finished work might be devoid of life. So did Hawthorne. Finally, however, Hawthorne's conviction that perfect appreciation of an artwork is rare, that excellence in art is rare, and that the creator may himself be doubt ridden does not mean that he denigrated the visual arts any more than he denigrated literature. Certainly he wavered about the value of *The Marble Faun*, as he wavered about all his other fiction. On some days he could perceive its greatness; on others he was not so sure. But he approached works of literature in the same spirit in which he approached paintings or statues, valuing them as productions of human beings who are radically imperfect yet capable of improvement of the mind, heart, and spirit as well as imagination and taste; and he wrote his last completed romance in the certainty that the value of a book, a painting, or a statue depends on its capacity to reflect and effect such improvement. Mere specificities were finally as delimiting as questions about Donatello's ears. For Hawthorne, the greatest value of an artwork was its suggestiveness.

NOTES

1. James R. Mellow in "Transcendental Admirers: Turner's American Friends," *Art News* (December 1980): 83 identifies John Naylor as a Manchester businessman and notes that Sophia had seen paintings by Turner at a Liverpool exhibition the year before and echoed Ruskin's praise.

2. Similar metaphors of ingestion, digestion, and assimilation recur in Hawthorne's notebooks, expressing problems of response to new experiences; for example, "like the anaconda, I need to lubricate any object a great deal, before I can swallow it and actually make it my own" (*EN:* 182). See Gollin's "Hawthorne on Perception, Lucubration, and Reverie," in *Nathaniel Hawthorne Journal, 1976* 6 (1978): 227-39, and "Hawthorne and the Anxiety of Aesthetic Response," *Centennial Review* 28, no. 4 and 29, no. 1 (Fall 1984-Winter 1985): 94-104.

3. See *The Art-Treasures Examiner: A Pictorial, Critical, and Historical Record of the Art-Treasures Exhibition, at Manchester, In 1857* (Manchester: A. Ireland, 1857). Hawthorne's copy of *A Handbook to the Gallery of British Paintings in the Art Treasures Exhibition* (London: Bradbury and Evans, 1857) is in the Berg Collection of the New York Public Library bound together with a supplemental catalogue of Old Masters, engravings, and photographs in the Manchester Exhibition, and also with an exhibition catalogue of artworks owned by the Bonaparte family (Liverpool: Davin Marples, 1855). See also the *Catalogue of the Art Treasures of the*

United Kingdom Collected at Manchester in 1857 (London: Bradbury and Evans, 1857). Winslow Ames in *Prince Albert and Victorian Taste* (New York: Viking, 1968) calls the exhibition superb, "the first really great general exhibition of works of art" (105-6). Both Prince Albert and Ruskin advised on selections; and living artists were invited to choose works they wanted included. The "Art Treasures Palace," which occupied over three acres, drew over a million viewers between its opening on May 5 and its closing on October 17. See the *Art-Journal* 3 (1857) for general commentaries, including complaints similar to Hawthorne's: for example, "There was absolutely a glut of Art-treasures" (66), and "there was so much to be seen that there was no time for studying" (362). Curiously, Sophia Hawthorne in *Notes in England and Italy* (New York: G. P. Putnam and Sons, 1869) said little about the art she saw in England and nothing at all about the Manchester Exhibition.

4. Hawthorne recalled the painting while writing *The Marble Faun* and alluded to it when he described some girls in Tuscany (IV: 291).

5. See Roger B. Stein, *John Ruskin and Aesthetic Thought in America, 1840-1900* (Cambridge: Harvard University Press, 1967): 2, and Marion L. Kesselring, *Hawthorne's Reading, 1828-1850* (New York: The New York Public Library, 1949).

6. Presumably the *Catalogue of the Sketches and Drawings by J.M.W. Turner, R. A., Exhibited in Marlborough House in the Year 1857-58* (London: Spottiswode, 1857).

7. His description focuses on "picturesque" details: Tennyson

> [was] rather slouching, dressed entirely in black, and with nothing white about him except the collar of his shirt, which methought might have been clean the day before. He had on a black wide-awake hat, with round crown and wide, irregular brim, beneath which came down his long black hair, looking terribly tangled; he had a long pointed beard, too, a little browner than the hair, and not so abundant as to incumber any of the expression of his face. His frock coat was buttoned across the breast, though the afternoon was warm. His face was very dark, and not exactly a smooth face, but worn, and expressing great sensitiveness, though not, at that moment, the pain and sorrow which is seen in his bust. His eyes were black. (*EN:* 553-54)

Hawthorne tried to capture Tennyson's character by describing his behavior—the way he paused before pictures "that interested him, with his hands folded behind his back"; his bass voice, "rather broken, as it were, and ragged about the edges, but pleasant to the ear"; his shy manner in conversation, suggesting "morbid painfulness"; his shuffling walk; the "wildness in his aspect"; and his "sallow, and unhealthy look." Yet it is a measure of Hawthorne's high standards for verbal portraiture that this meticulous and sensitive account did not satisfy him (as his description of the Salem apple dealer fifteen years earlier did not satisfy him). "How strange, that in these two or three pages I cannot get one single touch that may call him up hereafter!" he complained, and he finally abandoned the attempt, saying "I may as well leave him here; for I cannot touch the central point" (*EN:* 553-54).

8. According to Jeremy Maas, William Etty (1787-1849) "was the first and only painter before the present century for whom nude painting was essential to his

artistic creation. After 1811, his interest became obsessional," and his viewers were startled "by the literalness with which he painted his sensuous and full-blooded women" (164). Three weeks after the journal entry on Etty, after saying that he liked few of Titian's paintings except "some noble portraits," Hawthorne complained, "I am weary of naked goddesses, who never had any real life and warmth in the painter's imagination—or, if so, it was the impure warmth of the unchaste women who sat or sprawled for them" (EN: 560-61). Evidently Hawthorne felt that even Titian's nudes violated modesty and "nature"—of the painter, the sitter, and the spectator.

9. The painting is now attributed to Rosso Fiorentino. See Wonders of Italy, edited by Joseph Fattorusso (Florence: G. Fattorusso, 1930): 280.

10. See Paul R. Baker (29-30) and Neil Harris, The Artist in American Society: The Formative Years, 1790-1860 (New York: George Braziller, 1966).

11. See William H. Gerdts, American Neo-Classic Sculpture: The Marble Resurrection (New York: Viking, 1973) and The White Marmorean Flock: Nineteenth-Century American Women Neoclassical Sculptors (Poughkeepsie, N.Y.: Vassar College Art Gallery, 1972); Wayne Craven, Sculpture in America (New York: Crowell, 1968); and Sylvia E. Crane, White Silence: Greenough, Powers, and Crawford, American Sculptors in Nineteenth Century Italy (Coral Gables, Fla.: University of Miami Press, 1972).

12. Hillard, who shared the general opinion, dedicated his Six Months in Italy to Thomas and Laura Crawford.

13. He wrote to Ticknor about Lander on 14 April 1858, to Ticknor about Story on 10 February 1860, and to Fields the next day, to Ticknor about Thompson on 23 May 1859, and to Pierce about Powers on 27 October 1858.

14. On 15 April 1860, Story thanked Hawthorne "for that remarkable description of Cleopatra," which he thought better than the statue itself, saying, "It is very difficult to do with clay or marble what you yourself do with the airy material of language."

15. See Baker and Harris as well as the books themselves.

16. Anna Brownell Jameson (1794-1860) was an Englishwoman whose series of books on early Christian art, particularly its iconography—including Sacred and Legendary Art (1848), Legends of the Monastic Orders (1852), and Legends of the Madonna (1852)—were widely read in both England and America.

17. Here Hawthorne was praising George Loring Brown, and later in the same passage Cephas Thompson and Thomas Buchanan Read.

18. The painting is no longer attributed to Leonardo but simply to the Flemish School. See Leonardo da Vinci (186).

19. Earlier Kenyon saw divine majesty in the Tuscan landscape while Donatello saw only meaningless spots of sunshine and shadow; and as they looked at the same clouds, Kenyon saw the figure of Hilda while Donatello first saw the dead model and then Miriam.

20. Nina Baym in "The Marble Faun: Hawthorne's Elegy for Art" persuasively argues that Hilda accepted "the old masters as moral authorities" before witnessing murder, but she rejected them afterward because their paintings of the Virgin reveal that they are not moral patriarchs but "lovers" praising their mistresses' beauty (367). Hawthorne carefully qualifies Hilda's rejection of paintings of the Virgin, however; she realizes that "some" do not merit

devotion, but she does not reject the virgins of Raphael or Perugino. She values in them what she values in other paintings, a combination of the celestial and the earthly; thus she values Sodoma's *Christ Bound* for its reconciliations of "Divine Omnipotence and outraged, suffering Humanity" (IV: 340).

21. See Paul Brodtkorb, Jr. (254-67) for an analysis of Hawthorne's uncertainties about visual art and a reading of the novel as a "parable of art," "ideal" versus "existential"; Brodtkorb, however, overemphasizes Hawthorne's "denigration" of art.

22. Kenyon is not as interested in the broken statue of Venus as he is in continuing his search for Hilda, but that does not mean he is rejecting the power of Venus or renouncing art, as Baym suggests ("Hawthorne's Elegy for Art," 374). Hilda is "dearer to him than his art" (IV: 424), but Kenyon's love is at once physical, emotional, and spiritual, and marrying Hilda might make him a better artist. Hawthorne believed that for most artists, as for himself, participation in life is a prerequisite for reaching an audience. Although Millicent Bell assumes that after winning Hilda, Kenyon will give up "the wonder-working power of art," only anxiety about Hilda dispels Kenyon's love of art, and that anxiety is soon ended (169). Kenyon remains "the sculptor" to the end.

Afterword

LOOKING BACK TO ENGLAND AND AHEAD TO AMERICA'S FUTURE

Hawthorne settled once more at the Wayside after "getting a taste" for painting and sculpture in Europe and after his penetrating exploration of art and artists in *The Marble Faun*. Though he evidently did not lament the absence of a stimulating art colony or make efforts to visit museums, exhibitions, or churches with his wife and children, the walls of his Concord home were soon hung with Sophia's works and the family's growing collection of prints and original oils. As Sophia set to work on a copy of Guido's *Archangel Michael Subduing the Demon*, Hawthorne undertook to have Concord carpenters add to the Wayside a tower inspired by the Villa Montauto. It proved to be an artistic wart on the much cobbled house but did provide the solitude Hawthorne sought for his renewed literary efforts.

Encouraged by the critical and financial success of *The Marble Faun* and stocked with ideas for new romances, Hawthorne resumed his career as a romancer, though he never completed another piece of fiction. However hard he tried, he could not break his creative logjam. Meanwhile, his tower and home repairs depleted his savings. He needed cash, and one way to get it quickly was to write a series of articles for *The Atlantic Monthly*. At the suggestion of his publisher, James T. Fields, he mined his English notebooks for material on visits to English cathedrals, museums, and private homes. Some of the pieces in this series, notably "About Warwick," "Lichfield and Uttoxeter," "Pilgrimage to Old Boston," "A London Suburb," and "Up the Thames," included revised versions of his responses to art and architecture. As he had done for *The Blithedale Romance* and *The Marble*

Faun, Hawthorne simply lifted sentences and paragraphs from his notebooks and made minor changes as he put them to work in a new context. His descriptions of paintings, statues, and buildings largely serve to give a sense of place or to present art objects with enough detail to make them a felt presence. Like disciplined travel writers, Hawthorne refrains from dropping names of artists or titles of works. Some of his descriptions rely on a few broad strokes, but others, such as his depiction of Lichfield Cathedral, move toward a Ruskinian fullness of detail. Typically, when an art object engaged Hawthorne's eyes as well as his heart, he ruminated over it, seeking to understand the artist's conception and to open himself to a "spiritual possession" of the work. He never served up chunks of realistic descriptions but sought to help readers understand England as they saw it through his eyes. Though over the years he had more and more relished the solid "beef and ale" of such realistic writers as Dickens and Trollope, Hawthorne wanted something more than photographic exactness in these articles. If readers were to see through his eyes, they should also catch an occasional glimpse of higher and deeper truths as he perceived them. Carefully chosen details fused with authorial impressions would work best, Hawthorne evidently thought, especially for people who had seen the same sights. But he had read enough travel books and written enough travel sketches to know that he had to do more than simply jog the recollections of such travelers. Experienced travel writers know that many of their readers will be armchair travelers who will want more than impressions and ruminations, no matter how well expressed. Such readers prefer writing with pictorial and sensory exactitude, the kind of writing Hawthorne had done three decades earlier in his travel sketches, whether describing an Ontario steamboat, the ruins at Fort Ticonderoga, or his visit to Niagara Falls. But now he faced the challenge of doing justice to all the art objects and architectural styles he had seen. It was far more difficult to describe Westminster Abbey than a canal boat. He could not offer a mere catalogue of art objects or attempt in words what a photographer or engraver achieved through images. He had to use broad strokes, selecting the most salient traits to share with his readers.

While governed by this principle of selectivity, Hawthorne also decided to let his readers share his thoughts as he tried to comprehend the meaning and significance of the artworks he had seen. He therefore presented himself as an observant, responsive, thoughtful tourist rather than a connoisseur of art, someone whose judgment and taste might be relatively uninstructed but nonetheless sincere. A notebook entry on Lichfield Cathedral, later modified for the sophisticated readers of *The Atlantic Monthly*, exemplifies his technique:

> I have heretofore seen no cathedral save that of Chester, and one or two little ones, unworthy of the name, in Wales. No

doubt, there may be much more magnificent cathedrals, in England and elsewhere, than this of Lichfield; but if there were no other, I should be pretty well satisfied with this; such beautiful shapes it takes, from all points of view, with its peaks and pinnacles, and its three towers and their lofty spires, one loftier than its fellows; so rich it is with external ornament, of carved stone-work, and statues in a great many niches, though many more are vacant, which I suppose were once filled. I had no idea before (nor, possibly, have I now) what intricate and multitudinous adornment was bestowed on the front of a Gothic church. Above the chief entrance, there is a row of statues of saints, angels, martyrs, or kings, running along that whole front, to the number, no doubt, of more than a score, sculptured in red stone. Then there are such strange, delightful recesses in the great figure of the Cathedral; it is so difficult to melt it into one idea, and comprehend it in that way; and yet it is all so consonant in its intricacy—it seems to me a Gothic Cathedral may be the greatest work man has yet achieved—a great stone poem. I hated to leave gazing at it, because I felt that I did not a hundredth part take it in and comprehend it, and yet I wanted to leave off, because I knew I never should adequately comprehend its beauty and grandeur. Perhaps you must live with the Cathedral in order to know it. (*EN:* 149)

Though he generalizes momentarily and ruminates briefly, Hawthorne spent most of his energy here describing what he saw and acknowledging to himself that he was an innocent abroad. When he presented Lichfield Cathedral in the *Atlantic*, he sharply reduced the number of specific details and offered general impressions and ruminations. The notebook entry was the product of someone who had yet to see cathedrals in York, Lincoln, Paris, and Italy; the magazine treatment reflects much wider experience and thoughtful analysis of Gothic architecture:

I know not what rank the Cathedral of Lichfield holds among its sister-edifices in England, as a piece of magnificent architecture. Except that of Chester, (the grim and simple nave of which stands yet unrivalled in my memory,) and one or two small ones in North Wales, hardly worthy of the name of Cathedrals, it was the first that I had seen. To my uninstructed vision, it seemed the best object worth gazing at in the whole world; and now, after beholding a great many more, I remember it with less prodigal admiration only because others are as magnificent as itself. The traces remaining in my memory represent it as airy rather than massive. A multitude of beautiful shapes appeared to be comprehended within its single outline; it was a kind of kaleidoscopic mystery, so rich a variety of aspects did it assume from each altered point of view, through the presentation of a different face, and the rearrangement of its peaks and pinnacles and the three battlemented towers, with the spires that shot heavenward from all three, but one loftier than its fellows. Thus it impressed you, at every change, as a newly created structure of the passing moment, in which yet you lovingly recognized the half-vanished structure of the instant before, and felt, moreover, a joyful faith in the indestructible existence of all this cloudlike vicissitude. A Gothic Cathedral is surely the most wonderful work which mortal man has yet achieved, so vast, so intricate, and so profoundly simply, with such strange, delightful recesses in its grand figure, so difficult to comprehend within one idea, and yet all so consonant that it ultimately draws the beholder and his universe into its harmony. It is the only thing in the world that is vast enough and rich enough. (V: 124-25)

Here is a representative example of how art had assumed a potent role in Hawthorne's life, revealing a knowing and sensitive observer who found in art a means to peer into the heart of man and to grasp something of man's dreams of fixity and immortal beauty. A journalist fearing to expose himself as a dilettante no longer stands behind these words; yet Hawthorne, for all his newly instructed vision, proves himself no Ruskin. The splendor of the building could not be adequately or aptly conveyed by one whose receptive faculty was so easily exhausted and whose knowledge of architecture was so limited.

Not that I felt, or was worthy to feel, an unmingled enjoyment in gazing at this wonder. I could not elevate myself to its spiritual height, any more than I could have climbed from the ground to the summit of one of its pinnacles. Ascending but a little way, I continually fell back and lay in a kind of despair, conscious that a flood of uncomprehended beauty was pouring down upon me, of which I could appropriate only the minutest portion. After a hundred years, incalculably as my higher sympathies might be invigorated by so divine an employment, I should still be a gazer from below and at an awful distance, as yet remotely excluded from the interior mystery. But it was something gained, even to have that painful sense of my own limitations, and that half-smothered yearning to soar beyond them. (V: 125)

These disarmingly admitted limitations are Hawthorne's way of signifying his intent of leaving the work of art history and analysis to such experts as John Ruskin and Anna Jameson. He would speak to his readers in the first person but would occasionally address them in the second, acts at once endearing and confidential. What would ultimately emerge from this approach was testimony to his "spiritual possession" of much of England's art and architecture. But there was something more—a demonstration that a traveler must yield himself in both sympathy and faith if he is to understand the creative impulses that brought that art and architecture into being.

This critical stance helped Hawthorne to see another sight in Lichfield, R. C. Lucas's statue of Samuel Johnson. Recalling its massiveness, Hawthorne wrote, "You must look with the eyes of faith and sympathy or, possibly, you might lose the human being altogether, and find only a big stone within your mental grasp" (V: 132). How far he entered into the spirit of this statue appears in his words concerning the scene depicted in its bas-relief—Johnson doing penance in Uttoxeter for disobeying his father. Bearing in mind his recollection of the event as he had read about it as a boy and as he had later retold it for children, Hawthorne confided that he could not have been more deeply impressed if Michelangelo himself had carved the statue:

I had never heard of [this] piece of sculpture before; it appears to have no reputation as a work of art, nor am I at all positive that it deserves any. For me, however, it did as much as sculpture could, under the circumstances, even if the artist of the Libyan Sybil had wrought it, by reviving my interest in the sturdy old Englishman, and particularly by freshening my perception of a wonderful beauty and pathetic tenderness in the incident of the penance. (V: 132-33)

Whether Hawthorne stood before Shakespeare's tomb in Stratford, Burns's Grecian monument in Scotland, or Vanbrugh's Blenheim Palace, he refused to offer his readers "idealized nonsense" (V: 103), as he feared some painters and sculptors did, but sharply drawn detail and sincerely expressed personal response, though he did venture an occasional aesthetic pronouncement.

A clear illustration of how Hawthorne expressed his taste appears in a sentence added to his notebook passage about visiting John Cotton's church in Old Boston. Having extracted a passage on the church's "gargoyles of genuine Gothic grotesqueness, fiends, beasts, angels, and combinations of all three," he noted that "modern sculptors had tried to imitate these wild fantasies, but with little success" (V: 164). Hawthorne then added a Ruskin-like aphorism: "Extravagance and absurdity have still their law, and should pay as rigid obedience to it as the primmest things on earth" (V: 164). Such bold pronouncements are rare but do evince an instructed vision.

These pieces in *The Atlantic Monthly* and those added to make up *Our Old Home* reveal a man who weighed his notebook entries on British art and architecture, a man who sought to offer a sophisticated readership both concrete descriptions and informal observations, a man who proved himself capable of mentally grasping and spiritually possessing an artwork, and a man confident about his likes and dislikes of particular artists and works of art. A man with all these qualifications had been indeed justified in writing *The Marble Faun* and undertaking this magazine series, for he was helping Americans understand and appreciate the role of art and artists in the lives of cultivated men and women. This look backward to England was thus another of Hawthorne's lifelong attempts "to open an intercourse with the world" (IX: 6). These sketches of his old home prove to be more than "the talk of a secluded man with his own mind and heart" (IX: 6). They provided Hawthorne with the occasion to explore many of the nation's deepest cultural roots. They were means by which sensitive American readers could reclaim portions of an artistic heritage that Puritanism had denied.

Hawthorne stopped looking back upon his English travels long enough to visit Washington, D.C., with his publisher William Ticknor. The essay for the *Atlantic* resulting from that trip appeared as "Chiefly About War Matters" in the July 1862 issue and described Hawthorne's encounter with a living artist, Emanuel Leutze, then at work on a fresco entitled *Westward the Course of Empire* at the nation's Capitol. Hawthorne sought out Leutze, perhaps remembering that over a decade before his friend James T. Fields had told him of seeing Leutze's *Hester Prynne and Little Pearl*. Impressed by the artist and his wholehearted commitment to his work during troubled times and his unwavering faith in the nation's present and future greatness, Hawthorne offered his readers concrete details about the fresco and a sympathetic interpretation of its symbolic worth to a nation at war. A sketch and cartoon of the fresco and a talk with Leutze convinced Hawthorne that the new work would be superior to anything by John Trumbull in the Capitol's rotunda. To be sure, the fresco is today relatively unknown in contrast to Leutze's *Washington Crossing the Delaware*, but its suggestiveness fired Hawthorne's imagination as he pondered its implication for Americans and their perception of the nation's destiny:

> The work will be emphatically original and American, embracing characteristics that neither art nor literature have yet dealt with, and producing new forms of artistic beauty from the natural features of the Rocky Mountain region, which Leutze seems to have studied broadly and minutely. The garb of the hunters and wanderers of those deserts, too, under his free and natural management, is shown as the most picturesque of costumes. But it would be doing this admirable painter no kind office to

overlay his picture with any more of my colorless and uncertain words; so I shall merely add that it looked full of energy, hope, progress, irrepressible movement onward, all represented in a momentary pause of triumph; and it was most cheering to feel its good augury at this dismal time, when our country might seem to have arrived at such a deadly standstill.

. . . .

It was delightful to see him so calmly elaborating his design, while other men doubted and feared, or hoped treacherously, and whispered to one another that the nation would exist only a little longer, or that, if a remnant still held together, its centre and seat of government would be far northward and westward of Washington. But the artist keeps right on, firm of heart and hand, drawing his outlines with an unwavering pencil, beautifying and idealizing our rude, material life, and thus manifesting that we have an indefeasible claim to a more enduring national existence. (Riverside Edition, XVII: 369-71)

This passage raises an interesting point about Hawthorne's assumption about the artist in wartime and reflects, moreover, his sense that the Civil War would be a turning point in American art. Back home in Concord, Hawthorne had been unable to keep "right on, firm of heart and hand," as an artist, partly because the war and its ideological issues distracted him. Seeing Leutze's cartoon and hearing him speak of that push west, Hawthorne realized how just, how promising, the vision was: "The work will be emphatically original and American, embracing characteristics that neither art nor literature have yet dealt with, and producing new forms of artistic beauty from the natural features of the Rocky Mountain region." Indeed, after the Civil War was over, Leutze, Albert Bierstadt, Thomas Moran, and others would attempt to capture the beauty and grandeur of the Rocky Mountains in their paintings, even as Mark Twain, Bret Harte, Ned Buntline, and Owen Wister were opening up the West to literature. Speaking, therefore, with the sensitive perception of the artist who felt the pulse of the nation at a time of dis-ease, Hawthorne realized that the prognosis was good, that the nation indeed "looked full of energy, hope, progress, irrepressible movement onward."

As busy as Leutze was with this fresco and as eager as Hawthorne was to return to his family in Concord, Leutze persuaded him to sit for a portrait. As Hawthorne told Fields in explaining his delayed return home,

I stay here only while Leutze finishes a portrait—which I think will be the best ever painted of the same unworthy subject; and so does Ticknor. One charm it must needs have—an aspect of

immortal jollity and well-to-do-ness; for Leutze, when the
sitting begins, gives me a first-rate cigar, and when he sees me
getting tired, he brings out a bottle of splendid champagne; and
we quaffed and smoked, yesterday, in a blessed state of mutual
good-will, for three hours and a half, during which the picture
made a really miraculous progress. (XVIII: 445)

There is no way of knowing whether Hawthorne thought the finished
portrait was "the best ever of the same unworthy subject." His son
considered it "the least successful of them all" (Julian Hawthorne,
Hawthorne and His Circle, 312).

But Hawthorne's comments on this sitting for Leutze are his final
recorded words on a direct encounter with an artist. In an interlude of
well-being before Hawthorne's health drastically deteriorated, he
celebrated the "blessed state of mutual goodwill" as Leutze worked to
capture "an aspect of immortal jollity and well-to-do-ness." It was a
time to be a pleased and pleasant subject rather than an unbiased critic
or seeker of some profound truth about himself as perceived by Leutze.
It was a time to reflect upon Leutze's fresco as a picture prophetic of a
nation once again enjoying a "blessed state of mutual goodwill." And it
was a time to feel sympathetic identification with an artist dedicated to
the mission of keeping open "an intercourse with the world."

THE VISUAL ARTS IN THE INCOMPLETE ROMANCES

Although he sensed that the day of the romance was waning,
Hawthorne made several abortive attempts to reopen "intercourse with
the world" by developing subjects that had long haunted him. Putting
aside questions of the relationship of art and artists and of art and life,
he turned to what would be called "the international theme,"
dramatizing what might happen to a New England claimant to an
English estate, in manuscripts posthumously published as *The Ancestral
Footstep* and *Doctor Grimshawe's Secret*. Two other incomplete romances
examine the twined themes of immortality and the elixir of life, initially
entitled *The Dolliver Romance* and *Septimius Felton*. Flawed though they
are, these fragments are as pictorial as any of his finished pieces, and
there is no perceptible falling off in his use of iconic or emblematic
devices or scenes. As Hawthorne created characters and described
settings, he once more found the visual arts helpful and resumed many
of the practices he employed in his early tales and in the romances
preceding *The Marble Faun*.

In *Grimshawe*, as in *The House of the Seven Gables*, Hawthorne revealed
family resemblances through portraits, and, in fact, "the hanged man"
portrait in the unfinished romance has a couple of fresh touches. In one

of his studies for the American claimant material, he considered how he might use old portraits:

> Among the old gentleman's pictures, is one of a man of striking appearance, but in the habit of a bond-servant—coarse, and perhaps with the badge of servitude upon him. Afterwards, in England, the boy finds the same face, but in an old family-portrait gallery, and splendidly apparelled. He inquires about this latter portrait, and finds the original had mysteriously disappeared. Perhaps his guardian tells him the servitor's portrait is the likeness of an ancestor of his. It might afterwards come out, that he had been transported after the battle of Worcester. (XII: 483)

In *Grimshawe*, Ned hears the story of the portrait from Dr. Grimshawe:

> He led the boy by the hand into a corner of the room, where hung upon the wall a portrait, which Ned had often looked at. It seemed an old picture, but the Doctor had had it cleaned and varnished, so that it looked dim and dark; and yet it seemed to be the representation of a man of no mark, or such rank in life as would naturally leave his features to be transmitted for the interest of another generation; for he was clad in a mean dress, of old fashion, a leather jerkin, it appeared to be; and round his neck, moreover, was a noose of rope, as if he might have been on the point of being hanged. But the face of the portrait, nevertheless, was beautiful, noble, though sad, with a great development of sensibility, a look of suffering and endurance, amounting to triumph; peace through all. (XII: 359)

This passage is clearly meant to provide Ned with the image that would help him establish a family relationship. But Hawthorne also planned to use the portrait of the hanged man to characterize the viewers. An interjected note to himself reminded him to show that "the Doctor thinks the picture looks fierce & wicked; the boy and girl [Elsie] think it mild, sweet, sad" (XII: 359). Sad as it is that he must remind himself to be ambiguous, it is interesting nonetheless to see Hawthorne document a practice he had long followed. Perhaps the note should have been sent to a reviewer of *Grimshawe* for the *Athenaeum* (6 January 1883) who asked, "What is the meaning of the man with a noose around his neck?" (Crowley 431). Hawthorne would have recognized the reviewer as kinsman to the fact-demanding readers of *Transformation*.

In the Septimius Norton manuscript, a copperplate engraving of one of Septimius Norton's ancestors in a volume of sermons obviously was meant to function as the "hanged man portrait" does in *Grimshawe*—to help establish family identity. But in the "Septimius Felton" and "Septimius Norton" manuscripts a miniature plays a dramatic role in the plot when it is shattered by a bullet Septimius fires into the breast of his British cousin; it "passed directly through" a young woman's face on its way to her lover's heart, wholly destroying her face but leaving her arms and neck partially visible (XIII: 29, 236-37). Nothing further is made of that woman in the "Septimius Felton" manuscript, but in the "Septimius Norton" version the dying officer makes an emotionally charged statement after his last look at the shattered portrait:

> "Ah, it is a pity," said the young officer, but Septimius was struck by a shade of scorn that mingled with the pattern of his tones. "Her heart was broken," she told me,—and now her fair face is shattered too. But I repent, I repent! May Heaven forgive me. She was set as a snare for me, and I deemed it but a small crime to entangle her in her own devices. Yet the bullet pierced me through her. On second thoughts, bury her broken image in the grave along with me." (XIII: 237)

To his happiness and regret, Septimius Felton later meets that woman, Sybil Dacy, who enters the story and gradually changes from a vengeful *belle dame sans merci* into Septimius's self-sacrificing fiancée, a combined Beatrice Rappaccini and Eve, guilty of bringing poison into Septimius's elixir; however, she proves that she is strong enough to drain the last sip of death that a fearful Giovanni Guaconti might have been doomed to taste. Here is something far beyond Hawthorne's use of the Edward Malbone miniature of Clifford in *The House of the Seven Gables*, where Hepzibah's gaze upon Clifford's portrait serves mostly to remind her of her brother's earlier handsomeness. But Hawthorne uses the portrait here far less effectively than the portraits that helped him present leading characters in "Sylph Etherege" and "The Prophetic Pictures." If he had finished this romance, he surely would have more fully described Sybil's portrait to foreshadow her ambivalent nature. As he left matters, the portrait is a bulging, though suggestive, plot device.

As he resumed his practice of using art objects, Hawthorne considered whether to bring another artist into his fiction. Wondering what the character of Elsie should be, he wrote a note in a fragment entitled "Etherege": "She must be an artist—or may. A schoolmistress; a semptress. None of these" (XII: 332). Hawthorne allows her momentary existence as an artist. Elsie appears once with drawing materials (XII: 260) but later is described as taking lessons in "curious needlework" from Crusty Hannah (XII: 354). Perhaps his judgment told him that one Hilda or Hester was enough.

If uncertainties beset him about how and when to use art objects and whether to introduce yet another artist-figure, no such doubts arose when he took note of art treasures and architectural features when describing settings. No evidence of failing abilities occurs in his description of heraldic devices, crests, ornamental boxes, chairs, swords, goblets, carved chests, or tombstones. If anything, as Baym points out, Hawthorne's powers to render his scenes realistically improved in his last phase (252). Whether he is describing a leopard's head on a crest or a piece of Venetian glassware, Hawthorne had profited from his years of journalizing. His prose was more realistic, more like that of Dickens or Trollope, more certain to have pleased his outspoken English champion, Mary Russell Mitford (Idol, "Mary Russell Mitford: Champion of American Literature," 327-28). A passage from his English notebooks reworked for the Septimius Norton fragment shows undiminished descriptive powers:

> On one side, is a chapel, where the proud old family used to have their own priest, and their own worship, from time imme-morial; on the opposite side of the quadrangle, are state apart-ments, panelled with magnificent old oak, highly polished, carved in quaint devices, imitations of foliage, intricate puzzles of intersecting lines, sacred devices of Catholic times, anagrams of family names, portrait figures, all relics of a skill that the world has lost forever; a kind of magnificence that never will be equalled, because its richness is sombre, stately, and has a glow in it, being intended to last from age to age; whereas, in our times, to day is ashamed of the magnificence of yesterday. (XIII: 334-35)

Here is not the minuteness of his beloved Dutch masters, even though Rembrandt comes naturally to mind when you read Hawthorne's closing words on the sombre yet glowing house, but a generalized verbal sketch of the hall, idealized now because it represents the magnificence and glory of an earlier age. But here is skill enough to make Smithell's Hall, a Lancashire family seat he visited on 25 August 1855, a vivid fictional reality.

Perhaps because he had learned to depend more and more upon realistic details during all his years of journal keeping, Hawthorne rarely suggests an analogy between a character and painting or statue in the unfinished romances. Dropping the practice he had used in *The House of the Seven Gables* and *The Marble Faun*, he mentions no specific paintings or artists and problematically alludes just once to art in saying that Francis Norton's face appeared like marble as he lay in his hillside grave.

In his nonfiction, however, he combined realistic descriptions with reference to paintings, as he does in "Chiefly About War Matters" when describing guests lodged in Washington's Willard Hotel: "It is curious to observe what antiquated figures and costumes sometimes make their appearance at Willard's. You meet elderly men with frilled shirt-fronts, for example, the fashion of which adornment passed away from among the people of this world half a century ago. It is as if one of Stuart's portraits were walking abroad'' (*Works*, Riverside Edition, XVII: 414-15). How better enliven his description of old-fashioned clothes and the men in them than by referring to Gilbert Stuart's paintings of the heroes of the American republic? The allusion seems natural and just, indicating a mind grown confident enough in its knowledge of painting and other cultivated people's acquaintance with art to conjure up images by a well-known artist without apology or self-disparagement. Here, then, is a good example of how functional his knowledge of the visual arts had become.

Even though he now stood better prepared to integrate the visual arts into his nonfiction and romances, Hawthorne evidently preferred to return to natural objects for the symbolic trappings of the unfinished romances. Gone are the analogies of *The Marble Faun* between art objects and characters; back are objects from nature, specifically, spiders, a spider's web, and flowers.

He did, however, try to draw some distinctions between his English and American settings by showing that English households had a great many more art objects in them than did American homes. Typically, British homes had an accumulation acquired over centuries, whereas American homes, many of them dwellings of descendants of Cromwellian image-breakers, had fewer artworks.

Whenever he incorporated an art object into his pages during his last years, Hawthorne's abiding concern was whether it contributed to setting, characterization, plot, or symbolic pattern. He refrained from parading his hard-won knowledge of the visual arts or dropping names of artists and celebrated art objects to impress his readers. Knowledge, taste, comprehension, understanding, and experience in using art objects he had, but in the face of declining health he struggled to put them again to effective, suggestive use.

PICTORIALIST, EMBLEMATIST, REALIST, ROMANCER

Confessing how his routine at the Salem Custom House had dried up his creative juices so much that he ''cared not, at this period, for books'' (I: 26), Hawthorne explained, ''A gift, a faculty, if it had not departed, was suspended and inanimate within me. There would have been something sad, unutterably dreary, in all this, had I not been conscious that it lay within my own option to recall whatever was valuable in the past'' (I: 26). When he returned to writing, he pulled from the past exactly what he needed to write his masterpiece, *The Scarlet Letter*.

Part of his past, reckoned at different mileposts along his stop-and-go stream of creativity, was his immersion in the arts, literary and visual. His reading of works by Edmund Spenser, John Bunyan, Sir Walter Scott, John Keats, and others provided valuable lessons in the ways literary pictorialism enlivened and vivified writing. Emblems were everywhere, in books, shops, churches, and schools. Even as a child, Hawthorne saw portraits in homes and museums that stirred his interest in the "bewitchery of art." The small gallery at Bowdoin College, the paintings and statues in the Boston Athenaeum, and even prints and copies on restaurant walls prepared him for the great museums in Europe and led him to define a preference for the Dutch realists. Courtship and marriage brought him intimate knowledge of the mind and techniques of a practicing artist. But that knowledge was also grounded in wide reading in contemporary magazines, in books on art history and artists, in treatises on aesthetic theory, in travel accounts, and in volumes of art criticism. If his job as an editor of a magazine published by an engraving firm did not pay much, the duty of writing texts to accompany prints helped to tune his eye. Later, buying illustrated books to foster his children's appreciation of art pushed his acculturation along. A much greater push came in 1857 when he decided to attend the celebrated Manchester Exhibition of Art, where he and his family were immersed in art for days and days. But the greatest push came when he spent months in Italy visiting galleries, gardens, churches, and artists' studios and socializing with members of the English and American art colony.

The visual arts were at each stage a valuable part of his personal past even as he made them a part of the living present. He wanted to enjoy them, learn from them, share the creative mind that conceived them, and enlist their aid in the sketches, tales, and romances that he wrote (or tried to write). As Wendy Steiner has shown (91-120) and as our study has demonstrated, Hawthorne the romancer sometimes offered his readers pictures of characters or scenes to contemplate, pictures rich in iconic or emblematic suggestiveness, pictures inviting us to register the broad strokes and to fill in backgrounds and details. Sometimes those pictures were hung by a writer too much under the sway of Gothic novelists, but when things went right, as for example in "The Artist of the Beautiful" and The Marble Faun, Hawthorne lifted readers to new heights. Such cooperative experiences brought rare understanding and fuller enjoyment of the writer's craft.

Hawthorne acquired his "valuable past" in the visual arts with a mixture of pain and pleasure. And he acquired much of it relatively late in life. Unlike Henry James, whose childhood travels in Europe and friendship with John La Farge gave him an early taste for art, Hawthorne was well past the usual age of ready absorption before he had

ample opportunity to immerse himself in outstanding examples of the
visual arts. Hawthorne undertook something of a crash course and paid
the penalty.

When he was exhausted, few artworks pleased him; when he was
bone weary, he sometimes reacted like a captious Puritan, an intolerant
prude, or a relentless Cromwellian icon-breaker. He had to learn the
limits of his receptive faculty, believing that something in him limited
the number of works he could absorb. He wanted to see a work under
the best conditions of light. If that condition did not obtain, he
sometimes cried out for whitewash, fire, or flood. He often made the
same cry when he encountered dull, dingy, or begrimed paintings and
statues. With rare exceptions, he had a persistent problem with archaic
church art. And when he was tired, he groused, or worse.

But he had his moments. A painting or statue would catch his eye,
engage his mind, grab his heart. Such unpredictable moments usually
came during visits when he was already familiar with a work, and he
suddenly felt it come to life. Then he could be fully sympathetic,
insightful, understanding, and appreciative.

Underlying his lifelong interest in the visual arts was something more
profound than working up a taste for paintings and statuary. The visual
arts were means whereby other creative men and women attempted to
open intercourse with fellow humans. If somehow he could respond
sympathetically, appreciatively, insightfully to a painting, a statue, or,
better yet, a sketch, he might learn the deeper truths of human behavior
and catch glimpses of the terrestrial and celestial forces impelling human
conduct. Through the visual arts, therefore, he could aspire to a higher,
better, expression of his own art. That art—in notebooks, stories, and
novels—still impels readers to such glimpses and such truths.

Hawthorne's Comments on Art:
A Sampling

Hawthorne's responses to works of art consume many pages in his notebooks and spill over into his tales and romances. His comments on art also appear in his personal letters, in the *American Magazine of Useful and Entertaining Knowledge*, in *Our Old Home*, and in the *Atlantic Monthly*. They help to chronicle his development of taste and reflect his moods, his level of receptivity, his willingness or unwillingness to invest his creative energies in discovering the creative impulse behind a work of art, and his practice of dismissing a work out of hand or embracing it.

We offer the following extracts from Hawthorne's comments on art—and photographs of the artworks provoking his comments—with two chief goals in mind: to provide a representative sampling of Hawthorne's reactions to art objects both major and minor and to enable students and teachers to have quick and easy access to specific artworks figuring in the Hawthorne canon. (A fuller list, one citing nearly a hundred passages on art in his work, appeared in the Spring 1978 issue of the *Hawthorne Society Newsletter* [5-7]).

The following abbreviations have been used: AN (*The American Notebooks*), EN (*The English Notebooks*), FIN (*The French and Italian Notebooks*), HSG (*The House of the Seven Gables*), MF (*The Marble Faun*), MOM (*Mosses from an Old Manse*). With the exception of *The English Notebooks*, all of these Hawthorne works may be found in *The Centenary Edition of the Works of Nathaniel Hawthorne*. Publication information for *The English Notebooks* is listed separately in the bibliography.

With the extracts, we specify where and when Hawthorne saw a particular work of art. For pieces not presently displayed where Hawthorne saw them, we give their location.

Sir Francis Chantrey (Brit., 1781-1841), George Washington, Boston State House. June 1838. Statue of George Washington by Sir Francis Chantrey, Massachusetts State House, Boston. Courtesy of the Society for the Preservation of New England Antiquities, Boston. Photograph by Baldwin Coolidge, 1908.

York Cathedral (Gothic remodeling begun about 1226; completed in 1472). Interior view. July 14, 1857. Courtesy of B. T. Batsford Ltd. In Cathedrals of England and Wales *by John Hooper Harvey.*

After breakfast, we all went to the Cathedral; and no sooner were we within it, than we found how much our eyes had recently been educated, by the power of appreciating this magnificent interior; for it impressed both my wife and me with a joy that we never felt before. Julian felt it, too, and insisted that the Cathedral must have been altered and improved, since we were last here. But it is only that we have seen much splendid architecture, since then, and so have grown in some degree fitted to enjoy it. York Cathedral (I say it now, for it is my present feeling) is the most wonderful work that ever came from the hands of man. Indeed, it seems like a "house not made with hands," but rather to have come down from above, bringing an awful majesty and sweetness with it; and it is so light and aspiring, with all its vast columns and pointed arches, that one would hardly wonder if it should ascend back to heaven again, by its mere spirituality. Positively, the pillars and arches of the choir are so very beautiful that they give the impression of being exquisitely polished, though such is not the fact; but their beauty throws a gleam around them. I thank God that I saw this Cathedral again, and thank Him that he inspired the builder to make it, and that mankind has so long enjoyed it.

EN: 544-45

❧❦❧

William Hogarth (Brit., 1697-1764), March to Finchley. July 28, 1857, The Manchester Exhibition. From the collection of the Thomas Coram Foundation, London.

Day before yesterday, I paid a second visit to the Exhibition, and devoted the day mainly to seeing the works of British painters, which fill a very large space—two or three great saloons on the right side of the nave. Among the earliest are Hogarth's pictures, including the Sigismunda, which I remember to have seen before, with her lover's heart in her hand, looking like a monstrous strawberry; and the March to Finchley, than which nothing truer to English life and character was ever painted, nor ever can be; and a large, stately portrait of Captain Coram, and several others, all excellent in proportion as they come near to ordinary life, and are wrought out through its forms. All English painters seem to resemble Hogarth in this respect; they cannot paint anything high, heroic, and ideal, and their attempts in that direction are wearisome to look at; but they sometimes produce good effects by means of awkward figures in ill-made coats and small-clothes, and hard, coarse-complexioned faces, such as they might see anywhere in the street. They are strong in homeliness and ugliness; weak in their efforts at the beautiful. Sir Thomas Lawrence, for instance, attains a sort of grace, which you feel to be a trick, and therefore get disgusted with it. Reynolds is not quite genuine, though certainly he has produced some noble and beautiful heads. But Hogarth is the only English painter, except in the landscape department; there is no other (unless it be some of the modern pre-Raphaelites) who interprets life to me at all.

EN: 549

John Everett Millais (Brit., 1829-1896), Autumn Leaves, *Manchester City Art Galleries. July 28, 1857, The Manchester Exhibition. Courtesy Manchester City Art Galleries.*

I remember a heap of Autumn leaves, every one of which seems to have been stiffened with gum and varnish, and then put carefully down into the stiffly disordered heap. Perhaps these artists may hereafter succeed in combining their truth of detail with a broader and higher truth. Coming from such a depth as their pictures do, and having really an idea as the seed of them, it is strange that they should look like the most made-up things imaginable.

FIN: 550

A pre-Raphaelite artist (he, for instance, who painted so marvellously a windswept heap of autumnal leaves) might find an admirable subject in one of these Tuscan girls, stepping with a free, erect, and graceful carriage. The miscellaneous herbage and tangled twigs and blossoms of her bundle, crowning her head, (while her ruddy, comely face looks out between the hanging side-festoons like a larger flower,) would give the painter boundless scope for the minute delineation which he loves.

MF: 291

Gerard Dou (Dutch, 1613-1675), Woman Watering a Plant, *Buckingham Palace, London. August 9, 1857, The Manchester Exhibition. Copyright reserved to Her Majesty Queen Elizabeth II.*

Una and I spent an hour together, looking principally at the old Dutch Masters, who seem to me the most wonderful set of men that ever handled a brush. Such life-like representations of cabbages, onions, turnips, cauliflower, and peas; such perfect realities of brass kettles and kitchen crockery; such blankets, with the woolen fuzz upon them; such everything (except the human face, which moreover is fairly enough depicted) I never thought that the skill of man could produce. Even the photograph cannot equal their miracles. The closer you look, the more minutely true the picture is found to be; and I doubt if even the microscope could see beyond the painter's touch. Gerard Dow seems to be the master among these queer magicians. A straw mat, in one of his pictures, is the most miraculous thing that human art has yet accomplished; and there is a metal vase, with a dent in it, that is absolutely more real than reality. These painters accomplish all they aim at—a praise, methinks, which can be given to no other men since the world began. They must have laid down their brushes with perfect satisfaction, knowing that each one of their million touches had been necessary to the effect, and that there was not one too little or too much. And it is strange how spiritual, and suggestive the commonest household article—an earthen pitcher, for example—becomes when represented with entire accuracy. These Dutchmen get at the soul of common things, and so make them types and interpreters of the spiritual world.

EN: 556

❦

William Etty (Brit., 1787-1849), Aurora and Zephyr. August 9, 1857, The Manchester Exhibition. Courtesy of The Board of Trustees of the National Museums & Galleries on Merseyside [Lady Lever Art Gallery, Port Sunlight].

The most disagreeable of English painters is Etty, who had a diseased appetite for woman's flesh, and spent his whole life, apparently, in painting them with enormously developed bosoms and buttocks. I do not mind nudity, in a modest and natural way; but Etty's women really thrust their nakednesses upon you so with malice aforethought, and especially so enhance their posteriors, that one feels inclined to kick them. The worst of it is, they are not beautiful.

EN: 556

❧❦❧

John Mallord William Turner (Brit., 1775-1851), Shade and Darkness—The Evening of the Deluge, *Tate Gallery, London. August 9, 1857, Manchester Exhibition; December 8, 1857, Marlborough House, London (respectively). Courtesy of the Tate Gallery.*

From the Old Masters, I went among the English painters, and found myself more favorably inclined towards some of them, than at my previous visits; seeing something wonderful even in Turner's lights, and mists, and yeasty waves, although I should like him still better if his pictures looked in the least like what they typify.

EN: 556

I looked at all Turner's pictures, and at many of his drawings; and must again confess myself wholly unable to understand more than a very few of them. Even those few are tantalizing. At a certain distance, you discern what appears to be a grand and beautiful picture, which you shall admire and enjoy infinitely if you can get within the range of distinct vision. You come nearer, and find only blotches of color, and dabs of the brush, meaning nothing when you look closely, and meaning a mystery at the point where the painter intended to station you. Some landscapes there were, indeed, full of imaginative beauty, and of the better truth etherealized out of the prosaic truth of Nature; only it was still actually impossible to see it. There was a mist over it; or it was like a tract of beautiful dream-land, seen dimly through sleep, and glimmering out of sight if looked upon with wide-open eyes. . . . Now that I have done my best to understand them without an interpreter, I mean to buy Ruskin's pamphlet at my next visit, and look at them through his eyes.

EN: 614

*Bartolome Murillo (Span., 1617?-1682). St. John and the Lamb, National Gallery,
London. November 12 and December 8, 1857. Reproduced by Courtesy of the Trustees,
The National Gallery, London.*

Our final visit, to-day, was to the National Gallery, where I came to the conclusion that Murillo's Saint John was the most beautiful picture I have ever seen; and that there never was a painter who has really made the world richer, except Murillo.

. . . .

Nevertheless, I will not be quite certain that I really care a fig for any painter but Murillo, whose Saint John I should positively like to own. As far as my own pleasure is concerned, I could not say as much for any other picture; for I have always found an infinite weariness and disgust resulting from a picture being too frequently before my eyes. I had rather see a basilisk, for instance, than the very best of those old familiar pictures in the Boston Athenaeum; and most of those in the National Gallery would soon affect me in the same way.

EN: 596, 615

William Wetmore Story (Am., 1819-1895), Cleopatra, Metropolitan Museum, New York. February 14, 1858. The Metropolitan Museum of Art, Gift of John Taylor Johnston, 1888. All rights reserved, The Metropolitan Museum of Art.

Mr. [Cephas Giovanni] Thompson is a true artist, and whatever his pictures have of beauty comes from very far beneath the surface; and this, I suppose, is one great reason why he had but moderate success. I should like his pictures for the mere color even if they represented nothing. His Studio is in the Via Sistina, and at a little distance, on the other side of the same street, is William Story's, where we likewise went in, and found him at work on a sitting statue of Cleopatra. William Story looks thin and worn, already a little bald and a very little gray, but quite as vivid—in a graver way—as when I saw him last, a young man. He can yet, methinks, be scarcely thirty-seven. His perplexing variety of talents and accomplishments—a poet, a prose-writer, a lawyer, a painter, a sculptor—seems now to be concentrating itself into this latter vocation; and I cannot see why he should not achieve something very good. He has a beautiful statue, already finished, of Goethe's Margaret pulling a flower to pieces to discover whether Faust loves her; a very type of virginity and simplicity. The statue of Cleopatra, now only fourteen days advanced in the clay, is as wide a step from the little maidenly Margaret as any artist could take; it is a grand subject, and he appears to be conceiving it with depth and power, and working it out with adequate skill. He certainly is sensible of something deeper in his art than merely to make beautiful nudities and baptize them by classic names. By the by, he told us several queer stories about American visitors to his studio; one of them, after long inspecting Cleopatra (into which he has put all possible characteristics of her time and nation and of her own individuality) asked "Have you baptized your statue yet?" as if the sculptor were waiting till his statue were finished before he chose the subject of it; as, indeed, I should think many sculptors do.

FIN: 72-73

Albrecht Dürer (Ger., 1471-1528), Christ Among the Doctors, *Thyssen-Bornemisza Collection, Lugano, Switzerland. February 20, 1858.*

One that attracted our attention was a picture of Christ disputing with the Doctors, by Albert Durer, in which was represented the ugliest, most evil-minded, stubborn, pragmatical, and contentious old Jew, that ever lived under the law of Moses; and he and the child Jesus were arguing not only with their tongues, but making hieroglyphics, as it were, by the motion of their hands and fingers. It is a very queer, as well as a very remarkable picture.

FIN: 92

⋅§⋅

Marcus Aurelius *(Roman, gilded bronze), The Capitoline Hill, Rome. February 23 and April 25, 1858. Courtesy Alinari/Art Resource, New York.*

[W]e heartily admired the equestrian statue of Marcus Aurelius Antonius, which is full of grace and dignity, and makes the spectator love and reverence him even over this wide gap of ages—stretching forth his hand, as he does, with a gesture as if he were issuing a command that was in itself a benediction.

FIN: 101

They stood awhile to contemplate the bronze equestrian statue of Marcus Aurelius. The moonlight glistened upon traces of the gilding, which had once covered both rider and steed; these were almost gone; but the aspect of dignity was still perfect, clothing the figure as it were with an imperial robe of light. It is the most majestic representation of the kingly character that ever the world has seen. A sight of this old heathen Emperour is enough to create an evanescent sentiment of loyalty even in a democratic bosom; so august does he look, so fit to rule, so worthy of man's profoundest homage and obedience, so inevitably attractive of his love! He stretches forth his hand, with an air of grand beneficence and unlimited authority, but in which the obedient subject would find his highest interests consulted; a command, that was in itself a benediction.

"The sculptor of this statue knew what a King should be," observed Kenyon, "and knew, likewise, the heart of mankind, and how it craves a true ruler, under whatever title, as a child its father!"

MF: 165-66

Apollo Belvedere (*Roman marble copy of classical or Hellenistic Greek bronze*), *Vatican Museum. February 19, 1858, March 10, 1858, March 23, 1858.*

I acceded, and thus took my first view of those innumerable art-treasures, passing from one object to another, at an easy pace, pausing hardly a moment anywhere, and dismissing even the Apollo, and the Laocoon, and the torso of Hercules, in the space of half a dozen breaths. I was well enough content to do so, in order to get a general idea of the contents of the galleries, before settling down upon individual objects. Most of these world-famous sculptures presented themselves to my eye with a kind of familiarity, through the copies and casts which I had seen; but I found the originals were different than I anticipated. The Apollo, for instance, has a face which I have never seen in any cast or copy.

. . . .

On Monday, my wife, Una, Julian, and I, went to the Sculpture Gallery of the Vatican, and saw as much of the sculpture as we could in the three hours during which the public are admissible. There were a few things which I really enjoyed, and a few moments during which I really seemed to see them; but it is in vain to attempt giving the impression produced by masterpieces of art, and most in vain when we see them best. They are a language in themselves; and if they could be expressed any way except by themselves, there would have been no need of expressing those particular ideas and sentiments by sculpture. I saw the Apollo Belvidere as something ethereal and godlike; only for a flitting moment, however, and as if he had alighted from heaven, or shone suddenly out of the sunlight, and then had withdrawn himself again.

FIN: 86, 125

He [Kenyon] questioned, at that moment, whether Sculpture really ever softens and warms the material which it handles; whether carved marble is anything but limestone, after all; and whether the Apollo Belvedere itself possesses any merit above its physical beauty, or is beyond criticism even in that generally acknowledged excellence. In flitting glances, heretofore, he had seemed to behold this statue as something ethereal and godlike, but not now.

Nothing pleased him, unless it were the group of the Laocoon, which, in its immortal agony, impressed Kenyon as a type of the long, fierce struggle of Man, involved in the knotted entanglements of Errour and Evil, those two snakes, which (if no Divine help intervene) will be sure to strangle him and his children, in the end. What he most admired was the strange calmness, diffused through this bitter strife; so that it resembled the rage of the sea, made calm by its immensity, or the tumult of Niagara, which ceases to be tumult because it lasts forever. Thus, in the Laocoon, the horrour of a moment grew to be the Fate of interminable ages. Kenyon looked upon the group as the one triumph of Sculpture, creating the repose, which is essential to it, in the very acmé of turbulent effort; but, in truth, it was his mood of unwonted despondency that made him so sensitive to the terrible magnificence, as well as to the sad moral of this work.

MF: 391

❧

Laocoön (*About the middle of the second century* B.C., *School of Pergamum?*), *Vatican Museum. March 10, 1858.*

I felt the Laocoon, too, very powerfully, though very quietly; an immortal agony, with a strange calmness diffused through it, so that it resembles the vast rage of the sea, calm on account of its immensity, or the tumult of Niagara, which does not seem to be tumult because it keeps pouring on, forever and ever. I have not had so good a day as this (among works of art) since we came to Rome; and I impute it partly to the magnificence of the arrangements of the Vatican—its long vistas, and beautiful courts, and the aspect of immortality which marble statues acquire by being kept free from dust.

FIN: 125

❧

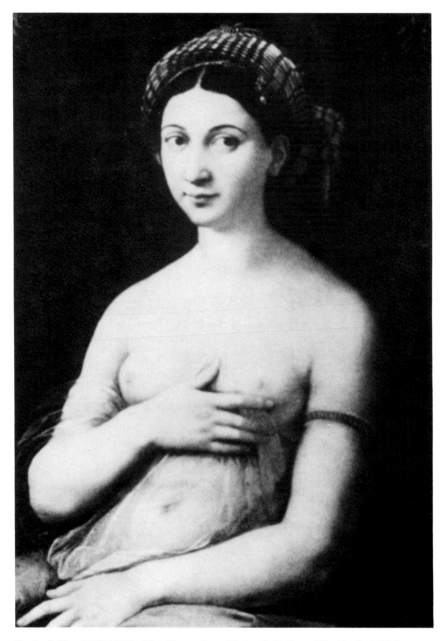

*Raphael (It., 1483-1520), The Fornarina, *National Gallery (The Barberini Museum, Rome). *February 20, 1858.*

Close beside Beatrice Cenci hangs the Fornarina, a brunette, with a deep, bright glow in her face, naked below the navel, and well pleased to be so for the sake of your admiration—ready for any extent of nudity, for love or money,—the brazen trollope that she is. Raphael must have been capable of great sensuality, to have painted this picture of his own accord and lovingly.

FIN: 93; see also *MF:* 337

❧

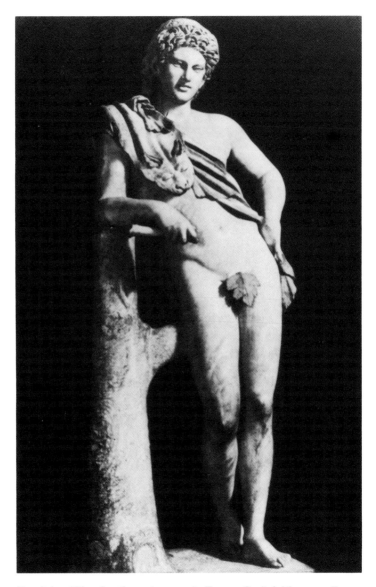

Praxiteles (Gk.. fourth century B.C.*),* Faun, *Capitol Museum, Rome.
April 18, 22, and 30, 1858.*

[A] Faun, copied from that of Praxiteles, and another, who seems to be dancing, are exceedingly pleasant to look at. I like these strange, sweet, playful, rustic creatures, almost entirely human as they are, yet linked so prettily, without monstrosity, to the lower tribes by the long, furry ears, or by a modest tail; indicating a strain of honest wildness in them. Their character has never, that I know of, been wrought out in literature; and something very good, funny, and philosophical, as well as poetic, might very likely be educed from them. In my mind, they connect themselves with that ugly, bearded woman, who was lately exhibited in England, and by some supposed to have been engendered betwixt a human mother and an orangoutang; but she was a wretched monster—the faun, a natural and delightful link betwixt human and brute life, and with something of a divine character intermingled.

. . . .

I likewise took particular note of the Faun of Praxiteles; because the idea keeps recurring to me of writing a little Romance about it, and for that reason I shall endeavor to set down a somewhat minutely itemized detail of the statue and its surroundings. The faun is the image of a young man, leaning with one arm upon the trunk or stump of a tree; he has a pipe, or some such instrument of music, in the hand which rests upon the tree, and the other, I think, hangs carelessly by his side. His only garment falls half way down his back, but leaves his whole front, and all the rest of his person, exposed, displaying a very beautiful form, but clad in more flesh, with more full and rounded outlines, and less developement of muscle, than the old sculptors were wont to assign to masculine beauty. The figure is not fat, but neither has it the attribute of slender grace. The face has a character corresponding with that of the form; beautiful and most agreeable features, but rounded, especially about the throat and chin; a nose almost straight, yet very slightly curving inward, a voluptuous mouth, that seems almost (not quite) to smile outright; in short, the whole person conveys the idea of an amiable and sensual nature, easy, mirthful, apt for jollity, yet not incapable of being touched by pathos. The faun has no principle, nor could comprehend it, yet is true and honest by virtue of his simplicity; very capable, too, of affection. He might be refined through his feelings, so that the coarser, animal part of his nature would be thrown into the back ground, though liable to assert itself at any time. Praxiteles has only expressed this animal nature by one (or rather two) definite signs—the two ears—which go up in a little peak, not likely to be discovered on slight inspection, and, I suppose, are covered with fine, downy fur. A tail is probably hidden under his garment. Only a sculptor of the finest imagination, most delicate taste, and sweetest feeling, could have dreamed of representing a Faun in this guise; and if you brood over it long enough, all the pleasantness of sylvan life, and all the genial and happy characteristics of the brute creation, seemed to be mixed in him with humanity—trees, grass, flowers, cattle, deer, and unsophisticated man.

FIN: 173-74, 191-92

Perhaps it is the very lack of moral severity, of any high and heroic ingredient in the character of the Faun, that makes it so delightful an object to the human

continued

eye and to the frailty of the human heart. The being, here represented, is endowed with no principle of virtue, and would be incapable of comprehending such. But he would be true and honest, by dint of his simplicity. We should expect from him no sacrifice nor effort for an abstract cause; there is not an atom of martyr's stuff in all that softened marble; but he has a capacity for strong and warm attachment, and might act devotedly through its impulse, and even die for it at need. It is possible, too, that the Faun might be educated through the medium of his emotions; so that the coarser, animal portion of his nature might eventually be thrown into the back-ground, though never utterly expelled.

The animal nature, indeed, is a most essential part of the Faun's composition; for the characteristics of the brute creation meet and combine with those of humanity, in this strange, yet true and natural conception of antique poetry and art. Praxiteles has subtly diffused, throughout his work, that mute mystery which so hopelessly perplexes us, whenever we attempt to gain an intellectual or sympathetic knowledge of the lower orders of creation. The riddle is indicated, however, only by two definite signs; these are the two ears of the Faun, which are leaf-shaped, terminating in little peaks, like those of some species of animals. Though not so seen in the marble, they are probably to be considered as clothed in fine, downy fur. In the coarser representations of this class of mythological creatures, there is another token of brute kindred—a certain caudal appendage—which, if the Faun of Praxiteles must be supposed to possess it at all, is hidden by the lion's skin that forms his garment. The pointed and furry ears, therefore, are the sole indications of his wild, forest nature.

MF: 8-10

꧁꧂

Guido Reni (It., 1575-1642), Judith, Samuel H. Kress Collection, Birmingham Museum of Art, Birmingham Alabama. May 21, 1858, Spada Palace. Produced by the courtesy of the Birmingham (Alabama) Museum of Art.

From the hall, we passed through several saloons containing pictures, some of which were by eminent artists; the Judith of Guido, a copy of which used to weary me to death, year after year, in the Boston Athenaeum, and many portraits of Cardinals of the Spada family, and other pictures, by the same.

FIN: 218

Raphael, The Transfiguration, *Vatican Museum. April 25, 1858.*

Before leaving the church, we went to look at the mosaic copy of the Transfiguration, because we were going to see the original, in the Vatican, and wished to compare the two. Going round to the entrance of the Vatican, we went first to the manufactory of mosaics, to which we had a ticket of admission. We found it a long series of rooms, in which the mosaic artists were at work, chiefly in making some medallions of the heads of saints, for the new church of St. Paul's. It was rather coarse work, and it seemed to me that the mosaic copy was somewhat stiffer and more wooden than the original, the bits of stone not flowing into color quite so freely as paint from a brush. There seemed to be no large picture now in process of being copied; but two or three artists were employed on small and delicate subjects; one had a holy family of Raphael in hand; and the Sybils of Guercino and Domenichino were hanging on the wall, apparently ready to be put into mosaic. Wherever great skill and delicacy, on the artist's part, were necessary, they seemed quite adequate to the occasion; but, after all, a mosaic from any celebrated picture is but a copy of a copy. The substance employed is a sort of stone paste, of innumerable different hues, and in bits of various sizes, quantities of which were seen in cases, along the whole series of rooms.

We next ascended an amazing height of staircases, and walked along I know not what extent of passages, under my wife's guidance, till we reached the picture gallery of the Vatican, into which I had never been before. There are but three rooms, all lined with red velvet, on which hang about fifty pictures, each one of them, no doubt, worthy to be considered a master-piece. In the first room, were three Murillos, all so beautiful that I could have spent the day happily in looking at either of them; for methinks, of all painters, he is the tenderest and truest. I could not enjoy these pictures now, however, because in the next room, and visible through the open door, hung the Transfiguration. Approaching it, I felt that the picture was worthy of its fame, and was far better than I could at once appreciate; admirably preserved, too, though, I fully believe, it must have possessed a charm when it left Raphael's hand that has now vanished forever. As an article of church furniture and external adornment, the mosaic copy is preferable to the original; but no copy could ever reproduce all the life and expression which we see here. It is useless to say any more about this picture. Opposite to it hangs the Communion of St. Jerome; the aged, dying Saint, half torpid with death already, partaking of the sacrament, and a sunny garland of cherubs in the upper part of the picture, looking down upon him, and quite comforting the spectator with the idea that the old man needs only to be quite dead in order to flit away with them. As for the other pictures, I did but glance at, and have forgotten them.

The Transfiguration is finished with great minuteness and detail; the weeds and blades of grass in the foreground being as distinct as if they were growing in a natural soil. A partly decayed stick of wood, with the bark, is likewise given in close imitation of nature. The reflection of one of the apostles' foot is seen in a pool of water, at the verge of the picture. One or two hands and arms seem almost to project from the canvass; there is great lifelikeness and reality, as well as higher qualities. The face of Jesus, being so high aloft, and so small in the distance, I could not well see, but am impressed with the idea that it looks too much like human flesh and blood to be in keeping with the celestial aspect of the

continued

Girl with a Dove (*Antique sculpture*), *Capitol Museum, Rome. April 30, 1858. Courtesy Alinari/Art Resource, New York.*

Round the walls, besides the Faun, stand other admirable statues, the Antinous, the Juno, a Minerva, an Apollo, a Roman matron, a little girl holding a dove and frightened by a snake.

FIN: 193

Here, likewise, is seen a symbol (as apt, at this moment, as it was two thousand years ago) of the Human Soul, with its choice of Innocence or Evil close at hand, in the pretty figure of a child, clasping a dove to her bosom, but assaulted by a snake.

MF: 5

❧❦❧

Vincenzio Danti (It., 1530-1576), Pope Julius III, *The Marketplace, Perugia. May 29, 1858.*

Within a short distance, there is a bronze statue of Pope Julius III, in his pontificals; one of the best statues, I think, that I ever saw in a public square. He seems to have life and observation in him, and impresses the spectator as if he might rise up from his chair, should any public exigency demand it, and encourage or restrain the people by the dignity and awe of his presence. I wish I could in any way catch and confine within words my idea of the venerableness and stateliness, the air of long-past time subsisting into the present, which remains upon my mind with the recollection of these mediaeval antiquities of Perugia. When I am absolutely looking at them, I do not feel it so much as when remembering them; for there is, of course, a good deal of the modern and common-place that obtrudes into the actual scene. The people themselves are not very picturesque; though there are some figures with cloaks (even in this summer weather) and broad-brimmed, slouching hats that a painter might make something of.

FIN: 260

It was the figure of a Pope, arrayed in his pontifical robes, and crowned with the tiara. He sat in a bronze chair, elevated high above the pavement, and seemed to take kindly, yet authoritative cognizance of the busy scene which was, at that moment, passing before his eyes. His right hand was raised and spread abroad, as if in the act of shedding forth a benediction, which every man (so broad, so wise, and so serenely affectionate, was the bronze Pope's regard) might hope to feel quietly descending upon the need, or the distress, that he had closest at his heart. The statue had life and observation in it, as well as patriarchal majesty. An imaginative spectator could not but be impressed with the idea, that this benignly awful representative of Divine and human authority might rise from his brazen chair, should any great public exigency demand his interposition, and encourage or restrain the people by his gesture, or even by prophetic utterances worthy of so grand a presence.

MF: 313-14

Venus de Medici (*A Roman copy of a fourth century B.C. Greek original ascribed to the sons of Praxiteles*), *Uffizi, Florence. June 8 and 15, 1858.*

I could not quite believe that I was not to find the Venus de Medici; and still, as I passed from one room to another, my breath rose and fell a little, with the half-hope, half-fear, that she might stand before me. Really, I did not know that I cared so much about Venus, or any possible woman of marble. At last—when I had come from among the Dutchmen, I believe, and was looking at some works of Italian artists, chiefly Florentines—I caught a glimpse of her, through the door of the next room. It is the best room of the whole series, octagonal in shape, and hung with red damask; and the light comes down from a row of windows passing quite round, beneath an octagonal dome. The Venus stands somewhat aside from the centre of the room, and is surrounded by an iron railing, a pace or two from her pedestal in front, and less behind. I think she might safely be left to the reverence her womanhood would win, without any other protection. She is very beautiful; very satisfactory; and has a fresh and new charm about her, unreached by any cast or copy that I have seen. The hue of the marble is just so much mellowed by time as to do for her all that Gibson tries, or ought, to try, to do for his statues by color; softening her, warming her almost imperceptibly, making her an inmate of the heart as well as a spiritual existence. I felt a kind of tenderness for her; an affection, not as if she were one woman, but all womankind in one. Her modest attitude—which, before I saw her, I had not liked, deeming that it might be an artificial shame—is partly what unmakes her as the heathen goddess, and softens her into woman. There is a slight degree of alarm, too, in her face; not that she really thinks anybody is looking at her, yet the idea has flitted through her mind and startled her a little. Her face is so beautiful and intellectual, that it is not dazzled out of sight by her body. Methinks this was a triumph for the sculptor to achieve. I may as well stop here. It is of no use to throw heaps of words upon her; for they all fall away, and leave her standing in chaste and naked grace, as untouched as when I began.

The poor little woman has suffered terribly by the mishaps of her long existence in the marble. Each of her legs had been broken into two or three fragments; her arms have been broken off; her body has been broken quite across at the waist; her head has been snapt off at the neck. Furthermore, there have been grievous wounds and losses of substance in various tender parts of her body. But, partly by the skill with which the statue has been restored, and partly because the idea is perfect and indestructible, all these injuries do not in the least impair the effect, even when you see where the dissevered fragments have been re-united. She is just as whole as when she left the hands of the sculptor. I am glad to have seen this Venus, and to have found her so tender and so chaste. On the wall of the room, and to be taken in at the same glance, is a painted Venus by Titian, reclining on a couch, naked and lustful.

The room of the Venus seems to be the treasure place of the whole Uffizzi palace, containing more pictures by famous masters than are to be found in all the rest of the gallery. There were several by Raphael, and the room was crowded with the easels of artists. I did not look half enough at anything, but merely took a preliminary taste, as a prophecy of enjoyment to come.

.   .   .   .

Yesterday, my wife and I went to the Uffizzi gallery; and of course I took the opportunity to look again at the Venus de Medici, after Powers' attack upon her face. Some of the defects he attributed to her I could not see in the statue; for instance, the ear appeared to be in accordance with his own rule; the lowest part of it being about in a straight line with the upper lip. The eyes must be given up, as not, when closely viewed, having the shape, the curve outwards, the formation of the lids, that eyes ought to have; but still, at a proper distance, they seemed to have intelligence in them, beneath the shadow cast by the brow, I cannot help thinking that the sculptor intentionally made every feature what it is, and calculated them all with a view to the desired effect. Whatever rules may be transgressed, it is a noble and beautiful face; more so, perhaps, than if all rules had been obeyed. I wish Powers would do his best to fit the Venus de Medici's figure (which he does not deny to be admirable) with a face which he would deem equally admirable, and in accordance with the sentiment of the form.

FIN: 297-99, 316

◈

Hiram Powers (Am. 1805-1873), The Greek Slave, Olive Louise Dann Fund, Yale University Art Gallery, New Haven, Connecticut. June 11, 1858. Courtesy Yale University Art Gallery.

I mean no disrespect to Gibson, or Powers, or a hundred other men who people the world with nudities, all of which are abortive as compared with [Venus de Medici]; but I think the world would be richer if their Venuses, their Greek Slaves, their Eves, were burnt into quick-lime, leaving us only this statue as our image of the beautiful. I observed to day (what my wife has already remarked) that the eyes of the statue are slightly hollowed out, in a peculiar way, so as to give them a look of depth and intelligence. She is a miracle. The sculptor must have wrought religiously, and have felt that something far beyond his own skill was working through his hand. I mean to leave off speaking of the Venus here-after, in utter despair of saying what I wish; especially as the contemplation of the statue will refine and elevate my taste, and make it continually more difficult to express my sense of its excellence, as the perception of it grows on me.

FIN: 308

✌ঠৡ৵

Peter Paul Rubens (Dutch, 1577-1640), Bacchus, The Hermitage, Leningrad. June 15, 1858, Uffizi, Florence. Courtesy Alinari/Art Resource, New York.

I looked with much pleasure at an ugly, old, fat, jolly Bacchus, astride on a barrel, by Rubens; the most natural and lifelike representation of a tipsy rotundity of flesh, that it is possible to imagine. And sometimes, amid these sensual images, I caught the divine pensiveness of a Madonna's face, or the glory and majesty of the babe Jesus in her lap, with his Father shining through him. This is a sort of revelation, whenever it comes.

FIN: 318

❦

Titian (It., 1487 or 1490-1576), The Magdalen, *Pitti Palace, Florence. June 21, 1858.*

The thunder muttered and grumbled; the lightning emitted now and then a flash; and a few raindrops pattered against the windows; but, for a long time, the shower held off. At last, it came down in a stream, and lightened the air to such a degree that we could see some of the pictures, especially those of Rubens, and the illuminated parts of Salvator Rosa's, and best of all, Titian's Magdelene, the one with the golden hair clustering round her naked body. The golden hair, indeed, seemed to throw out a glory of its own. This Magdelene is very coarse and sensual, with only an impudent assumption of penitence and religious sentiment, scarcely so deep as the eyelids; but it is a splendid picture, nevertheless, with those naked, lifelike arms, and the hands that press the rich locks about her, and so carefully let those two voluptuous breasts be seen. She a penitent! She would shake off all pretence to it, as easily as she would shake aside that clustering hair and offer her nude front to the next comer. Titian must have been a very good-for-nothing old man.

FIN: 333-34

❧❦❧

Michelangelo (It., 1475-1564), Lorenzo de Medici, *San Lorenzo, Medici Chapel, Florence. June 19, 1858. Courtesy Alinari/Art Resource, New York.*

But the statue that sits above these two latter allegories, Morning and Evening, is like no other that ever came from a sculptor's hand; it is the one work worthy of Michael Angelo's reputation, and grand enough to vindicate for him all the genius that the world gave him credit for. And yet it seems a simple thing enough to think of, or to execute; merely a sitting figure, the face partly overshadowed by a helmet, one hand supporting the chin, the other resting on the thigh. But after looking at it a little while, the spectator ceases to think of it as a marble statue; it comes to life, and you see that this princely figure is brooding over some great design, which, when he has arranged in his own mind, the world will be fain to execute for him. No such majesty and grandeur has elsewhere been put into human shape. It is all a miracle; the deep repose, and the deep life within it; it is as much a miracle to have achieved this, as to make a statue that would rise up and walk. The face, when one gazes earnestly into it, beneath the shadow of its helmet, is seen to be calmly sombre, a mood which I think is generally that of the rulers of mankind except in moments of vivid action. This statue is one of the things which I look at with highest enjoyment, but also with grief and impatience, because I feel that I do not come at all which it involves, and that by-and-by I must go away and leave it forever. How wonderful! To take a block of marble and convert it wholly into thought; and to do it through all the obstructions and impediments of drapery; for there is nothing nude in this statue but the face and hands. The rest is the costume of Michael Angelo's century. This is what I always thought that a sculptor of true genius should be able to do—to show the man of whatever epoch nobly and heroically through the costume which he might actually have worn.

It is a shame for me to write about such a great work, and leave out everything that really characterizes it; its naturalness, for example, as if it came out of the marble of its own accord, with all its grandeur hanging heavily about it, and sat down there beneath its weight. I cannot describe it. It is like trying to stop the ghost of Hamlet's father by crossing a spear before it.

FIN: 327-28

I asked Powers what he thought of Michael Angelo's statue of Lorenzo de Medici. He allowed that its effect was very grand and mysterious; but added that it owed this to a trick—the effect being produced by the arrangement of the hood, as he called it, or helmet, which throws the upper part of the face into shadow. The niche in which it sits has, I suppose, its part to perform in throwing a still deeper shadow. It is very possible that Michael Angelo may have calculated upon this effect of sombre shadow, and legitimately, I think; but it really is not worthy of Mr. Powers to say that the whole effect of this mighty statue depends, not on the positive efforts of Michael Angelo's chisel, but on the absence of light in a space of a few inches. He wrought the whole statue in harmony with that little part of it which he leaves to the spectator's imagination, and if he had erred at any point, the miracle would have been a failure; so that, working in marble, he has positively reached a point of excellence above the capability of marble, sculpturing his highest touches upon air and duskiness.

FIN: 336

Perugino (It., 1445-1523), Compianto su Cristo Morto, *Uffizi, Florence. September 3, 1858. Courtesy Alinari/Art Resource, New York.*

The drawings hang on the walls, framed and glazed, and number perhaps from one to two hundred in each room; but this is only a small portion of the collection, which amounts, it is said, to twenty-five thousand, and is reposited in portfolios. The sketches on the walls are changed, from time to time, so as to exhibit all the most interesting ones in turn. Their whole charm is artistic, imaginative, and intellectual, and in no degree of the upholstery kind; their outward presentment being, in general, a design hastily shadowed out, by means of light-colored crayons, on tinted paper; or perhaps scratched rudely in pen-and-ink; or drawn in pencil, or charcoal, and half-rubbed out;—very rough things indeed, in many instances, and the more interesting on that account; because as it seems as if the artist had bestirred himself to catch the first glimpse of an image that did but reveal itself, and vanish. The sheets—or sometimes scraps—of paper on which they are drawn, are discolored with age, creased, soiled; but yet you are magnetized by the hand of Raphael, Michael Angelo, Leonardo, or whoever may have jotted down those rough-looking master-touches. They certainly possess a charm that is lost in the finished picture; and I was more sensible of forecasting thought, skill, and prophetic design, in these sketches, than in the most consummate works that have been elaborated from them. There is something more divine in these; for, I suppose, the first idea of a picture is real inspiration, and all the subsequent elaboration of the master serves but to cover up the celestial germ with something that belongs to himself. At any rate, the first sketch is the more suggestive, and sets the spectator's imagination at work; whereas, the picture, if a good one, leaves him nothing to do; if bad, it confuses, stupefies, disenchants, and disheartens him. First thoughts have an aroma and fragrance in them that they do not lose in three hundred years; for so old, and a good deal more, are some of these sketches.

None interested me more than some sketches, on separate pieces of paper, by Perugino, for his picture of the mother and friends of Jesus round his dead body, now at the Pitti palace. The attendant figures are distinctly made out, as if the Virgin, and John, and Mary Magdalen, had each favored the painter with a sitting; but the body of Jesus lies in the midst, dimly hinted with a few pencil-marks.

FIN: 401-3

❧

Guido Reni or Francesco Albani (It., 1578-1660), Beatrice Cenci, National Gallery of Ancient Art, Rome. February 20, 1858 and May 15, 1859.

But we passed hastily by this, and almost all the other pictures, being eager to see the two which chiefly make the collection famous.—These are Raphael's Fornarini, and Guido's portrait of Beatrice Cenci. These we found in the last of the three rooms: and as regards Beatrice Cenci, I might as well not try to say anything, for its spell is indefinable, and the painter has wrought it in a way more like magic than anything else I have known. It is a very youthful, girlish, perfectly beautiful face, with white drapery all around it, and quite enveloping the form. One or two locks of auburn hair stray out. The eyes are large and brown, and meet those of the spectator; and there is, I think, a little red about the eyelids, but it is very slightly indicated. The whole face is perfectly quiet; no distortion nor disturbance of any single feature; nor can I see why it should not be cheerful, nor why an imperceptible touch of the painter's brush should not suffice to brighten it into joyousness. Yet it is the very saddest picture that ever was painted, or conceived; there is an unfathomable depth and sorrow in the eyes; the sense of it comes to you by a sort of intuition. It is a sorrow that removes her out of the sphere of humanity; and yet she looks so innocent, that you feel as if it were only this sorrow, with its weight and darkness, that keeps her down upon the earth and brings her within our reach at all. She is like a fallen angel, fallen, without sin. It is infinitely pitiful to meet her eyes, and feel that nothing can be done to help or comfort her; not that she appeals to you for help and comfort, but is more conscious than we can be that there is none in reserve for her. It is the most profoundly wrought picture in the world; no artist did it, or could do it again. Guido may have held the brush, but he painted better than he knew. I wish, however, it were possible for some spectator, of deep sensibility, to see the picture without knowing anything of its subject or history; for no doubt we bring all our knowledge of the Cenci tragedy to the interpretation of the picture.

FIN: 92-93

Yesterday afternoon, my wife, Julian, & I, went to the Barberini picture-gallery, to take a farewell look at the Beatrice Cenci, which I have twice visited before. I attempted a description of it at my first visit, more than a year ago; but the picture is quite indescribable, inconceivable, and unaccountable in its effect; for if you attempt to analyze it, you can never succeed in getting at the secret of its fascination. Its peculiar expression eludes a straightforward glance, and can only be caught by side glimpses, or when the eye falls upon it casually, as it were, and without thinking to discover anything; as if the picture had a life and consciousness of its own, and were resolved not to betray its secret of grief or guilt, though it wears the full expression of it when it imagines itself unseen. I think no other such magical effect can ever have been wrought by pencil. I looked close into its eyes, with a determination to see all that there was in them, and could see nothing that might not have been in any young girl's eyes; and yet, a moment afterwards, there was the expression (seen aside, and vanishing in a moment) of a being unhumanized by some terrible fate, and gazing at me out of a remote and inaccessible region, where she was frightened to be alone, but

continued

where no sympathy could reach her. The mouth is beyond measure touching; the lips apart, looking as innocent as a baby's after it has been crying. The picture never can be copied. Guido himself could not have done it over again. The copyists get all sorts of expression, gay as well as grievous; some copies have a coquettish air, a half-backward glance, thrown alluringly at the spectator; but nobody ever did catch, or ever will, the vanishing charm of that sorrow. I hated to leave the picture, and yet was glad when I had taken my last glimpse, because it so perplexed and troubled me not to be able to get hold of its secret.

FIN: 520-21

"There has been one exquisite copy, I have heard," said Hilda, "by an artist capable of appreciating the spirit of the picture. It was Thompson, who brought it away piece-meal, being forbidden (like the rest of us) to set up his easel before it. As for me, I knew the Prince Barberini would be deaf to all entreaties; so I had no resource but to sit down before the picture, day after day, and let it sink into my heart. I do believe it is now photographed there. It is a sad face to keep so close to one's heart; only, what is so very beautiful can never be quite a pain. Well; after studying it in this way, I know not how many times, I came home, and have done my best to transfer the image to canvas."

"Here it is then," said Miriam, contemplating Hilda's work with great interest and delight, mixed with the painful sympathy that the picture excited. "Everywhere we see oil-paintings, crayon-sketches, cameos, engravings, lithographs, pretending to be Beatrice, and representing the poor girl with blubbered eyes, a leer of coquetry, a merry look, as if she were dancing, a piteous look, as if she were beaten, and twenty other modes of fantastic mistake. But here is Guido's very Beatrice; she that slept in the dungeon, and awoke betimes, to ascend the scaffold. And now that you have done it, Hilda, can you interpret what the feeling is, that gives this picture such a mysterious force? For my part, though deeply sensible of its influence, I cannot seize it."

"Nor can I, in words," replied her friend. "But, while I was painting her, I felt all the time as if she were trying to escape from my gaze. She knows that her sorrow is so strange, and so immense, that she ought to be solitary forever, both for the world's sake and her own; and this is the reason we feel such a distance between Beatrice and ourselves, even when our eyes meet hers. It is infinitely heart-breaking to meet her glance, and to feel that nothing can be done to help or comfort her; neither does she ask help or comfort, knowing the hopelessness of her case better than we do. She is a fallen angel, fallen, and yet sinless; and it is only this depth of sorrow, with its weight and darkness, that keeps her down upon earth, and brings her within our view even while it sets her beyond our reach."

"You deem her sinless?" asked Miriam. "That is not so plain to me. If I can pretend to see at all into that dim region, whence she gazes so strangely and sadly at us, Beatrice's own conscience does not acquit her of something evil, and never to be forgiven."

"Sorrow so black as hers oppresses her very nearly as sin would," said Hilda.

"Then," inquired Miriam, "do you think that there was no sin in the deed for which she suffered?"

"Ah," replied Hilda shuddering, "I really had quite forgotten Beatrice's history, and was thinking of her only as the picture seems to reveal her character. Yes, yes; it was terrible guilt, an inexpiable crime, and she feels it to be so. Therefore it is that the forlorn creature so longs to elude our eyes, and forever vanish away into nothingness! Her doom is just."

"Oh, Hilda, your innocence is like a sharp steel sword," exclaimed her friend. "Your judgments are often terribly severe, though you seem all made up of gentleness and mercy. Beatrice's sin may not have been so great; perhaps it was no sin at all, but the best virtue possible in the circumstances. If she viewed it as a sin, it may have been because her nature was too feeble for the fate imposed upon her. Ah," continued Miriam passionately, "if I could only get within her consciousness! If I could but clasp Beatrice Cenci's ghost, and draw it into myself! I would give my life to know whether she thought herself innocent, or the one great criminal since time began!"

As Miriam gave utterance to these words, Hilda looked from the picture into her face, and was startled to observe that her friend's expression had become almost exactly that of the portrait; as if her passionate wish and struggle to penetrate poor Beatrice's mystery had been successful.

"Oh, for Heaven's sake, Miriam, do not look so!" she cried. "What an actress you are! And I never guessed it before! Ah; now you are yourself again," she added, kissing her. "Leave Beatrice to me, in future."

"Cover up your magical picture then," replied her friend; "else I never can look away from it. It is strange, dear Hilda, how an innocent, delicate, white soul, like yours, has been able to seize the subtle mystery of this portrait; as you surely must, in order to reproduce it so perfectly. Well; we will not talk of it any more. Do you know, I have come to you, this morning, on a small matter of business? Will you undertake it for me?"

MF: 65-67

❧❦❧

Sodoma (It., 1477-1549), Christ Bound to the Pillar, *National Art Museum, Siena. October 5, 21, 1858, Institute of the Fine Arts.*

At last we came to a picture by Sodoma, the most illustrious representative of the Sienese school. It was a fresco, but perfectly well preserved; Christ, bound to the pillar, after having been scourged. I do believe that painting has never done anything better, so far as expression is concerned, than this figure; in all these generations, since it was painted, it must have softened thousands of hearts—drawn down rivers of tears—been more effectual than a million of sermons. It is inexpressibly touching; so weary is the Savior, and utterly worn out with suffering, that his mouth has fallen apart from mere exhaustion; his eyes seem to be set; he tries to lean his head against the pillar, and is only kept from sinking down upon the ground by the cords that bind him. Really, it is a thing to stand and weep at; and yet, by nothing less than miracle, the great painter has not suffered the Son of God to be merely an object of pity, though depicting him in a state so profoundly pitiful. He is redeemed by a diviner majesty and beauty, I know not how, and is as much our Redeemer as if he sat on his throne in Heaven. Sodoma, I believe, was earlier than Perugino; and neither the latter, nor any other painter, has done anything that can deserve to be compared to this.

. . . .

Looking over what I have said of Sodoma's picture of Christ bound, at Siena, I see that I have omitted to notice what seems to me one of its most striking characteristics—its loneliness. You feel as if the Savior was deserted, both in Heaven and earth; the despair is in him, which made him say, "My God, why hast thou forsaken me!" Even in this extremity, however, he is still divine; and Sodoma almost seems to have reconciled the impossibilities of combining an Omnipotent Divinity with a suffering and outraged humanity. But this is one of the cases in which the spectator's imagination completes what the artist merely hints at.

FIN: 451-52, 491-92

Guido Reni, Archangel Michael, *Santa Maria della Concezione, Rome. May 15, 1859.*

Thence we went to the church of the Capuchins, and saw Guido's Archangel, in the first chapel on the right of the entrance. I have been several times to this church, but never saw the picture before, though I am familiar with the mosaic copy at St. Peters, and had supposed the latter to be an equivalent representation of the original. It is nearly, or quite so, as respects the general effect; but there is a beauty in the archangel's face that immeasurably surpasses the copy. The expression is of heavenly severity, and a degree of pain, trouble, or disgust, at being brought in contact with sin, even for the purpose of quelling and punishing it. There is something finical in the copy, what I do not find in the original; the sandalled feet are here those of an angel; in the mosaic, they are those of a celestial coxcomb, treading daintily, as if he were afraid they would be soiled by the touch of Lucifer.

FIN: 521

"What an expression of heavenly severity in the Archangel's face! There is a degree of pain, trouble, and disgust at being brought in contact with sin, even for the purpose of quelling and punishing it; and yet a celestial tranquillity pervades his whole being."

"I have never been able," said Miriam, "to admire this picture nearly so much as Hilda does, in its moral and intellectual aspect. If it cost her more trouble to be good—if her soul were less white and pure—she would be a more competent critic of this picture, and would estimate it not half so high. I see its defects to-day more clearly than ever before."

"What are some of them?" asked Kenyon.

"That Archangel, now!" Miriam continued. "How fair he looks, with his unruffled wings, with his unhacked sword, and clad in his bright armour, and that exquisitely fitting sky-blue tunic, cut in the latest Paradisaical mode. What a dainty air of the first celestial society! With what half-scornful delicacy he sets his prettily sandalled foot on the head of his prostrate foe! But, is it thus that Virtue looks, the moment after its death-struggle with Evil? No, no! I could have told Guido better. A full third of the Archangel's feathers should have been torn from his wings; the rest all ruffled, till they looked like Satan's own! His sword should be streaming with blood, and perhaps broken half-way to the hilt; his armour crushed, his robes rent, his breast gory; a bleeding gash on his brow, cutting right across the stern scowl of battle! He should press his foot hard down upon the old Serpent, as if his very soul depended upon it, feeling him squirm mightily, and doubting whether the fight were half-over yet, and how the victory might turn! And, with all this fierceness, this grimness, this unutterable horrour, there should still be something high, tender, and holy, in Michael's eyes, and around his mouth. But the battle never was such child's play as Guido's dapper Archangel seems to have found it!"

"For Heaven's sake, Miriam," cried Kenyon, astonished at the wild energy of her talk, "paint the picture of man's struggle against sin, according to your own idea! I think it will be a master-piece."

"The picture would have its share of truth, I assure you," she answered; "but I am sadly afraid the victory would fall on the wrong side. Just fancy a smoke-blackened, fiery-eyed Demon, bestriding that nice young angel, clutching his white throat with one of his hinder claws, and giving a triumphant whisk of his scaly tail, with a poisonous dart at the end of it! That is what they risk, poor souls, who do battle with Michael's enemy."

MF: 183-85

⋘⋙

Emanuel Leutze (Ger.-Am., 1816-1868), Westward the Course of Empire Takes Its Way, *National Capitol, United States House of Representatives Collection (in the House wing, west staircase), Washington, D.C. Late March, 1862. Courtesy Architect of the Capitol.*

The work will be emphatically original and American, embracing characteristics that neither art nor literature have yet dealt with, and producing new forms of artistic beauty from the natural features of the Rocky Mountain region, which Leutze seems to have studied broadly and minutely. The garb of the hunters and wanderers of those deserts, too, under his free and natural management, is shown as the most picturesque of costumes. But it would be doing this admirable painter no kind office to overlay his picture with any more of my colorless and uncertain words; so I shall merely add that it looked full of energy, hope, progress, irrepressible movement onward, all represented in a momentary pause of triumph; and it was most cheering to feel its good augury at this dismal time, when our country might seem to have arrived at such a deadly standstill.

. . . .

It was delightful to see him so calmly elaborating his design, while other men doubted and feared, or hoped treacherously, and whispered to one another that the nation would exist only a little longer, or that, if a remnant still held together, its centre and seat of government would be far northward and westward of Washington. But the artist keeps right on, firm of heart and hand, drawing his outlines with an unwavering pencil, beautifying and idealizing our rude, material life, and thus manifesting that we have an indefeasible claim to a more enduring national existence.

Works, Riverside Edition, XVII: 369-71

Select Bibliography

Abel, Darrel. *The Moral Picturesque: Studies in Hawthorne's Fiction*. West Lafayette, Ind.: Purdue University Press, 1988.

Alison, Archibald. *Essay on the Nature and Principle of Taste*. New York: Harper and Bros., 1856.

Ames, Winslow. *Prince Albert and Victorian Taste*. New York: Viking, 1968.

"Art in the Provinces." *Art-Journal* 3 (1857): 66.

Arthos, John. "Hawthorne in Florence." *Michigan Alumnus Quarterly* 59 (Winter 1953): 118-29.

The Art-Treasures Examiner: A Pictorial, Critical, and Historical Record of the Art-Treasures Exhibition, at Manchester, In 1857. Manchester: A. Ireland, 1857.

Askew, Melvin W. "The Pseudonymic American Hero." *Bucknell Review* 10 (March 1962): 224-31.

_____. "The Wounded Artist and His Work." *Kansas Magazine* 4 (1961): 73-77.

Aubrey, Max. "Hawthorne's Study in Clay." *Xavier University Studies* 11 (1972): 1-5.

Auerbach, Jonathan. "Executing the Model: Painting, Sculpture, and Romance-Writing in Hawthorne's *The Marble Faun*." *English Literary History* 47, no. 1 (Spring 1980): 103-20.

Bailey, Brigette. "Pictures of Italy: American Aesthetic Response to the Development of the Nineteenth-Century American Travel Sketch." Ph.D. diss., Harvard University, 1986.

Baker, Paul R. *The Fortunate Pilgrims: Americans in Italy, 1800-1860*. Cambridge: Harvard University Press, 1964.

Bales, Kent. "Nathaniel Hawthorne's Use of the Sublime." Ph.D. diss., University of California-Berkeley, 1967.

Barnett, Gene A. "Art as Setting in *The Marble Faun*." *Transactions of the Wisconsin Academy of Sciences, Arts, and Letters* 54 (1965): 231-47.

Barnett, Louise K. "American Novelists and the 'Portrait of Beatrice Cenci.'" *New England Quarterly* 53, no. 2 (June 1980): 160-83.

Bass, Eben. "The Sculptor of the Beautiful." *Colby Library Quarterly* 14 (1978): 28-35.

Baxter, Annette K. "Independence vs. Isolation: Hawthorne and James on the
    Problem of the Artist." *Nineteenth Century Fiction* 10 (December 1955):
    225-31.

Baym, Nina. "Hawthorne's Holgrave: The Failure of the Artist-Hero." *Journal of
    English and Germanic Philology* 69 (1970): 584-98.

_____. "*The Marble Faun*: Hawthorne's Elegy for Art." *New England Quarterly* 44
    (1971): 355-76.

_____. *The Shape of Hawthorne's Career*. Ithaca: Cornell University Press, 1976.

Beidler, Peter G. "The Theme of the Fortunate Fall in *The Marble Faun*." *Emerson
    Society Quarterly* 47 (1967): 56-62.

Bell, Millicent. *Hawthorne's View of the Artist*. Albany: State University of New
    York Press, 1962.

Bercovitch, Sacvan. "Hawthorne's 'Seven-Branched Allegory': An Echo from
    Cotton Mather in *The Marble Faun*." *Early American Literature* 1 (Summer
    1966): 5-6.

_____. "Of Wise and Foolish Virgins: Hilda Versus Miriam in Hawthorne's *The
    Marble Faun*." *New England Quarterly* 41 (1966): 281-86.

Berthold, Dennis. "Hawthorne, Ruskin, and the Gothic Revival: Transcendent
    Gothic in *The Marble Faun*." *ESQ* 20 (First quarter 1974): 15-32.

_____. "A Literary and Pictorial Iconography of Hawthorne's Tour [of 1832]."
    In *Hawthorne's American Travel Sketches*, edited by Alfred Weber. Hanover,
    N.H.: University Press of New England, 1989.

_____. "A Transcendentalist Aesthetics of Imperfection." *American Transcendental
    Quarterly* 50 (Spring 1981): 139-48.

Bicknell, John W. "*The Marble Faun* Reconsidered." *University of Kansas City
    Review* 10 (Spring 1954): 193-99.

Billy, Ted. "Time and Transformation in 'The Artist of the Beautiful.'" *American
    Transcendental Quarterly* 29 (1976): 17-24.

Blair, Walter. "Color, Light, and Shadow in Hawthorne's Fiction." *New England
    Quarterly* 15 (March 1942): 74-94.

Blow, Suzanne. "Pre-Raphaelite Allegory in *The Marble Faun*." *American
    Literature* 44 (1972): 122-27.

Bochner, Jay. "Life in the Picture Gallery: Things in *The Portrait of a Lady* and
    The Marble Faun." *Texas Studies in Language and Literature* 11 (1969): 761-77.

Brancaccio, Patrick. "The Ramble and the Pilgrimage: A Critical Reading of
    Hawthorne's *The Marble Faun*." Ph.D. diss., Rutgers University, 1967.

Brand, Dana. "The Panoramic Spectator in America: A Re-reading of Hawthorne's
    Sketches." *American Transcendental Quarterly* 59 (March 1986): 5-17.

Brill, Lesley W. "Conflict and Accommodation in Hawthorne's 'The Artist of
    the Beautiful.'" *Studies in Short Fiction* 12 (1985): 381-86.

Brodtkorb, Paul, Jr. "Art Allegory in *The Marble Faun*." *PMLA* 77 (June 1962):
    254-67.

Brooks, Van Wyck. *The Dream of Arcadia: American Writers and Artists in Italy,
    1760-1915*. New York: Dutton, 1958.

Brown, Merle E. "The Structure and Significance of *The Marble Faun*." Ph.D.
    diss., University of Michigan, 1953.

_____. "The Structure of *The Marble Faun*." *American Literature* 28 (November
    1956): 302-13.

Budick, Emily Miller. *Fiction and Historical Consciousness: The American Romance Tradition.* New Haven, Conn.: Yale University Press, 1989.

Budz, Judith Kaufman. "Cherubs and Humblebees: Nathaniel Hawthorne and the Visual Arts." *Criticism* 17 (1975): 168-81.

_____. "Nathaniel Hawthorne and the Visual Arts." Ph.D. diss., Northwestern University, 1973.

Bunge, Nancy L. "Unreliable Artist-Narrators in Hawthorne's Short Stories." *Studies in Short Fiction* 14 (Spring 1977): 145-50.

Buscaroli, Piero. "Hawthorne's Italy." *L'Italia* 205 (1965): 26-39.

Butts, Leonard C. "Diorama, Spectroscope, or Peepshow: The Question of the Old German's Showbox in Nathaniel Hawthorne's 'Ethan Brand.'" *Studies in Short Fiction* 20 (Fall 1983): 320-22.

Caldwell, Wayne T. "The Emblem Tradition and the Symbolic Mode: Clothing Imagery in *The House of the Seven Gables.*" *Emerson Society Quarterly* 19 (1973): 32-42.

C[alhoun], C[harles] C. "The Borrowed Faun." *Bowdoin* 61, no. 3 (Spring 1988): 2-7.

Calhoun, Thomas O. "Hawthorne's Gothic: An Approach to the Four Last Fragments." *Genre* 3 (1970): 222-41.

Cameron, Kenneth W. "Prints of American Authors." *Emerson Society Quarterly* 28 (1962): 77-106.

_____. "Twenty Pictures of Hawthorne." *Emerson Society Quarterly* 39 (1965): 2-12.

Carlson, Patricia A. *Hawthorne's Functional Settings: A Study of Artistic Method.* Atlantic Highlands, N.J.: Humanities Press, 1977.

Carton, Evan. *The Rhetoric of American Fiction: Dialectic and Identity in Emerson, Dickinson, Poe, and Hawthorne.* Baltimore: Johns Hopkins University Press, 1985.

Catalogue of the Art Treasures of the United Kingdom Collected at Manchester in 1857. London: Bradbury and Evans, 1857.

Catalogue of the Sketches and Drawings by J.M.W. Turner, R. A. Exhibited in Marlborough House in the Year 1857-58. London: Spottiswode, 1857.

Cavanaugh, Miriam Katherine. "The Romantic Hero in Byron, Hawthorne, and Melville." Ph.D. diss., University of Massachusetts, 1978.

Channing, William Ellery. *Conversations in Rome: Between an Artist, a Catholic, and a Critic.* Boston: William Crosby and H. P. Nichols, 1867.

Clark, C. E. Frazer, Jr. "A Lost Miniature of Hawthorne." *Nathaniel Hawthorne Journal* 6 (1976): 80-85.

Clark, Harry Hayden. "Hawthorne's Literary and Aesthetic Doctrines as Embodied in His Tales." *Transactions of the Wisconsin Academy of Sciences, Arts, and Letters* 50 (1961): 251-75.

Clarke, Graham. "To Transform and Transfigure: The Aesthetic Play of Hawthorne's *The Marble Faun.*" In *Nathaniel Hawthorne: New Critical Essays,* edited by A. Robert Lee, 131-47. Totowa, N.J.: Barnes and Noble, 1982.

Cook, William A. "Hawthorne's Artistic Theory and Practice." Ph.D. diss., Lehigh University, 1971.

Cooke, Alice L. "The Shadow of Martinus Scriblerus in Hawthorne's 'The Prophetic Pictures.'" *New England Quarterly* 17 (December 1944): 597-604.

Crane, Sylvia E. *White Silence: Greenough, Powers, and Crawford, American Sculptors in Nineteenth Century Italy.* Coral Gables, Fla.: University of Miami Press, 1972.

Craven, Wayne. *Sculpture in America.* New York: Crowell, 1968.

Crews, Frederick C. *The Sins of the Fathers: Hawthorne's Psychological Themes.* New York: Oxford University Press, 1966.

Crowley, J. Donald. *Hawthorne: The Critical Heritage.* New York: Barnes and Noble, 1970.

Curran, Ronald T. "Irony: Another Thematic Approach to 'The Artist of the Beautiful.'" *Studies in Romanticism* 6 (August 1966): 34-45.

Curtis, Jessie K. "*The Marble Faun:* An Interpretation." *Andover Review* 18 (August 1982): 139-47.

Darnell, Donald G. "Doctrine by Ensample: The Emblem and *The Marble Faun.*" *Texas Studies in Language and Literature* 15 (1973): 301-10.

_____. "Hawthorne's Emblematic Method." Ph.D. diss., University of Texas, 1964.

_____. "*The Scarlet Letter:* Hawthorne's Emblem Book." *Studies in American Fiction* 7, no. 2 (1979): 153-62.

Dauber, Kenneth M. *Re-discovering Hawthorne.* Princeton: Princeton University Press, 1977.

Davidson, Edward H. *Hawthorne's Last Phase.* New Haven, Conn.: Yale University Press, 1949.

Davis, Sarah I. "Hawthorne and the Revision of American Art History." *Nathaniel Hawthorne Journal* 7 (1977): 124-37.

_____. "Hawthorne's Pygmalion and William Rush." *Studies in Short Fiction* 19 (Fall 1982): 343-49.

_____. "Margaret Fuller's 'Canova' and Hawthorne's 'Drowne's Wooden Image.'" *American Transcendental Quarterly* 49 (Winter 1981): 73-78.

Dawson, Hugh. "Discovered in Paris: An Earlier First Illustrated Edition of *The Scarlet Letter.*" In *Studies in the American Renaissance*, edited by Joel Myerson. Charlottesville: University Press of Virginia, 1988.

_____. "The Triptych Design of *The Scarlet Letter.*" *Nathaniel Hawthorne Review* 13, no. 1 (Spring 1987): 12-14.

Delaune, Henry M. "The Beautiful of 'The Artist of the Beautiful.'" *Xavier University Studies* 1 (December 1961): 94-99.

Detlaff, Shirley M. "The Concept of Beauty in 'The Artist of the Beautiful' and Hugh Blair's Rhetoric." *Studies in Short Fiction* 13 (1976): 512-15.

Dichmann, Mary E. "Hawthorne's 'Prophetic Pictures.'" *American Literature* 23 (May 1951): 188-202.

Dolis, John J., Jr. "Hawthorne's Metonymic Gaze: Image and Object." *American Literature* 56 (March 1984): 362-78.

_____. "Hawthorne's Ontological Models: Daguerreotype and Diorama." Ph.D. diss., Loyola University (of Chicago), 1978.

Donohue, Agnes McNeill. *Hawthorne: Calvin's Ironic Stepchild.* Kent, Ohio: Kent University Press, 1985.

Doubleday, Neal Frank. *Hawthorne's Early Tales.* Durham, N.C.: Duke University Press, 1972.

_____. "Hawthorne's Use of Three Gothic Patterns." *College English* 7 (February 1946): 250-62.

Dryden, Edgar A. *Nathaniel Hawthorne: The Poetics of Enchantment.* Ithaca, N.Y.: Cornell University Press, 1977.

Duerksen, Roland A. "The Double Image of Beatrice Cenci in *The Marble Faun.*" *Michigan Academician* 1 (1969): 47-55.

Earnest, Ernest. "The Ambivalent Puritan: Nathaniel Hawthorne." *Expatriates and Patriots: American Artists, Scholars, and Writers in Europe.* Durham, N.C.: Duke University Press, 1968.

Eisiminger, Sterling K. and John L. Idol, Jr. "Nathaniel Hawthorne and Emanuel Leutze." *Essex Institute Historical Collections* 118, no. 1 (January 1982): 67-71.

Elder, Marjorie J. "Hawthorne's *The Marble Faun:* A Gothic Structure." *Costerus* 1 (1972): 81-88.

_____. *Nathaniel Hawthorne: Transcendental Symbolist.* Athens, Ohio: Ohio University Press, 1969.

Eldred, Janet M. "Gender and Creativity: Female Artist." Ph.D. diss., University of Illinois, 1988.

Fairbanks, Henry G. "Hawthorne Amid the Alien Corn." *College English* 17 (February 1956): 263-68.

_____. *The Lasting Loneliness of Nathaniel Hawthorne: A Study of the Sources of Alienation in Modern Man.* Albany, N.Y.: Magi Books, 1965.

Fay, Stephanie. "American Pictorial Rhetoric: Describing Works of Art in Fiction and Art Criticism, 1820-1875." Ph.D. diss., University of California-Berkeley, 1982.

_____. "Lights from Dark Corners: Works of Art in 'The Prophetic Pictures' and 'The Artist of the Beautiful.'" *Studies in American Fiction* 13, no. 1 (Spring 1985): 15-29.

Feidelson, Charles, Jr. *Symbolism and American Literature.* Chicago: Chicago University Press, 1953.

Fields, James T. Letter to Nathaniel Hawthorne, 21 August 1851, Berg Collection, New York Public Library.

_____. *Yesterdays with Authors.* Boston: Houghton, Mifflin and Company, 1871.

Fisher, Marvin. "Portrait of the Artist in America: 'Hawthorne and His Mosses.'" *Southern Review* 11 (1975): 156-66.

Fogle, Richard H. *Hawthorne's Fiction: The Light and the Dark.* Norman: University of Oklahoma Press, 1952.

_____. "Hawthorne's Pictorial Unity." *Emerson Society Quarterly* 55 (1969): 71-76.

Folsom, James K. *Man's Accidents and God's Purposes: Multiplicity in Hawthorne's Fiction.* New Haven, Conn.: College and University Press, 1963.

Forsyth, Joseph. *Remarks on the Antiquities, Art, and Letters during an Excursion to Italy in the Years 1802 and 1803.* Boston: Wells and Lilly, 1818.

Franklin, Rosemary F. "The Cabin by the Lake: Pastoral Landscapes of Poe, Cooper, Hawthorne, and Thoreau." *Emerson Society Quarterly* 22 (1976): 59-70.

Friedl, Herwig. "Problemgeschichtliche Überlegungen zum Stellenwert der Kunst in Amerikanischen Kunstlerzählungen." *Anglia* 97 (1979): 153-67.

Gale, Martha Tyler. "*The Marble Faun*, an Allegory, with a Key to Its Interpretation." *New Englander* 19 (October 1861): 860-70.

Gale, Robert L. "*The Marble Faun* and *The Sacred Fount*: A Resemblance." *Studi Americani* 8 (1962): 21-33.

Gargano, James W. "Hawthorne's 'The Artist of the Beautiful.'" *American Literature* 35 (May 1963): 225-30.

Gerdts, William H. *American Neo-Classic Sculpture: The Marble Resurrection*. New York: Viking, 1973.

_____. *The White Marmorean Flock: Nineteenth-Century American Women Neoclassical Sculptors*. Poughkeepsie, N.Y.: Vassar College Art Gallery, 1972.

Gergits, Julia Marie. "Women Can Paint—Sometimes: Women Painters in Nineteenth-Century Novels." Ph.D. diss., University of Minnesota, 1987.

Gollin, Rita K. "'Getting a Taste for Pictures': Hawthorne and the Manchester Exhibition." *Nathaniel Hawthorne Journal* 7 (1977): 80-97.

_____. "Hawthorne and the Anxiety of Aesthetic Response." *Centennial Review* 28, no. 4 and 29, no. 1 (Fall 1984-Winter 1985): 94-104.

_____. "Hawthorne on Perception, Lucubration, and Reverie." *Nathaniel Hawthorne Journal, 1976* 6 (1978): 227-39.

_____. *Nathaniel Hawthorne and the Truth of Dreams*. Baton Rouge: Louisiana State University Press, 1979.

_____. "Painting and Character in *The Marble Faun*." *Emerson Society Quarterly* 21 (1976): 1-10.

_____. *Portraits of Nathaniel Hawthorne: An Iconography*. Dekalb: Northern Illinois University Press, 1983.

Gombrich, E. H. *Art and Illusion*. New York: Pantheon, 1960.

Goodspeed, Charles E. *Nathaniel Hawthorne and the Museum of the Salem East India Society: or the Gathering of a Virtuoso's Collection*. Salem, Mass.: Peabody Museum, 1946.

Grayson, Robert C. "Hawthorne's Early Interest in Portraits." *Hawthorne Society Newsletter* 8, no. 2 (Fall 1982): 7-8.

Greenwood, Douglas. "The Heraldic Device in *The Scarlet Letter*: Hawthorne's Symbolic Use of the Past." *American Literature* 46 (1974): 207-10.

Gupta, Raj Kumar. "Hawthorne's Theory of Art." *American Literature* 40 (1968): 309-24.

_____. "Hawthorne's Treatment of the Artist." *New England Quarterly* 45 (1972): 65-80.

Gysin, Fritz. "Paintings in the House of Fiction: The Example of Hawthorne." *Word & Image* 5, no. 2 (April-June 1989): 159-72.

[Hall, Samuel Carter]. Rev. of *Transformation*, *Art-Journal* 1 April 1860, p. 127.

Hall, Spencer. "Beatrice Cenci: Symbol and Vision in *The Marble Faun*." *Nineteenth Century Fiction* 25 (1970): 85-95.

Hall, William F. "Henry James and the Picturesque Mode." *English Studies in Canada* 1 (Fall 1975): 326-43.

Harris, Kenneth Marc. *Hypocrisy and Self-Deception in Hawthorne's Fiction*. Charlottesville: University Press of Virginia, 1988.

Harris, Neil. *The Artist in American Society: The Formative Years, 1790-1860*. New York: George Braziller, 1966.

Hasselmayer, Louis A. "Hawthorne and Cenci." *Neophil* 27 (1941): 59-64.

Hawthorne, Julian. *Hawthorne and His Circle.* New York: Harper & Brothers, 1903.

_____. *Hawthorne and His Wife.* 2 vols. 1884. Reprint. New York: Archon Books, 1968.

_____. *Memoirs of Julian Hawthorne.* New York: Macmillan, 1938.

Hawthorne, Manning. "A Glimpse of Hawthorne's Boyhood." *Essex Institute Historical Collections* 83 (April 1947): 178-84.

_____. "Nathaniel Hawthorne at Bowdoin." *New England Quarterly* 13 (June 1940): 246-79.

Hawthorne, Nathaniel. *The Centenary Edition of the Works of Nathaniel Hawthorne,* edited by William Charvat, Roy Harvey Pearce, Claude Simpson, Thomas Woodson, and others. 19 vols. Columbus: Ohio State University Press, 1962 and continuing.

_____. *The Complete Works of Nathaniel Hawthorne.* Riverside Edition. 12 vols. Boston: Houghton Mifflin, 1883.

_____. *The English Notebooks,* edited by Randall Stewart. Reprint. New York: Russell and Russell, 1962.

Hawthorne, Sophia Peabody. *Notes in England and Italy.* New York: G. P. Putnam and Sons, 1869.

Heinitz, Kenneth L. "Nathaniel Hawthorne's Theory of Art." Ph.D. diss., Loyola University (of Chicago), 1963.

Hennelley, Mark M., Jr. "'Alice Doane's Appeal': Hawthorne's Case Against the Artist." *Studies in American Fiction* 6 (1978): 125-40.

Herndon, Jerry A. and Sidney P. Moss. "The Identity and Significance of the German-Jewish Showman in Hawthorne's 'Ethan Brand.'" *College English* 23 (February 1962): 362-63.

Hillard, George Stillman. "The English Note-Books of Nathaniel Hawthorne." *Atlantic Monthly* (September 1870): 257-72.

_____. *Six Months in Italy.* Boston: Ticknor, Reed, and Fields, 1853.

Hoeltje, Hubert H. "A Forgotten Hawthorne Silhouette." *American Literature* 27 (January 1957): 516-21.

_____. *The Inward Sky: The Mind and Art of Nathaniel Hawthorne.* Durham, N.C.: Duke University Press, 1962.

Holland, J. Gill. "Hawthorne and Photography: *The House of the Seven Gables.*" *Nathaniel Hawthorne Journal* 8 (1978): 1-10.

Holmes, Oliver Wendell. "Exhibition of Pictures Painted by Washington Allston at Harding's Gallery, School Street." *North American Review* 50 (April 1840): 358-81.

Howard, June. "The Watch Maker, the Artist, and the Iron Accents of History: Notes on Hawthorne's 'The Artist of the Beautiful.'" *Emerson Society Quarterly* 28 (1982): 1-10.

[Howells, William Dean]. "Recent Literature." *Atlantic Monthly* 29 (May 1872): 624-26.

Hudleston, Eugene L. and Douglas A. Noverr. *The Relationship of Painting and Literature: A Guide to Information Sources.* Detroit: Gale Research Company, 1978.

Hutcheson, Francis. *An Inquiry Concerning Beauty, Order, Harmony, Design,* edited by Peter Kivy. The Hague: Martinus Nijhoff, 1973.

Hutner, Gordon. *Secrets and Sympathy: Forms of Discourse in Hawthorne's Novels.* Athens: University of Georgia Press, 1988.

Huzzard, John A. "Hawthorne's *The Marble Faun.*" *Italica* 35 (June 1958): 119-24.

Idol, John L., Jr. "Clifford Pyncheon's Soap Bubbles." *American Notes & Queries* 23, no. 3, no. 4 (1984): 38-41.

———. "Hawthorne on Sophia's Paintings of Lake Como." *Hawthorne Society Newsletter* 10, no. 2 (Fall 1984): 11.

———. "Hawthorne's Biographical Sketch of Benjamin West." *Re:Artes Liberales* 7, no. 2 (Spring 1981): 1-7.

———. "Mary Russell Mitford: Champion of American Literature." In *Studies in the American Renaissance,* edited by Joel Myerson. Charlottesville: University Press of Virginia, 1983.

———. "Nathaniel Hawthorne and Harriet Hosmer." *Nathaniel Hawthorne Journal* 6 (1976): 120-28.

———. "A Show of Hands in 'The Artist of the Beautiful.'" *Studies in Short Fiction* 22, no. 4 (Fall 1985): 455-60.

———. "Why Hawthorne Chose to Write a Sketch of Benjamin West." *Hawthorne Society Newsletter* 7, no. 2 (Fall 1981): 4-5.

Idol, John L., Jr., and Sterling K. Eisiminger. "Hawthorne Sits for a Bust by Maria Louisa Lander." *Essex Institute Historical Collections* 114, no. 4 (October 1978): 207-12.

Idol, John L., Jr., Sterling K. Eisiminger and Rita K. Gollin. "Prophetic Pictures: A Working List of Art Objects." *Hawthorne Society Newsletter* 4, no. 1 (Spring 1978): 5-7.

Irwin, John T. *American Hieroglyphics: The Symbol of the Egyptian Hieroglyphics in the American Renaissance.* New Haven, Conn.: Yale University Press, 1982.

Jacobson, Richard J. *Hawthorne's Conception of the Creative Process.* Cambridge: Harvard University Press, 1965.

Jaffe, David. "The Miniature That Inspired Clifford Pyncheon's Portrait." *Essex Institute Historical Collections* 78 (October 1962): 278-82.

James, Henry. *Hawthorne.* London: Macmillan, 1879.

———. "Hawthorne's French and Italian Notebooks." *Nation* 14 (March 1872): 172-73.

Jameson, Anna. *Legends of the Madonna.* London: Longman, Brown Green and Longmans, 1852.

———. *Legends of the Monastic Orders.* London: Longman, Brown, Green and Longmans, 1852.

———. *Sacred and Legendary Art.* London: Longman, Brown, Green and Longmans, 1848.

Jehlen, Myra. *American Incarnation: The Individual, The Nation, and the Continent.* Cambridge: Harvard University Press, 1986.

Jones, Buford. "The Faery Land of Hawthorne's Romances." *Emerson Society Quarterly* 48 (1967): 106-24.

———. "'The Man of Adamant' and the Moral Picturesque." *American Transcendental Quarterly* 14 (1972): 33-41.

Jones, Marga C. "The Marble Faun and a Writer's Crisis." *Studi Americani* 16 (1970): 81-123.

Kaftan, Robert A. "A Study of the Gothic Technique in the Novels of Nathaniel

Hawthorne." Ph.D. diss., Michigan State University, 1976.

Kane, Robert J. "Hawthorne's 'The Prophetic Pictures' and James' 'The Liar.'" *Modern Language Notes* 65 (1950): 257-58.

Kesselring, Marion L. *Hawthorne's Reading, 1828-1850*. New York: The New York Public Library, 1949.

Kimbrough, Robert. "The Actual and the Imaginary: Hawthorne's Concept of Art in Theory and Practice." *Transactions of the Wisconsin Academy of Sciences, Arts, and Letters* 50 (1961): 277-93.

Kinkead-Weekes, Mark. "The Letter, the Picture, and the Mirror: Hawthorne's Framing of *The Scarlet Letter*." In *Nathaniel Hawthorne: New Critical Essays*, edited by A. Robert Lee, 68-87. Totowa, N.J.: Barnes and Noble, 1982.

Kisner, Madeleine. "Color in Worlds and Works of Poe, Hawthorne, Crane, Anderson, and Welty." Ph.D. diss., University of Michigan, 1975.

Kleitz, Katherine Agnes. "The Italian World of Art in Nineteenth-Century English and American Literature." Ph.D. diss., Tufts University, 1988.

Koisumi, Ichiro. "The 'Artist' in Hawthorne." *Studies in English Literature* 40 (February 1964): 35-43.

Kouwenhoven, John. *Made in America: The Arts in Modern Civilization*. New York: Norton, 1967.

Krieger, Murray. "Afterword." *The Marble Faun: or the Romance of Monte Beni*. New York: New American Library, 1961.

Kruse, Horst. "The Museum Motif in English and American Fiction of the Nineteenth Century." *Amerikastudien* 31, no. 1 (1986): 71-79.

Lasser, Michael L. "Mirror Imagery in *The Scarlet Letter*." *English Journal* 56 (February 1967): 274-77.

Lathrop, Rose Hawthorne. *Memories of Hawthorne*. Boston: Houghton Mifflin, 1897.

Lease, Benjamin. "Diorama and Dream: Hawthorne's Cinematic Vision." *Journal of Popular Culture* 5 (1971): 315-23.

_____. "Hawthorne and the Archaeology of the Cinema." *Nathaniel Hawthorne Journal* 6 (1976): 133-71.

Leib, Amos P. "Nathaniel Hawthorne as Scenic Artist." Ph.D. diss., Tulane University, 1963.

Levin, Harry. "Statues from Italy: *The Marble Faun*." *Refractions: Essays in Comparative Literature*. New York: Oxford University Press, 1966.

Levy, Leo B. "The Landscape Modes of *The Scarlet Letter*." *Nineteenth Century Fiction* 23 (1969): 377-92.

_____. "'Lifelikeness' in Hawthorne's Fiction." *Nathaniel Hawthorne Journal* 5 (1975): 141-45.

_____. "*The Marble Faun*: Hawthorne's Landscape of the Fall." *American Literature* 42 (1970): 139-56.

_____. "Picturesque Style in *The House of the Seven Gables*." *New England Quarterly* 39 (June 1966): 147-60.

Liebman, Sheldon W. "The Design of *The Marble Faun*." *New England Quarterly* 40 (1967): 61-78.

_____. "Hawthorne's Romanticism: 'The Artist of the Beautiful.'" *Emerson Society Quarterly* 22 (1976): 85-95.

Leonardo da Vinci. New York: Reynal, 1956.

Lister, Paul A. "Some New Light on Hawthorne's *The Marble Faun*." *Nathaniel Hawthorne Journal* 8 (1978): 79-86.

Lloyd, Michael. "Hawthorne, Ruskin, and the Hostile Tradition." *English Miscellany* 6 (1955): 109-33.

Lloyd-Smith, Allan G. "The Elaborated Sign of the Scarlet Letter." *American Transcendental Quarterly*, n.s., no. 1 (March 1987): 69-82.

_____. *Eve Tempted: Writing and Sexuality in Hawthorne's Fiction*. Totowa, N.J.: Barnes and Noble, 1984.

Loring, George B. "Hawthorne's *Scarlet Letter*." *The Massachusetts Quarterly Review* 3 (September 1850): 484-500.

Lucke, Jessie R. "Hawthorne's Madonna Image in *The Scarlet Letter*." *New England Quarterly* 38 (September 1965): 391-92.

Luedtke, Luther. "Hawthorne on Architecture: Sources for Parley's *Universal History* and *The American Notebooks*." *Papers of the Bibliographical Society of America* 71 (1977): 88-98.

Lundblad, Jane. *Nathaniel Hawthorne and the European Literary Tradition*. Cambridge: Harvard University Press, 1947.

_____. "Nathaniel Hawthorne and the Tradition of Gothic Romance." *Studia Neophilologica* 19 (1946): 1-92.

Maas, Jeremy. *Victorian Painters*. New York: Putnam, 1969.

McCarthy, Harold T. "Hawthorne's Dialogue with Rome: *The Marble Faun*." *Studi Americani* 14 (1968): 97-112.

McCullen, Joseph T., Jr. "Influences on Hawthorne's 'The Artist of the Beautiful.'" *Emerson Society Quarterly* 50 (1968): 43-46.

McDonald, John J. "A Sophia Hawthorne Journal, 1843-1844." *Nathaniel Hawthorne Journal* 4 (1974): 1-30.

Mack, Stanley T. "Portraits and Portraitists in Hawthorne and James." Ph.D. diss., Lehigh University, 1976.

MacKay, Carol H. "Hawthorne, Sophia, and Hilda as Copyists: Duplication and Transformation in *The Marble Faun*." *Browning Institute Studies* 12 (1984): 93-120.

McKinsey, Elizabeth. *Niagara Falls: Icon of the American Sublime*. Cambridge: Cambridge University Press, 1985.

Maggins, Mary A. "Hawthorne on Church Architecture." *Florida State University Studies* 11 (1963): 54-74.

_____. "Hawthorne's Comments on the Arts as Evidence of an Aesthetic Theory." Ph.D. diss., University of North Carolina, 1948.

Mahan, Helen R. "Hawthorne's *The Marble Faun*: A Critical Introduction and Annotation." Ph.D. diss., University of Rochester, 1965.

Marks, Alfred H. "Hawthorne's Daguerreotypist: Scientist, Artist, Reformer." *Ball State Teachers College Forum* 3 (Spring 1962): 61-74.

Marovitz, Sanford E. "Roderick Hudson: James' *Marble Faun*." *Texas Studies in Language and Literature* 11 (1970): 1427-43.

Martin, Terence. *The Instructed Vision: Scottish Commonsense Philosophy and the Origin of American Fiction*. Bloomington: Indiana University Press, 1961.

_____. *Nathaniel Hawthorne*. Twayne's United States Authors Series. New Haven, Conn.: College and University Press, 1965.

Matthiessen, F. O. *American Renaissance: Art and Expression in the Age of Emerson and Whitman.* New York: Oxford University Press, 1941.

Meixsell, Anne B. "Symbolism in *The Marble Faun.*" Ph.D. diss., Pennsylvania State University, 1966.

Mellow, James. *Nathaniel Hawthorne in His Times.* Boston: Houghton Mifflin, 1980.

_____. "Transcendental Admirers: Turner's American Friends." *Art News* (December 1980): 80-83.

Merivale, Patricia. "The Raven and the Bust of Pallas: Classical Artifacts and the Gothic Tale." *PMLA* 89 (1974): 960-66.

Meyers, Jeffrey. *Painting and the Novel.* New York: Barnes and Noble, 1975.

Michael, John. "History and Romance, Sympathy and Uncertainty: The Moral of the Stones in Hawthorne's *The Marble Faun.*" *PMLA* 103, no. 2 (March 1988): 150-61.

Miller, William B. "A New Review of the Career of Paul Akers, 1825-1861." *Colby Library Quarterly* 7 (1966): 227-56.

Moore, L. Hugh, Jr. "Hawthorne's Ideal Artist as Presumptuous Intellectual." *Studies in Short Fiction* 2 (Spring 1965): 278-83.

Moss, Sidney P. "The Problem of Theme in *The Marble Faun.*" *Nineteenth Century Fiction* 18 (March 1966): 393-99.

_____. "The Symbolism of the Italian Background in *The Marble Faun.*" *Nineteenth Century Fiction* 28 (1968): 332-36.

Moyer, Patricia. "Time and the Artist in Kafka and Hawthorne." *Modern Fiction Studies* 4 (Winter 1958): 295-306.

Murray, Elizabeth W. "George Inness Painting." *Hawthorne Society Newsletter* 3, no. 1 (Spring 1977): 6.

Myers, Joan S. "Dualism and Duplicity in the Works of Nathaniel Hawthorne." Ph.D. diss., Rutgers University, 1970.

Myerson, Joel. "Sarah Clarke's Reminiscences of the Peabodys and Hawthorne." *Nathaniel Hawthorne Journal* 3 (1973): 130-33.

"Nathaniel Hawthorne." *North British Review* (September 1868): 173-208.

Normand, Jean. *Nathaniel Hawthorne: An Approach to an Analysis of Artistic Creation,* translated by Derek Cox. Cleveland, Ohio: The Press of the Case Western Reserve University, 1970.

O'Donnell, Charles R. "The Mind of the Artist: Cooper, Thoreau, Hawthorne, Melville." Ph.D. diss., Syracuse University, 1956.

Ossoli, Margaret Fuller. "A Record of the Impressions Produced by the Exhibition of Mr. Allston's Pictures in the Summer of 1839." In *Papers on Literature and Art.* Two vols. in one. London: Wiley & Putnam, 1846.

Pancost, David W. "Washington Irving's *Sketch Book* and American Literature to the Rise of Realism: Framed Narrative, the Pictorical Mode, and Irony in the Fiction of Irving, Longfellow, Kennedy, Poe, Hawthorne, Melville, Howells, Twain, James, and Others." Ph.D. diss., Duke University, 1977.

Paris, Bernard J. "Optimism and Pessimism in *The Marble Faun.*" *Boston University Studies in English* 2 (Summer 1956): 95-112.

Peabody, Elizabeth Palmer. "Exhibition of Allston's Paintings in Boston in 1839." In *Last Evening with Allston and Other Papers,* 30-62. Boston: D. Lothrop and Company, 1886.

_____. "The Genius of Hawthorne." *Atlantic Monthly* 22 (September 1868): 359-74.

Pearce, Roy Harvey, ed. *Hawthorne Centenary Essays*. Columbus: Ohio State University Press, 1964.

Pearson, Norman Holmes. "Elizabeth Peabody on Hawthorne." *Essex Institute Historical Collections* 94 (July 1958): 256-76.

Perkins, Robert T. and William J. Gavin. *The Boston Athenaeum Art Exhibition Index, 1827-1874*. Boston: The Library of the Boston Athenaeum, 1980.

Person, Leland S. *Aesthetic Headaches: Women and a Masculine Poetics in Poe, Melville, & Hawthorne*. Athens: University of Georgia Press, 1988.

Pierce, H. Winthrop. *Early Days of the Copley Society*. Boston: Rockwell and Churchill Press, 1903.

Ponder, Melinda Mowry. *Hawthorne's Narrative Art: Its Origins in Eighteenth-Century Anglo-Scottish Aesthetics*. Lewiston, N.Y.: Edwin Mellen Press, 1990.

Porte, Joel. *The Romance in America: Studies in Cooper, Poe, Hawthorne, Melville, and James*. Middletown, Conn.: Wesleyan University Press, 1969.

Predmore, Richard. "Thoreau's Influence in 'The Artist of the Beautiful.'" *American Transcendental Quarterly* 40 (Fall 1978): 329-34.

Rees, Abraham. *The Cyclopaedia; or, Universal Dictionary of Arts, Sciences, and Literature*. Philadelphia: S. F. Bradford, 1810-1842.

Rees, John O., Jr. "Nathaniel Hawthorne and the Emblem." Ph.D. diss., Iowa State University, 1964.

Reynolds, Donald M. *Hiram Powers and His Ideal Sculpture*. New York: Garland, 1977.

Robinson, Danny Lee. "Hawthorne's 'April Fools': Source and Significance." *American Transcendental Quarterly* 53 (1982): 67-72.

Rucker, Mary. "Science and Art in Hawthorne's 'The Birth-Mark.'" *Nineteenth Century Fiction* 41, no. 4 (March 1987): 445-61.

Rupp, Richard H. "Introduction." *The Marble Faun*. Indianapolis: Bobbs-Merrill, 1971.

Ryan, Thomas J. "'Scenes Well Worth Gazing At': The Effects of Hawthorne's Touristic Vision in *The Marble Faun*." Ph.D. diss., York University, 1976.

St. Armand, Barton L. "The Golden Stain of Time: Ruskinian Aesthetics and the Ending of *The House of the Seven Gables*." *Nathaniel Hawthorne Journal* 3 (1973): 143-53.

_____. "Hawthorne, Art, and *The Marble Faun*: Some Literary Gossip." *Hawthorne Society Newsletter* 6, no. 2 (Fall 1980): 6-7.

Sanborn, Frank B., ed. *Hawthorne and His Friends: Reminiscence and Tribute*. Cedar Rapids, Iowa: Torch, 1902.

Sanders, Charles. "A Note on Metamorphosis in Hawthorne's 'The Artist of the Beautiful.'" *Studies in Short Fiction* 4 (Fall 1966): 82-83.

Scheick, William. "The Hieroglyphic Rock in Hawthorne's 'Roger Malvin's Burial.'" *Emerson Society Quarterly* 24 (1978): 72-76.

Schriber, Mary Sue. "Emerson, Hawthorne and 'The Artist of the Beautiful.'" *Studies in Short Fiction* 8 (1971): 607-16.

Schubert, Leland. *Hawthorne the Artist: Fine-Art Devices in Fiction*. Chapel Hill:

University of North Carolina Press, 1944.

Schuyler, Eugene. *Italian Influences*. New York: Scribners, 1901.

Sharf, Frederick A. "Charles Osgood: The Life and Times of a Salem Portrait Painter." *Essex Institute Historical Collections* 102 (July 1966): 203-12.

_____. "'A More Bracing Morning Atmosphere': Artistic Life in Salem, 1856-1859." *Essex Institute Historical Collections* 95 (April 1959): 149-64.

Shinn, Thelma J. "A Fearful Power: Hawthorne's Views on Art and the Artist as Expressed in His Sketches and Short Stories." *Nathaniel Hawthorne Journal* 8 (1978): 121-35.

Shloss, Carol. *In Visible Light: Photography and the American Writer: 1840-1940*. Oxford: Oxford University Press, 1987.

Shumaker, Conrad. "A Daughter of the Puritans: History in Hawthorne's *The Marble Faun*." *New England Quarterly* 57 (March 1984): 65-83.

Smith, Charles R., Jr. "The Structural Principle of *The Marble Faun*." *Thoth* 3 (Winter 1962): 32-38.

Smyth, A. H. "Hawthorne's *The Marble Faun*." *Chautauquan* 30 (February 1900): 523-26.

Sparks, Jared. *The Library of American Biography*. Boston: Hilliard, Gray & Co., 1837.

Spicer, Harold. "Hawthorne's Credo of 'The Beautiful.'" *Yearbook of English Studies* 4 (1974): 190-96.

Steegman, John. *Victorian Taste: A Study of the Arts and Architecture from 1830 to 1870*. 1950. Reprint. London: Thomas Nelson, 1970.

Stein, Roger B. *John Ruskin and Aesthetic Thought in America, 1840-1900*. Cambridge: Harvard University Press, 1967.

Stein, William Bysshe. "'The Artist of the Beautiful': Narcissus and the Thimble." *American Imago* 18 (Spring 1961): 35-44.

Steiner, Wendy. *Pictures of Romance: Form Against Context in Painting and Literature*. Chicago: University of Chicago Press, 1988.

Stevens. Rosemary. "'A' is for 'Art' in *The Scarlet Letter*." *American Transcendental Quarterly* 1 (1969): 23-27.

Stewart, Dugald. *The Collected Works of Dugald Stewart*. Edinburgh: Thomas Constable, 1854.

Stewart, Randall. *Nathaniel Hawthorne: A Biography*. New Haven, Conn.: Yale University Press, 1946.

Stocking, D. M. "An Embroidery on Dimmesdale's Scarlet Letter." *College English* 13 (March 1952): 336-37.

Strandberg, Victor. "The Artist's Black Veil: Hawthorne." *New England Quarterly* 41 (December 1968): 567-74.

Stubbs, John Caldwell. "The Ideal in the Literature and Art of the American Renaissance." *Emerson Society Quarterly* 55 (1969): 55-63.

_____. "A Note of the Source of Hawthorne's Heraldic Device in *The Scarlet Letter*." *Notes and Queries* 15 (1968): 175-76.

_____. *The Pursuit of Form: A Study of Hawthorne and the Romance*. Urbana: University of Illinois Press, 1970.

Sutherland, Judith L. *The Problematic Fictions of Poe, James, and Hawthorne*. Columbia: University of Missouri Press, 1984.

Swann, Charles. "Hawthorne's *The Marble Faun* and Michelangelo's Bust of Brutus." *Oxford Notes and Queries* n.s. 36 [o.s. 234], no. 2 (June 1989): 185-86.

Tanner, Tony. "Problems and Roles of the American Artist as Portrayed by the American Artist." *Proceedings of the British Academy* 57 (1971): 159-79.

_____. *Scenes of Nature, Signs of Men.* Cambridge: Cambridge University Press, 1987.

Tharp, Louise H. *The Peabody Sisters of Salem.* Boston: Little, Brown, 1950.

Tintner, Adeline R. "'The Impressions of a Cousin': Henry James' Transformation of *The Marble Faun.*" *Nathaniel Hawthorne Journal* 6 (1976): 205-13.

Tommasini, Margaret C. "*The Marble Faun:* Eden Re-visited and Reexamined." Ph.D. diss., Brown University, 1971.

Toulouse, Teresa. "Spatial Relations in 'The Old Manse.'" *Emerson Society Quarterly* 28 (1982): 154-66.

Travis, Mildred K. "Of Hawthorne's 'The Artist of the Beautiful' and Spenser's 'Muioptomos.'" *Philological Quarterly* 54 (1975): 537.

Tripathy, Biyot K. "Hawthorne, Art, and the Artist: A Study of 'Drowne's Wooden Image' and 'The Artist of the Beautiful.' " *Indian Journal of American Studies* 1 (1971): 63-71.

Turner, Arlin. *Nathaniel Hawthorne: A Biography.* New York: Oxford University Press, 1980.

_____. *Nathaniel Hawthorne: An Introduction and an Interpretation.* New York: Barnes and Noble, 1961.

_____. "Park Benjamin on the Author and Illustrator of 'The Gentle Boy.'" *Nathaniel Hawthorne Journal* 4 (1974): 85-91.

_____, ed. *Hawthorne as Editor: Selections from His Writings in* The American Magazine of Useful Entertaining Knowledge. Baton Rouge: Louisiana State University Press, 1972.

Valenti, Patricia Dunlavy. "The Frozen Art or the Ethereal Domain: Hawthorne's Concept of Sculpture." *Studies in Short Fiction* 22 (1985): 323-30.

_____. "Hawthorne's Use of Visual Elements." Ph.D. diss., University of North Carolina, 1977.

_____. "Viewing 'The Prophetic Pictures' During Its First One Hundred and Fifty Years." *Nathaniel Hawthorne Review* 13, no. 2 (Fall 1987): 13-15.

Vance, William L. "The Sidelong Glance: Victorian Americans and Baroque Rome." *New England Quarterly* 58 (1985): 501-32.

Von Abele, Rudolph. "Baby and Butterfly." *Kenyon Review* 15 (1953): 280-92.

_____. *The Death of the Artist: A Study in Hawthorne's Disintegration.* The Hague: Martinus Nijhoff, 1955.

_____. "*The Scarlet Letter:* A Reading." *Accent* 11 (August 1951): 211-17.

Wagenknecht, Edward C. *Nathaniel Hawthorne: The Man, His Tales and Romances.* New York: Continuum, 1989.

_____. *Nathaniel Hawthorne: Man and Writer.* New York: Oxford University Press, 1961.

Waggoner, Hyatt H. *Hawthorne: A Critical Study.* Rev. ed. Cambridge: Harvard University Press, 1963.

Walters, Charles T. "Hawthorne in Relation to Art: *The Marble Faun* and the Sculptural Aesthetic." *Indian Journal of American Studies* 8 (1978): 36-45.

Waples, Dorothy. "Suggestions for Interpreting *The Marble Faun.*" *American Literature* 13 (November 1941): 224-39.

Weber, Alfred, Beth L. Leuck and Dennis Berthold. *Hawthorne's American Travel Sketches and His Northern Tour of 1832.* Lebanon, N.H.: University Press of New England, 1989.

Wegelin, Christof. "Europe in Hawthorne's Fiction." *English Literary History* 14 (September 1947): 219-45.

West, Harry C. "Hawthorne's Magic Circle: 'The Artist as Magician.'" *Criticism* 16 (1974): 311-25.

_____. "The Sources for Hawthorne's 'The Artist of the Beautiful.'" *Nineteenth Century Fiction* 30 (1975): 105-11.

Wheelock, Alan S. "Architecture's Moral Dimension: The House Image in Hawthorne's Fiction." Ph.D. diss., SUNY, Albany, 1972.

Whelan, Robert E., Jr. "*The Marble Faun:* Rome as Hawthorne's Mansoul." *Research Studies* [Washington State University] 40 (1972): 163-75.

Winner, Viola Hopkins. "The American Pictorial Vision: Objects and Ideas in Hawthorne, James, and Hemingway." *Studies in Short Fiction* 15 (1977): 143-59.

Wohlpart, A. James. "The Status of the Artist in Hawthorne's 'The Artist of the Beautiful.'" *American Transcendental Quarterly* n.s. 3, no. 3 (September 1989): 245-56.

Wonders of Italy. Edited by Joseph Fattorusso. Florence: G. Fattorusso, 1930.

Woodberry, George. *Nathaniel Hawthorne.* Boston: Houghton Mifflin, 1902.

Wright, Nathalia. *American Novelists in Italy.* Philadelphia: University of Pennsylvania Press, 1965.

_____. "The Influence of Italy on *The Marble Faun.*" *Tennessee Studies in Literature* special number (1961): 141-49.

Yoder, Ralph A. "Hawthorne and His Artist." *Studies in Romanticism* 7 (1968): 193-206.

Ziff, Larzer. "The Artist and Puritanism." In *Hawthorne Centenary Essays,* edited by Roy Harvey Pearce. Columbus: Ohio State University Press, 1964.

Index

About the Authors

RITA K. GOLLIN is Professor of English at the State University of New York at Geneseo. Her previous books include *Portraits of Nathaniel Hawthorne: An Iconography* (1983) and *Nathaniel Hawthorne and the Truth of Dreams* (1979). She is the author of numerous articles on Nathaniel Hawthorne and is a past president of the Nathaniel Hawthorne Society.

JOHN L. IDOL, JR., is Professor of English at Clemson University. His previous works include *A Thomas Wolfe Companion* (Greenwood Press, 1987). He is the editor of the *Nathaniel Hawthorne Review* and a past president of the Nathaniel Hawthorne Society.

STERLING K. EISIMINGER is Professor of English at Clemson University. He is the author of *The Consequence of Error and Other Essays* (1991) and *Wordspinner* (1991), and a past associate editor of the *Nathaniel Hawthorne Review*.

Recent Titles in
Contributions in American Studies

The Course of American Democratic Thought
Third Edition with Robert H. Walker
Ralph Henry Gabriel

The Golden Sword: The Coming of Capitalism to the Colorado Mining Frontier
Michael Neuschatz

Corporations and Society: Power and Responsibility
Warren J. Samuels and Arthur S. Miller, editors

Abortion, Politics, and the Courts: *Roe v. Wade* and Its Aftermath
Revised Edition
Eva R. Rubin

The Secret Constitution and the Need for Constitutional Change
Arthur S. Miller

Business and Religion in the American 1920s
Rolf Lundén

Modular America: Cross-Cultural Perspectives on the Emergence of an
American Way
John G. Blair

The Social Christian Novel
Robert Glenn Wright

The Urbanists, 1865-1915
Dana F. White

In the Public Interest: The League of Women Voters, 1920-1970
Louise M. Young

The Rhetoric of War: Training Day, the Militia, and the Military Sermon
Marie L. Ahearn

Restrained Response: American Novels of the Cold War and Korea, 1945-1962
Arne Axelsson

In Search of America: Transatlantic Essays, 1951-1990
Marcus Cunliffe

WITHDRAWN